EL LIBERTADOR

Writings of Simón Bolívar

EL LIBERTADOR

Writings of Simón Bolívar

Translated from the Spanish by
FREDERICK H. FORNOFF

EDITED WITH AN INTRODUCTION AND NOTES
BY DAVID BUSHNELL

OXFORD
UNIVERSITY PRESS

2003

OXFORD

UNIVERSITY PRESS

Oxford New York
Auckland Bangkok Buenos Aires Cape Town Chennai
Dar es Salaam Delhi Hong Kong Istanbul Karachi Kolkata
Kuala Lumpur Madrid Melbourne Mexico City Mumbai Nairobi
São Paulo Shanghai Taipei Tokyo Toronto

Copyright © 2003 by Oxford University Press, Inc.

Published by Oxford University Press, Inc.
198 Madison Avenue, New York, New York 10016

http://www.oup.com

Oxford is a registered trademark of Oxford University Press

Library of Congress Cataloging-in-Publication Data
Bolívar, Simón, 1783–1830.
[Selections. English]
El Libertador : writings of Simón Bolívar/
translated from the Spanish by Frederick H. Fornoff ;
edited with an introduction and notes by David Bushnell.
p. cm. — (Library of Latin America)
Includes bibliographical references.
ISBN 0-19-514481-3 (pbk.) — ISBN 0-19-514480-5 (cloth)
1. South America—History—Wars of Independence, 1806–1830—Sources.
2. Latin America—History—Wars of Independence, 1806–1830—Sources.
I. Fornoff, Frederick H.   II. Bushnell, David, 1923–   III. Title.   IV. Series.
F2235.3 .A5 2003
980'.02'092—dc21
2002011540

1 3 5 7 9 8 6 4 2

Printed in the United States of America
on acid-free paper

Contents

SERIES EDITORS' GENERAL INTRODUCTION   ix

CHRONOLOGY OF SIMÓN BOLÍVAR   xiii

AN OVERVIEW OF THE BOLIVARIAN SOURCES   xviii

TRANSLATOR'S NOTE   xxiii

INTRODUCTION   xxvii

I THE MAJOR POLITICAL STATEMENTS

The Cartagena Manifesto: Memorial Addressed to the
    Citizens of New Granada by a Citizen from Caracas
    (15 December 1812)   3

The Jamaica Letter: Response from a South American to a
    Gentleman from This Island (6 September 1815)   12

The Angostura Address (15 February 1819)   31

The Bolivian Constitution (1826)   54
    I. Address to the Constituent Congress (25 May 1826)   54
    II. Draft of a Constitution for Bolivia   64

Message to the Convention of Ocaña
    (29 February 1828)   86

A Glance at Spanish America (1829)   95

Address to the "Congreso Admirable": Message to the
    Constituent Congress of the Republic of Colombia
    (20 January 1830)   103

II LESSER BOLIVARIAN TEXTS

1. *Political and Military*

Oath Taken in Rome (15 August 1805)   113

Decree of War to the Death (15 June 1813)   115

Manifesto to the Nations of the World
    (20 September 1813)   117

Manifesto of Carúpano (7 September 1814)   126

Manifesto on the Execution of General Manuel Piar
    (17 October 1817)   130

Declaration of Angostura (20 November 1818)   132

My Delirium on Chimborazo (1822)   135

Letter to José Antonio Páez: "Nor Am I Napoleon"
    (6 March 1826)   137

A Soldier's Death Penalty Commuted (26 January 1828)   139

Manifesto Justifying the Dictatorship (27 August 1828)   141

Manifesto Concerning the Installation of the Constituent
    Congress, the End of the Dictatorship, and Announcing
    the End of His Political Career (20 January 1830)   143

Letter to General Juan José Flores: "Ploughing the Sea"
    (9 November 1830)   145

Final Proclamation of the Liberator
    (10 December 1830)   150

2. *International Affairs*

Letter to Sir Richard Wellesley: An Appeal for Support
    (27 May 1815)   153

Letter to Baptis Irvine, Agent of the United States of
    America to Venezuela: Debating Neutral Rights
    (20 August 1818)   156

Invitation to the Governments of Colombia, Mexico, Río de la Plata, Chile, and Guatemala to Hold a Congress in Panama (7 December 1824)   159

Letter to General Francisco de Paula Santander: The Brazilian Empire, Upper Peru, North Americans, and Other Problems (30 May 1825)   162

Thoughts on the Congress to Be Held in Panama (1826)   169

Letter to General Lafayette: On George Washington (20 March 1826)   171

Letter to Colonel Patrick Campbell, British Chargé d'Affaires: "Plague America with Miseries" (5 August 1829)   172

3. *Social and Economic Affairs*

Decree for the Emancipation of the Slaves (2 June 1816)   177

Redistribution of Properties as Compensation for Officers and Soldiers (10 October 1817)   179

Letter to General Francisco de Paula Santander: On Slave Recruitment (18 April 1820)   182

Decrees on Indian Rights, Lands, and Tribute

   I. Decree Abolishing Personal Service Imposed on the Native Peoples: New Statute Governing Their Work (20 May 1820)   184

   II. Proclamation of the Civil Rights of Indians and Prohibition of Their Exploitation by Officials, Priests, Local Authorities, and Landowners (4 July 1825)   187

   III. Resolution on the Redistribution of Communal Lands (4 July 1825)   189

   IV. Resolution That Colombian Indians Pay a Tax Called "a Personal Tribute from Indigenous Peoples" (15 October 1828)   191

Application of Capital Punishment to Officials Who Have Taken Money from Public Funds (12 January 1824)   197

Measures for the Protection and Wise Use of the Nation's Forest Resources: Bolívar As Ecologist (31 July 1829)   199

4. *Education and Culture*

Method to Be Employed in the Education of My Nephew
Fernando Bolívar (1822?)   205

Decree on the Installation of Several Normal Schools Based
on the Lancasterian System (31 January 1825)   207

Letters to José Joaquín de Olmedo: Critique of the
"Victoria de Junín"

   I.   27 June 1825   209

   II.   12 July 1825   211

Circular on Educational Reform: Bentham Treatises
Banned from All Colombian Universities
(12 March 1828)   214

Prohibition of Secret Societies (8 November 1828)   216

NOTES   219

SELECT BIBLIOGRAPHY   233

Series Editors'
General Introduction

The Library of Latin America series makes available in translation
major nineteenth-century authors whose work has been neglected
in the English-speaking world. The titles for the translations from the
Spanish and Portuguese were suggested by an editorial committee that
included Jean Franco (general editor responsible for works in Spanish),
Richard Graham (series editor responsible for works in Portuguese), Tulio
Halperín Donghi (at the University of California, Berkeley), Iván Jaksić
(at the University of Notre Dame), Naomi Lindstrom (at the University
of Texas at Austin), Eduardo Lozano of the Library at the University of
Pittsburgh, and Francine Masiello (at the University of California,
Berkeley). The late Antonio Cornejo Polar of the University of Califor-
nia, Berkeley, was also one of the founding members of the committee.
The translations have been funded thanks to the generosity of the Lampadia Foundation and the Andrew W. Mellon Foundation.

During the period of national formation between 1810 and into the
early years of the twentieth century, the new nations of Latin America
fashioned their identities, drew up constitutions, engaged in bitter struggles over territory, and debated questions of education, government, eth-
nicity, and culture. This was a unique period unlike the process of nation
formation in Europe and one that should be more familiar than it is to
students of comparative politics, history, and literature.

The image of the nation was envisioned by the lettered classes—a minority in countries in which indigenous, mestizo, black, or mulatto peasants and slaves predominated—although there were also alternative nationalisms at the grassroots level. The cultural elite were well educated in European thought and letters, but as statesmen, journalists, poets, and academics, they confronted the problem of the racial and linguistic heterogeneity of the continent and the difficulties of integrating the population into a modern nation-state. Some of the writers whose works will be translated in the Library of Latin America series played leading roles in politics. Fray Servando Teresa de Mier, a friar who translated Rousseau's *The Social Contract* and was one of the most colorful characters of the independence period, was faced with imprisonment and expulsion from Mexico for his heterodox beliefs; on his return, after independence, he was elected to the congress. Domingo Faustino Sarmiento, exiled from his native Argentina under the dictatorship of Rosas, wrote *Facundo: Civilización y barbarie,* a stinging denunciation of that government. He returned after Rosas' overthrow and was elected president in 1868. Andrés Bello was born in Venezuela, lived in London, where he published poetry during the independence period, settled in Chile, where he founded the University, wrote his grammar of the Spanish language, and drew up the country's legal code.

These post-independence intelligentsia were not simply dreaming castles in the air, but vitally contributed to the founding of nations and the shaping of culture. The advantage of hindsight may make us aware of problems they themselves did not foresee, but this should not affect our assessment of their truly astonishing energies and achievements. It is still surprising that the writing of Andrés Bello, who contributed fundamental works to so many different fields, has never been translated into English. Although there is a recent translation of Sarmiento's celebrated *Facundo,* there is no translation of his memoirs, *Recuerdos de provincia (Provincial Recollections).* The predominance of memoirs in the Library of Latin America series is no accident—many of these offer entertaining insights into a vast and complex continent.

Nor have we neglected the novel. The series includes new translations of the outstanding Brazilian writer Joaquim Maria Machado de Assis' work, including *Dom Casmurro* and *The Posthumous Memoirs of Brás Cubas.* There is no reason why other novels and writers who are not so well known outside Latin America—the Peruvian novelist Clorinda Matto de Turner's *Aves sin nido,* Nataniel Aguirre's *Juan de la Rosa,* José de Alencar's *Iracema,* Juana Manuela Gorriti's short stories—should not be read with as much interest as the political novels of Anthony Trollope.

A series on nineteenth-century Latin America cannot, however, be limited to literary genres such as the novel, the poem, and the short story. The literature of independent Latin America was eclectic and strongly influenced by the periodical press newly liberated from scrutiny by colonial authorities and the Inquisition. Newspapers were miscellanies of fiction, essays, poems, and translations from all manner of European writing. The novels written on the eve of Mexican Independence by José Joaquín Fernández de Lizardi included disquisitions on secular education and law, and denunciations of the evils of gaming and idleness. Other works, such as a well-known poem by Andrés Bello, "Ode to Tropical Agriculture," and novels such as *Amalia* by José Mármol and the Bolivian Nataniel Aguirre's *Juan de la Rosa*, were openly partisan. By the end of the century, sophisticated scholars were beginning to address the history of their countries, as did João Capistrano de Abreu in his *Capítulos de história colonial.*

It is often in memoirs such as those by Fray Servando Teresa de Mier or Sarmiento that we find the descriptions of everyday life that in Europe were incorporated into the realist novel. Latin American literature at this time was seen largely as a pedagogical tool, a "light" alternative to speeches, sermons, and philosophical tracts—though, in fact, especially in the early part of the century, even the readership for novels was quite small because of the high rate of illiteracy. Nevertheless, the vigorous orally transmitted culture of the gaucho and the urban underclasses became the linguistic repertoire of some of the most interesting nineteenth-century writers—most notably José Hernández, author of the "gauchesque" poem "Martín Fierro," which enjoyed an unparalleled popularity. But for many writers the task was not to appropriate popular language but to civilize, and their literary works were strongly influenced by the high style of political oratory.

The editorial committee has not attempted to limit its selection to the better-known writers such as Machado de Assis; it has also selected many works that have never appeared in translation or writers whose work has not been translated recently. The series now makes these works available to the English-speaking public.

Because of the preferences of funding organizations, the series initially focuses on writing from Brazil, the Southern Cone, the Andean region, and Mexico. Each of our editions will have an introduction that places the work in its appropriate context and includes explanatory notes.

We owe special thanks to the late Robert Glynn of the Lampadia Foundation, whose initiative gave the project a jump start, and to Richard

Ekman of the Andrew W. Mellon Foundation, which also generously supported the project. We also thank the Rockefeller Foundation for funding the 1996 symposium "Culture and Nation in Iberoamerica," organized by the editorial board of the Library of Latin America. We received substantial institutional support and personal encouragement from the Institute of Latin American Studies of the University of Texas at Austin. The support of Edward Barry of Oxford University Press has been crucial, as has the advice and help of Ellen Chodosh of Oxford University Press. The first volumes of the series were published after the untimely death, on July 3, 1997, of Maria C. Bulle, who, as an associate of the Lampadia Foundation, supported the idea from its beginning.

—*Jean Franco*
—*Richard Graham*

Chronology of Simón Bolívar

1783	24 July. Simón Bolívar is born at Caracas, the youngest of two brothers and two sisters.
1786	Death of his father, Juan Vicente Bolívar y Ponte, wealthy creole planter and militia colonel and heir to the title of marquis of San Luis, although he never used it.
1792	Death of his mother, María de la Concepción Palacios y Blanco, whose family also formed part of the colonial aristocracy. Primary responsibility for Simón's upbringing passes to a maternal uncle, Esteban Palacios, but as he is living in Spain, it is exercised in practice by another uncle, Carlos Palacios.
1795	Bolívar goes to live in the house of Simón Rodríguez, the most influential of his teachers.
1798	Bolívar is commissioned *subteniente* in the colonial militia.
1799–1802	Bolívar's first visit to Europe. He stays principally in Spain but makes an excursion to France early in 1802.

1802   26 May. In Madrid, Bolívar marries María Teresa
        Rodríguez del Toro, daughter of a noble family of Cara-
        cas. Shortly afterward, the couple returns to Venezuela.

1803   22 January. Death of Bolívar's wife.

1803–1806   Bolívar's second stay in Europe. He travels more widely
        but spends most of his time in Paris, where he meets
        Alexander von Humboldt and other notables and renews
        his acquaintance with Simón Rodríguez.

1805   15 August. Accompanied by Rodríguez, Bolívar makes a
        vow at Rome to liberate Spanish America.

1807   1 January (apparently). Bolívar lands in Charleston, South
        Carolina, on his return from Europe. He visits other
        major cities before finally sailing from Philadelphia back
        to Venezuela.

1807–1810   Living in Venezuela and occupied with agricultural and
        commercial activities, Bolívar takes part, as still a relative-
        ly minor figure, in the revolutionary ferment that arose
        in Spanish America following the Napoleonic invasion
        of Spain and the overthrow of the legitimate monarch,
        Fernando VII.

1810   On 19 April Caracas revolutionists depose the Spanish
        captain-general and establish a junta to govern ostensibly
        in the name of Fernando VII, but in practice autonomous.
        The junta names Bolívar commissioner to London to
        seek the sympathy and support of Great Britain for the
        new regime.

1811   On 5 July an elected Venezuelan congress formally de-
        clares independence. Shortly afterward, Bolívar receives
        his baptism of fire in the campaign to suppress a coun-
        terrevolutionary outbreak at Valencia.

1812   Bolívar helps to rally a demoralized populace after the
        disastrous Holy Thursday earthquake in Caracas, but on
        6 July he is forced to evacuate the strategic position of
        Puerto Cabello, which had been entrusted to his com-
        mand. On 31 July, embittered at the surrender agreed to
        by Francisco de Miranda as dictator of Venezuela's "First
        Republic," Bolívar is one of the leaders who arrest him
        and thereby prevent his escape from Venezuela. Bolívar

subsequently goes to Cartagena in New Granada to resume the struggle and on 15 December issues the Cartagena Manifesto, his first major political text.

1813   With backing from the revolutionary government of New Granada, Bolívar conducts the "Admirable Campaign," which again delivers most of Venezuela into patriot hands.

1814   The "Second Republic," in which Bolívar held supreme civil and military power, proves unable to gain wide popular backing and is defeated, in large part by the action of royalist irregulars.

1814–1815   Again a fugitive in New Granada, Bolívar helps the federal authorities subdue the recalcitrant state of Cundinamarca (Bogotá), but in the face of continuing internal dissensions he withdraws to the West Indies, where on 6 September 1815 he publishes the Jamaica Letter.

1816   With help from Haiti, Bolívar in the second of two attempts reestablishes a foothold in Venezuela. At Carúpano on 2 June he issues his first decree against slavery.

1817   Bolívar establishes a provisional government at Angostura on the lower Orinoco River.

1818   Bolívar joins forces with the chief of Venezuela's *llaneros* (plainsmen), José Antonio Páez, and with him consolidates control over much of the interior Orinoco Basin.

1819   On 15 February at Angostura, Bolívar inaugurates a new Venezuelan congress and delivers another of his key political statements, the Angostura Address. Later in the year he launches a campaign for the liberation of New Granada, crowned with success at the Battle of Boyacá (7 August). On 17 December the Congress of Angostura votes to establish the Republic of Colombia, comprising both Venezuela and New Granada as well as Quito (modern Ecuador).

1821   24 June. Bolívar defeats royalist forces in the Battle of Carabobo, the last major engagement of the war in Venezuela. The Colombian constituent congress, meeting at Cúcuta, adopts a formal constitution and elects Bolívar first president to serve under it, with Francisco de

Paula Santander as vice president. Santander is left as acting chief executive in Bogotá, the national capital, when Bolívar leaves to continue directing the military struggle against Spain.

1822   The Battle of Pichincha on 24 May, won by Bolívar's lieutenant, Antonio José de Sucre, seals the liberation of Ecuador and paves the way for Bolívar's entry to Quito three weeks later. On 26–27 July, at Guayaquil, Bolívar meets the Argentine Liberator, José de San Martín, and fails to reach agreement on plans for completing the liberation of Peru or on the future political order of Spanish America.

1823   1 September. At the invitation of Peruvian authorities, Bolívar lands in Callao to assume leadership of the independence struggle in Peru.

1824   On 6 August, at the Battle of Junín, Bolívar scores a major victory in the Peruvian highlands. On 7 December, from Lima, Bolívar invites other Spanish American nations to a conference at Panama City for the purpose of creating a permanent alliance. Two days later, in the Battle of Ayacucho, Sucre defeats the Peruvian viceroy and for all practical purposes completes the war of independence in Spanish South America.

1825   The former territory of Upper Peru, where royalist resistance crumbled before the advance of Sucre following the Battle of Ayacucho, takes the name of Bolivia and invites Bolívar, who proceeded there from Lima, to write its first constitution.

1826   On 25 May Bolívar submits his draft constitution for Bolivia. Its central feature is a president serving for life. In June–July the Congress of Panama meets but fails to produce lasting results. On 3 September Bolívar finally leaves Peru to return to Colombia.

1827   Bolívar makes a peaceful arrangement with Páez to end the revolt that he had begun in Venezuela the year before. However, he is increasingly estranged from Vice President Santander and the liberals of New Granada, who object both to his leniency toward Páez and to the seeming betrayal of republican principles in his constitution for Bolivia.

1828   Failure of the Convention of Ocaña, called to reform the Colombian constitution, leads Bolívar to establish a conservative military dictatorship in a desperate attempt to maintain internal stability and, if possible, the unity of Colombia. On 25 September he survives an assassination attempt in Bogotá; believing Santander responsible, even in the absence of clear-cut proof, he sends the former vice president into exile.

1829   While Bolívar is in Ecuador, primarily to deal with a conflict between Colombia and Peru, a monarchist scheme floated by his supporters in Bogotá arouses widespread hostility, especially in Venezuela.

1830   Faced with the secession of Venezuela from the Colombian union and the unrelenting opposition of New Granadan liberals, Bolívar resigns the presidency and on 8 May leaves Bogotá, intending to go into foreign exile. However, he dies on 17 December at Santa Marta on the coast.

An Overview of
the Bolivarian Sources

The extant private and official writings of Simón Bolívar are voluminous, and virtually all have found their way into print, but new items
of generally minor significance still turn up from time to time.[1] Bolívar
conscientiously accumulated an archive that eventually filled ten trunks;
it included messages received, copybooks of outgoing orders and messages, and other items as well. In his will, he gave instructions that this
archive be burned, but at the time of his death it was already on its way
to Jamaica in the care of a trusted friend, the Frenchman Jean Pavageau.
There the documents were ultimately divided into three sections. Most
of the papers relating to the years 1813–18 were sent to Pedro Briceño
Méndez, a close military collaborator of Bolívar who proposed to write a
history of the period in question; those from 1819 to 1830 were mainly
consigned to Bolívar's former aide, Daniel F. O'Leary, who intended to
write the history of the later period; and the remainder stayed with Juan
de Francisco Martín, a New Granadan who had been a fervent civilian
supporter of Bolívar and was one of his executors.[2]

The portions of Bolívar's archive consigned to Briceño Méndez and
O'Leary would become the nuclei of two major printed compilations
that appeared in Venezuela in the second half of the nineteenth century,
in combination with other documents collected by the two original cus-

todians and others who collaborated in or continued their work. The papers kept by Juan de Francisco Martín ended up in Paris, where he lived for many years, part of the time in diplomatic service. They returned to Venezuela in the early twentieth century and along with the other two sections of Bolívar's archive and much else of related significance became part of the present Archivo del Libertador, located in the Casa Natal in Caracas. This repository, whose principal creator was the indefatigable Bolivarianist Vicente Lecuna, contains the most important collection anywhere in the world of documents generated by or concerned in some way with Simón Bolívar. It was directed by Lecuna himself until his death in 1954 and over the years has been steadily enriched through further acquisitions. But it is not, of course, the only archive holding Bolivarian materials, whether in Venezuela or in other countries. No doubt the most important of the other repositories is Colombia's Archivo Histórico Nacional in Bogotá, although the Fundación John Boulton in Caracas microfilmed most of its documents of Bolivarian interest, which can thus be consulted—in that form—at the office of the Fundación in the Venezuelan capital. [3]

Even though there is still much material relating to Bolívar and his associates that has not been published, there can be little surviving documentation signed or dictated by Bolívar himself that has not appeared in print. Indeed, most of his major texts and many lesser ones were quickly circulated in printed form in the press of the period or in pamphlet form. Not only that, but in his own lifetime a first multivolume compilation of Bolivarian materials had already been published by the Venezuelan patriots Francisco Javier Yanes and Cristóbal Mendoza, under the title *Colección de documentos relativos a la vida pública del Libertador de Colombia y del Perú, Simón Bolívar para servir a la historia de la Independencia de Sur América*. It comprised twenty-two small volumes, printed in Caracas from 1826 to 1829, with an appendix volume appearing in 1833. This was, in the words of Manuel Pérez Vila, "the point of departure" for all subsequent collections of documents concerning independence of the Bolivarian nations.[4] In the second half of the century, two more major compilations were added. The first of these, compiled by the patriot warrior-priest José Félix Blanco and Ramón Azpurúa, was published in Caracas in 1875 as *Documentos para la historia de la vida pública del Libertador de Colombia, Perú y Bolivia*, in fourteen large volumes of double-column format. Its nucleus was the part of Bolívar's original archive that had been given to Briceño Méndez, but it incorporated other documents already included in the Yanes-Mendoza series, and still others gathered by the two compilers (of whom Blanco had died before the collection appeared).[5] The other was the misleadingly titled but even more important *Memorias del General O'Leary*, published from 1879 to 1888. In this case, of course, the nucleus of the collection was the part of the Liberator's own archive entrusted to Daniel F. O'Leary. He had died in 1854, but his son Simón Bolívar O'Leary took responsibility for the publication. Two of the volumes contained the actual memoirs ("Narración") of Bolívar's Irish-born aide and confidant; the rest were filled with the supporting documents, naturally including many that had been added to what O'Leary initially received.[6] There are some errors and omissions in the Blanco and Azpurúa compilation and that of O'Leary, but they remain essential resources for all scholars studying the independence period and have both been reprinted in recent years.[7]

Although the work of those nineteenth-century compilers was certainly admirable, the most eminent of all collectors and publishers of Bolivarian materials was without question Vicente Lecuna, who worked mainly in the first half of the twentieth century. Lecuna produced a steady stream of compilations of Bolívar's own writings and related documents as well as original research and syntheses on all aspects of the Liberator's career. He was at the same time the most learned and most active guardian of Venezuela's Bolívar cult, as can be seen from the title itself of just one of his many works: *Catálogo de errores y calumnias en la historia de Bolívar* (3 vols., New York, 1956–58). In 1929–30, Lecuna brought forth a definitive collection of Bolívar's letters, the ten-volume series *Cartas del Libertador,* which included (and when necessary corrected) all those previously published and added some more, along with an analytical index. In 1947 he produced an eleventh volume, published in New York, as addendum to the series, and a twelfth was added in 1959 by the Fundación John Boulton. Lecuna also published, among much else, a two-volume *Documentos referentes a la creación de Bolivia* (1924) that includes Bolívar's draft of a constitution for Bolivia as well as other materials related to the beginnings of the country that bore his name.[8]

Not least, we have Lecuna to thank for the *Obras completas* of Bolívar published initially in 1947 in two volumes, by Editorial Lex of Havana, Cuba, though by order of the Venezuelan government. A three-volume set of the same was also published in Havana in 1950 and later reprinted in Caracas, in an undated edition but about 1963.[9] It was reprinted one more time in 1984, in six volumes and in Spain, but still conserving Lecuna's original text.[10] The two three-volume editions—Havana 1950 and Caracas 1963(?)—are the most widely available. Fortunately, they have identical pagination and will be the version cited in the present work. The *Obras completas* were not, of course, truly *completas*. Quite apart from the failure to include items that came to light after the initial publication, they do not include, for example, something as essential for the study of Bolívar's career as his Bolivian constitution or all the decrees that he issued over the years. Fortunately, however, there is no lack of other places to find the text of the constitution,[11] and the *Decretos del Libertador, 1813–1830*, were published in 1961 by the Sociedad Bolivariana de Venezuela.

The *Obras completas* continue to be the single most convenient and accessible compilation, but for purposes of academic research it is being superseded by the *Escritos del Libertador*, launched in 1964 by the Sociedad Bolivariana de Venezuela. The latter series not only includes items newly come to light but gives more detailed information on provenance, prior publication, and differing versions of the documents, along with introductory essays and research aids prepared by such qualified specialists as Pérez Vila, whose general survey of the source materials appears at the front of the first volume. Pérez Vila was the driving force behind the publication project until the time of his death in 1991. Unfortunately, by century's end the series still had not been completed.[12]

Needless to say, there are also many compilations of Bolívar's writings that do not even pretend to be complete but present instead a selection either of those concerning a particular topic or of whatever the compilers considered most important. Two that deserve mention here are *Doctrina del Libertador*, published in Venezuela in 1976 under the editorship of Pérez Vila, which is notable for the quantity and quality of its explanatory notes,[13] and the two-volume *Bolívar documental* compiled by the Venezuelan historian Germán Carrera Damas.[14] Nor is there a lack of English-language compilations and anthologies. Of these much the most complete, in two volumes, is Simón Bolívar, *Selected Writings*, compiled by Vicente Lecuna, and edited by Harold A. Bierck Jr. The set was published by the Banco de Venezuela (of which Lecuna was a director) in New York in 1951 and widely distributed to U.S. libraries and Latin American specialists.[15] An example of the various shorter and more specialized compilations available is Gerald E. Fitzgerald, *The Political Thought of Bolívar: Selected Writings*.[16] The present volume will, of course, include numerous items that have already appeared more than once in the English language, but it also contains some that have never before been translated, and the intent is to offer all the documents in a version that is contemporary and accurate.

NOTES

1. By far the most authoritative survey of the sources for the study of Bolívar is that by Manuel Pérez Vila, "Contribución a la bibliografía de los escritos del Libertador, manuscritos y ediciones," published in Sociedad Bolivariana de Venezuela, *Escritos del Libertador*, vol. I, *Introducción general* (Caracas, 1964–), 61–290. Except where otherwise specified, this note is based directly on that survey.

2. Pérez Vila, "Contribución," 63, 68–70.

3. Ibid., 70–85, 257.

4. Ibid., 160–61.

5. Ibid., 187–91.

6. Ibid., 224–27.

7. The Blanco and Azpurúa compilation was reprinted by the Comité Ejecutivo del Bicentenario de Simón Bolívar, Caracas, in 15 vols., 1977–79. The *Memorias del General O'Leary* were republished by the Ministerio de la Defensa in 34 vols. in 1981, the last two volumes containing the index to the entire collection; unfortunately, this edition was not widely distributed.

8. Pérez Vila, "Contribución," 231–43, 247–49.

9. Ibid., 243–47.

10. Madrid: Maveco de Ediciones, 1984.

11. For example, in vol. 1 of *El pensamiento constitucional hispanoamericano hasta 1830* (Caracas, 1961; Biblioteca de la Academia Nacional de la Historia, 40), 171–221.

12. By 1996 the series had reached vol. 27, with documents of January–February 1824.

13. Caracas: Biblioteca Ayacucho, 1976.

14. Caracas: Monte Avila, 1993.

15. The translation is by Lewis Bertrand; publisher was the Colonial Press.

16. The Hague: M. Nijhoff, 1971.

Translator's Note

In translating these political addresses, letters, manifestos, and decrees, I had two goals. First, I sought to reproduce the sense of Simón Bolívar's writings as accurately as possible. In this endeavor I must acknowledge the assistance of David Bushnell, editor of this volume, who selected the texts and coached me through numerous fine points of Spanish–American administrative and constitutional terminology. He also made available his earlier translation of extensive portions of Bolívar's draft of the constitution for Bolivia. For some of the pieces I was also able to consult the earlier translation by Lewis Bertrand in the two-volume *Selected Writings of Bolívar* (New York: Colonial Press, 1951), compiled by Vicente Lecuna and edited by Harold A. Bierck Jr. Bertrand's translation is quite accurate, if somewhat dated in tone.

My second task was to try to convey the stylistic spectrum of Bolívar's writing, which ranges from genteel prodding in letters to close friends and colleagues, fierce clarity in the political texts and manifestos, to lyric effusiveness in a piece such as his delirium on Chimborazo. In his letter to J. J. Olmedo, we sense his gratification at being the protagonist of an epic poem and his concern to reassure Olmedo of their friendship, even as he gently damns the poem with faint praise.

Given who he was and what he was working so hard to accomplish, it is inevitable that in all of these texts Bolívar's awareness of his own persona as a maker of history is always front and center. He is not so much egotistical as he is dedicated to his vision for America and aware of his own importance to that vision. By following Bolívar's writing from the turn of the century until his death in 1830, we can follow the shifts in his enthusiasm for his American project. What a difference in tone from "Oath Taken in Rome" (1805):

> This nation [the nation of Romulus and Numa] has examples for everything, except for the cause of humanity: corrupt Messalinas, gutless Agrippas, great historians, distinguished naturalists, heroic warriors, rapacious consuls, unrestrained sybarites, golden virtues, and foul crimes; but for the emancipation of the spirit, the elimination of cares, the exaltation of man, and the final perfectibility of reason, little or nothing. The civilization blowing in from the East has shown all its faces here, all its parts; but the resolution of the great problem of man set free seems to have been something inconceivable, a mystery that would only be made clear in the New World.
>
> I swear before you; I swear by the God of my fathers; I swear on their graves; I swear by my Country, that I will not rest body or soul until I have broken the chains binding us to the will of Spanish might!

to the near tragic resignation he voices in his last letter, addressed to General J. J. Flores (November 9, 1830):

> Nations are like children, who soon throw away what they have wept to attain. Neither you nor I nor anyone else knows the will of the people. . . . Use the past to predict the future. You know that I have ruled for twenty years and derived from these only a few sure conclusions: (1) America is ungovernable for us; (2) Those who serve revolution plough the sea; (3) The only thing one can do in America is emigrate; (4) This country will fall inevitably into the hands of the unrestrained multitudes, and then into the hands of tyrants so insignificant they will be almost imperceptible, of all colors and races; (5) Once we've been eaten alive by every crime and extinguished by ferocity, the Europeans won't even bother to conquer us; (6) If it were possible for any part of the world to revert to primitive chaos, it would be America in her last hour.

The dispirited tone of this last letter serves as coda to the tragedy of the man known as the Liberator, and reflects a gradual shift of mood that is perhaps inevitable in a man who identified his persona with a continent full of people whose will he could not decipher.

Introduction

With the possible exception of Fidel Castro, Simón Bolívar is by far the most widely known of Latin American historical figures. Books and articles written about him in his native region are very numerous, and works both translated and original abound in English and other major languages. Bolívar enjoys a degree of name recognition around the world even among people who have read none of the works concerning him or anything else that deals expressly with Latin America. Yet much of what people know or think they know about Bolívar is superficial or even erroneous. As Venezuelan historian Germán Carrera Damas shrewdly observed, the sheer accumulation of writings on Bolívar's life has served as much to obscure as to clarify his historical significance.[1]

Part of the problem in understanding Bolívar is the sheer breadth of his thought and action. He was one of the few leaders of Latin American independence who remained fully engaged in the struggle from beginning to end, or more precisely from immediate antecedents to early aftermath. But he was more than just a soldier and founder of new nations, or "Liberator" to use his preferred title. He was a thinker who probed the meaning of what he was doing in historical perspective and in a wide international context. He analyzed past and present conditions of his part of the world and speculated, sometimes with uncanny prescience, concerning its future. He drafted constitutions, orders, and decrees that he hoped would make that future more bearable. Amid all this, Bolívar found time to offer his ideas on questions of literary usage and educational method and a great deal more. Fortunately, his voluminous writings have been preserved, and the vigor of his prose style—almost always lucid even when presenting questionable theses, often trenchant or ironic, but never dull—must be included among his claims to fame.

From Caracas to Santa Marta

Bolívar may or may not have been sent to earth by Divine Providence, as his nineteenth-century biographer Felipe Larrazábal insisted,[2] but it is still fair to say that both the geographic locale and the social circumstances of his birth were propitious for his later emergence as the preeminent leader of Latin American independence. His life began in the year 1783 at Caracas, in Venezuela, which would be the first Spanish colony to gain de facto autonomy (1810) and also first to declare outright independence from the mother country (1811). Both distinctions were due in part to the geographic accident of being situated at the northeast extremity of Spanish South America. Of all the principal Spanish colonies, Venezuela was closest to Europe, and Caracas in particular, situated a mere day's journey from the Caribbean coast, was normally the first Spanish colonial capital to receive news from the other side of the Atlantic. Thus in 1810 Venezuelans had early notice of the fact that most of Spain had fallen under the control of Napoleon and his allies and that a new Spanish resistance government, the Council of Regency, had emerged—requiring Spanish Americans to decide either to recognize its authority or to strike out on their own, as Venezuela now did. But it was also the Spanish colony closest to the still-loyal West Indian territories of Cuba and Puerto Rico, so its fledgling revolutionary government was the one most directly exposed to counterrevolutionary attack and least able to maintain the fiction of an autonomous status short of actual separation from Spain.

Venezuela's economic role also prepared it to become a key player in the independence movement. It was an agroexporting region, with extensive slave-worked landholdings that made it, after Cuba, the most successful of Spain's plantation colonies. By far the principal commodity was cacao, grown in valleys and slopes of the Andean coastal range and in the narrow strip between that range and the Caribbean. On the eve of independence, cacao represented almost half the colony's exports, even though its relative importance was tending to decline, resulting from competition on the world market of cheaper cacao from Guayaquil and the rise within Venezuela itself of indigo and coffee cultivation. It is impossible, for lack of adequate statistical data, to calculate exactly what proportion of Venezuela's Gross Colonial Product was contributed by the external sector of the economy, but it was substantially greater than in neighboring New Granada (or present-day Colombia), which had 50 percent more inhabitants yet traded less. Hence Spanish imperial trade policy, whose theoretical objective was to prohibit all interchange between Spanish colonial and non-Spanish ports, had considerable relevance for Venezuela—and it was a distinct inconvenience.

The level of commercial activity (both legal and in the form of contraband) was naturally facilitated by Venezuela's relative ease of access to the outside world. These same factors together facilitated the movement of persons, whether on private or official business or engaging in early forms of tourism, and likewise favored the penetration of new ideas, fads, and fashions from abroad. Until 1808 Venezuela did not even have a printing press, but Spanish and to a lesser extent other foreign publications were available to those who wanted them, and they brought among other things the latest news of world events. To be sure, the reception accorded to such outside stimuli was uneven. As most people were illiterate, they were not stimulated at all by the printed word—at least not directly. And such major events as the Anglo-American, French, and Haitian Revolutions evoked widely differing reactions. Liberty in moderation, as appeared to be practiced in the United States, was widely viewed as a good thing, but the violence and active anticlericalism of the French Revolution were a different matter; and while some Venezuelans saw the eradication of white domination and human slavery in Haiti as an example worth following in their country, for that very same reason the Haitian Revolution evoked a diametrically opposite reaction among most Venezuelan whites, slaveowners or not.

Although Bolívar belonged to the creole landowning elite and owned slaves, one cannot take for granted that he shared the fear of a Haitian-style slave uprising that consumed other members of his class nor that he showed the same repugnance at the social and economic advancement achieved by select members of the free colored population. We have no record of his early thinking on such matters, and his later views, at least, were significantly more enlightened than those of a majority of his social peers. Moreover, his practice as a teenager of wandering off through the streets of Caracas, mingling freely with his social inferiors—much to the displeasure of his older sister María Antonia—suggests the possible early appearance of the ease in relationships with all sorts and conditions of people that he would display in later life and that would, among other things, make him a commander genuinely popular with his ragtag armies. Bolívar's superior social position did, of course, in itself foster a degree of self-confidence and relieve him of the need to be always on guard to protect his status. In any case, through the circle of extended family and personal acquaintances, that position gave him exposure to whatever trends and ideas were currently making the rounds at the upper level of colonial society. And it naturally guaranteed him some formal education, even if while growing up in Caracas he was not a particularly dedicated student. His favorite tutor, Simón Rodríguez, was a man of unconventional behavior and a devotee of Rousseau, whose influence probably lay more in the encouragement of an open and inquiring mind than in any concrete notions he may have implanted.

The social environment in which Bolívar grew up was ultimately the result of his family's economic role, as leading landowners and agroexporters, and at certain intervals—mainly brief—of his adult life he would devote himself personally to his business interests. Initially, there were others who took care of those interests for him, but it was still the Bolívar family fortune that made possible the period of living and traveling in Europe. Actually, there were two such periods, the first spent principally in Spain and the second in France, separated by an abortive return to Venezuela that was cut short by the death of the wife he had just married in Madrid. It was while residing in Europe that Bolívar developed the voracious appetite for reading that led him to take along cases of books even on military campaigns. As he wrote later, his tastes were broad, including "Locke, Condillac, Buffon, D'Alembert, Helvétius, Montesquieu, Mably, Filangieri, Lalande, Rousseau, Voltaire, Rollin, Berthot, and all the classics of antiquity, whether philosophers, historians, orators, or poets, and all the modern classics of Spain, France, Italy, and a great many of the English."[3] The list was not exhaustive, and it is probable that Bolívar read the English authors and the ancients mainly in French translation, that being the one foreign language of which he had full mastery. We do not necessarily know just what works he read by a given author, or whether he read them from first page to last, but more than one acquaintance noted his fondness for Voltaire, and his interest in, say, ancient history is well attested by the historical examples cited in his political addresses. At the very least, Bolívar's fondness for good reading endowed him with a breadth of intellectual culture matched by few if any of his fellow liberators.

While in Europe Bolívar also met some famous authors, among them Alexander von Humboldt, and he renewed his relationship with Simón Rodríguez, now an expatriate since fleeing Caracas under suspicion of subversive activity. During a sidetrip to Italy, accompanied by Rodríguez, he made his celebrated vow of 1805 on one of the hills of Rome to liberate Spanish America. Much less is known about Bolívar's subsequent visit to the United States, which occupied the first part of 1807; he could only have been an interested observer of the newly independent English America, yet there is even some doubt as to his precise itinerary. He was then back in Venezuela before the Napoleonic invasion of Spain and forced abdication of the Spanish royal family triggered the general imperial crisis whose outcome in Spanish America was the war for independence. Bolívar was a minor actor in developments leading up to the creation in 1810 of a self-governing junta in Caracas, but he served the junta as head of a diplomatic mission to London and eventually took part in the military struggle in Venezuela itself—suffering one of the most embarrassing setbacks of his career when he lost the strategic fortress of Puerto Cabello to a counterrevolutionary uprising.

Only after the collapse of Venezuela's First Republic did Bolívar finally assume supreme command. He had initially taken refuge in Cartagena, where he produced the first of the documents included in this volume: the so-called Cartagena Manifesto, which was both his explanation of the defeat of the Venezuelan patriots and a call for joint action between New Granada and Venezuela to regain Caracas. And regain it he did. As head of the Second Republic, with dictatorial powers, Bolívar was less concerned with building institutions and formulating political doctrine than with military defense against the royalist counteroffensive that was not long in coming. Particularly troublesome was the degree of support obtained by bands of royalist irregulars among the free pardos (of part African descent) and mestizos who formed a majority of the population of Venezuela and clearly did not yet feel a sense of solidarity with the upper-class creoles who thus far led the republican cause. Bolívar was one of the men who would take that lesson to heart, but before he could do anything about it he had to seek refuge once more in New Granada and—when the New Granadan patriots' internal dissensions doomed their republic, too—in the British colony of Jamaica and the independent black republic of Haiti.

Bolívar's West Indian interlude of 1815-16 was critically important both for his use of the enforced leisure time to organize and communicate his thinking about the independence struggle and the future of Spanish America—above all, in his "Jamaica Letter"—and for his marshaling of defeated and dispirited South American patriots for an ultimately successful effort, with Haitian help, to regain a foothold in Venezuela. And it was then that Bolívar refined what might be called a form of military populism. On returning to Venezuela he took pains to recognize and promote soldiers of pardo or other lower-class origin, although he did not hesitate to execute the brilliant pardo officer Manuel Piar, whom he believed guilty of conspiring to exploit racial tensions in a challenge to Bolívar's own leadership. Of particular importance was Bolívar's achievement in gaining the confidence and support of José Antonio Páez, a man of little or no formal education but the quintessential caudillo of the Orinoco plains who brought with him his fiercely loyal following of mounted lancers. Then, too, while the mere fact that Bolívar had returned to Venezuela with the aid of Haiti and now incorporated abolition of slavery among his revolutionary objectives alarmed many of his own class, it further contributed to giving the independence movement a more popular aura. For the military in particular, there was a pledge of bonuses for everyone engaged in the fighting and, of rather more symbolic than practical importance, a decree granting in principle the right to vote to all common soldiers even if they did not meet the standard social and economic conditions for voting.[4]

Once Bolívar in close collaboration with Páez had established republican control over the greatest part of the Orinoco Basin, he made one more of his major political statements, to the Congress of Angostura, which he inaugurated in February 1819. In the address he repeated his plea for the eradication of slavery and insisted again on the need to justly reward the veterans of independence. On the other hand, the constitutional prescriptions that he presented before the deputies tended more toward aristocracy than democracy, although an aristocracy that would include patriot heroes of modest social origin alongside others of his own class, suggesting that he still did not consider the population at large to be ready for self-government. But national independence from Spain was a different matter, so that shortly afterward Bolívar embarked on the first of a series of military campaigns that would effectively end Spanish rule in South America. His initial objective was Santafé, soon to be renamed Bogotá, which he entered three days after decisively defeating the royalists in the Battle of Boyacá (7 August 1819). This victory delivered to the republicans not only the former viceregal capital but the greatest part of Andean New Granada. Not quite two years later, in the Battle of Carabobo (24 June 1821), Bolívar broke the back of royalist resistance in Venezuela and was able to return in triumph to Caracas, his hometown. In the following year, the presidency of Quito or modern Ecuador was liberated by forces under the command of Bolívar's favorite lieutenant, Antonio José de Sucre, but Bolívar's own advance through southern New Granada, culminating in the pyrrhic victory of Bomboná, had increased the pressure on Quito's royalist defenders. In 1823, Bolívar finally accepted an invitation from Peru to complete the unfinished independence struggle there. Having achieved a major victory at Junín in the Peruvian highlands in August 1824, he left Sucre to deliver the coup de grace in the Battle of Ayacucho (9 December 1824). Bolívar also let Sucre do the mopping up of royalist resistance in Upper Peru, to which he made his own way in mid-1825 and received not just all the usual honors but the less usual one of having the new nation assume the name of Bolivia.

This unbroken series of successes was made possible in the last analysis by the gross disproportion in area, population, and resources between Spain and its American colonies. Demoralization and disarray in the enemy camp, stemming in part from the bitter rivalry between Spanish liberals and absolutists, was an important contributing factor. Even so, it was Bolívar who in the end mobilized the republicans' assets for victory, with his political sagacity quite as much as with the military skill in which he was largely self-taught (but obviously a good learner). Above all, perhaps, he never lost sight of the need for military and political unity among the Spanish Americans themselves. In his original theater of operations, northern South America, this meant indiscriminately combining and using forces from both Venezuela and New Granada, and the process of unification between those two ex-colonies reached a seemingly inevitable conclusion after the Battle of Boyacá, when Bolívar induced the Congress of Angostura to proclaim the creation of the Republic of Colombia, which included both ex-colonies (and is generally known as Gran Colombia to distinguish it from the smaller Colombia of today). The measure that established Colombia further incorporated the presidency of Quito or modern Ecuador, even though none of it had yet been freed from Spain. But when Bolívar arrived on the scene, as both conquering general and first constitutional president of Colombia, he made sure that the decision was properly implemented. In the one province of Guayaquil, many of whose people were tempted either to become an autonomous city-state or to join Peru, Bolívar's followers applied the needed pressure to head off either alternative. In this way, Bolívar thwarted the aim of the Argentine Liberator, José de San Martín, lately serving as Protector of Peru, to make Guayaquil Peruvian. By the time San Martín reached Guayaquil to meet with Bolívar in July 1822, that issue was in effect decided. Instead, the two leaders appear to have discussed only the state of the war in Peru and plans for the future of Spanish America, and though both were strong proponents of close alliance among all the newly independent nations, there was no meeting of minds on much else.

When Bolívar himself moved on to Peru, after San Martín resigned his position as Protector and departed for self-imposed exile, he inherited the remains of San Martín's Argentine-Chilean force, which he molded together with native Peruvian units and his own Colombians for the final campaign against the royalists. And as the military struggle drew to a close, he turned his attention not only to organizing republican institutions in Peru, where the Congress had named him Dictator, but also to larger projects of Spanish American unity. One of these was his proposal for the Congress of Panama, intended to be a gathering of former Spanish colonies for the purpose of adopting agreements of permanent cooperation and alliance. Bolívar sent out invitations from Lima in December 1824, for a meeting to take place in 1826. The other was his concept of a Federation of the Andes, in which would be subsumed not only Gran Colombia itself but Peru and Bolivia. For this creation he envisaged a looser union than the Colombian (which was at least on paper a highly centralized state), though with its component parts bound more closely together than the members of the general league that he hoped would emerge from the Congress of Panama. The number of member states of the proposed Andean Federation was indeterminate, since Gran Colombia might first be divided into its three major sections and Peru into separate northern and southern states. But whatever the precise number, Bolívar hoped that the constitution he had been commissioned to draft for Bolivia could serve as model, in some form, for the governments to be established in each of the other member states—and presumably also the overall government of the Federation. The distinctive feature of the constitution as finally drafted was a president serving for a life term and with the right to name his successor, so that inevitably the scheme was assailed as nothing but a constitutional monarchy in republican disguise. Bolívar, who had always disliked the conventional republican constitution adopted by Colombia in 1821, considered the

Bolivian project to be the product of his mature political thinking, indeed his masterpiece.

Unfortunately for Bolívar, neither of his latest projects found wide acceptance. The Congress of Panama did meet, in June and July 1826, and though the vice president and foreign secretary he had left behind in Bogotá invited both the United States and Brazil, in violation of his express wishes, in practice it was a meeting only of Spanish American nations. (One United States delegate died on the way; another arrived late; no Brazilian even set forth.) Yet not all of the Spanish American governments sent representatives to Panama, and only Colombia ratified the resulting agreements. Hence there was no league of Spanish American nations—and neither, of course, did the Andean Federation come into being. Bolivia adopted Bolívar's constitution, with some minor changes such as deleting the provision for immediate abolition of slavery, and so did Peru, but they did not join together at that point in federal union. In Gran Colombia itself, even many of Bolívar's close supporters were skeptical of both his constitutional masterpiece and the Federation of the Andes.

Instead, internal tensions that had been incubating for some time within Colombia now reached a critical stage. In Venezuela, the fact of subordination to a central government in Bogotá had long rankled, and José Antonio Páez gave expression to this regional disaffection when he rebelled against the authorities in Bogotá—even while still professing ultimate allegiance to Bolívar—in April 1826. Venezuela's defiance turned out to be the signal that people in Ecuador had been waiting for to give vent to their own resentment, rather more clearly justified than in the case of Venezuela, over the neglect of their regional interests at the national capital; they launched no outright rebellion but in various places adopted manifestos demanding ill-defined reforms and calling on the Liberator to return from Peru to direct the process. In Bogotá itself, Vice President Santander had been managing the national executive with considerable success in Bolívar's absence, but intermittent frictions had arisen between the two men, with Bolívar complaining over Santander's failure to send him all necessary reinforcements when he wanted them and Santander suffering hurt feelings over Bolívar's apparent lack of appreciation for the efforts he actually made. Moreover, Santander and his political faction, typically composed of New Granadan liberals, felt a personal and ideological identification with the existing constitutional order that Bolívar hoped to replace by means of his Bolivian constitution or something similar. They were identified, too, with the program of generally moderate fiscal and ecclesiastical reforms that the national congress and administration had been adopting, whereas Bolívar increasingly made clear that even though he generally agreed with the objectives of the reforms, he considered them premature, thus bound to stir dissension and undermine internal stability.

When Bolívar finally returned to Gran Colombia in the latter part of 1826, he quickly pacified Venezuela by the simple expedient of granting Páez and his partisans a full pardon for their rebellion. It was a practical solution but one that offended Santander and his friends, who had been trying as best they could to uphold legality. He offended them further by continuing to lend an ear to anyone with a complaint against the existing constitution and laws and by holding out the promise of a convention for constitutional reform in technical violation of an existing provision that prohibited any such reform before the year 1831. But the Santanderistas did their part in widening the gap between president and vice president by making intemperate attacks on Bolívar in the press and by their delighted celebration of an uprising by Colombian troops still stationed in Lima against Venezuelan higher officers whom they accused of plotting to foist the Bolivian constitution on Gran Colombia. In March 1827, from Caracas where he was still settling affairs after the revolt of Páez, Bolívar broke off correspondence with Santander, and by September he had resumed personal control of the central administration, permanently displacing Santander from his role as acting chief executive.

The promised convention for constitutional reform took place at Ocaña between April and June 1828 but was so divided between the supporters of Bolívar and Santander and assorted independents that it took no action at all. Bolívar concluded that he had no alternative but to accept the dictatorship his supporters now offered him. He made clear that it was only temporary, until such time as another convention could be held to revamp the nation's institutions. It was also a relatively mild dictatorship, at least until the unsuccessful attempt on Bolívar's life in September 1828 that sparked a round of harsher repression, including the exile of Santander for alleged complicity. Bolívar sought to satisfy the demands of Venezuela and Ecuador by placing them under the direct administration of high-ranking generals—Páez in the case of Venezuela—with broad discretionary power in the local implementation of national policies. He gave the military heightened influence at all levels of government and increased independence from civilian authority. He sought favor with the church through the expedient rollback of controversial anticlerical measures, and he adopted a generally conservative approach in economic and social affairs, with the primary exception of slavery, as he tried to strengthen rather than weaken the manumission law enacted by Colombia's constituent congress in 1821.

In the short term Bolívar's dictatorship obtained at least tacit acceptance from most people. However, its conservative bent did not sit well with Venezuela, which was ideologically the most liberal part of the country, particularly when members of Bolívar's cabinet began sounding out opinion at home and abroad over the possibility that Bolívar might ultimately be succeeded by a European prince. This occurred while Bolívar himself had gone to the south of the country to deal with a brief armed conflict with Peru, but rightly or wrongly he received the blame, and it did not hurt him only in Venezuela. The Peruvian war was unpopular, too, if only for the taxes and recruitment it entailed, and though a new constitutional convention did meet, in January 1830, by then Venezuela was already preparing to go its way as a separate nation; the repressed followers of Santander were regaining confidence and returning to the fray, and with Bolívar himself visibly ailing, his leadership was increasingly ignored even by his own supporters.

After finally resigning the presidency, he departed Bogotá in May 1830 for the Caribbean, intending to go into foreign exile as San Martín had done earlier. He never got there. He died at Santa Marta on the Colombian coast in December 1830 before he had a chance to take ship but not before penning one of his most memorable lines: "He who serves a revolution ploughs the sea."

Bolívar and the Art of Government

Regardless of the exact source of Bolívar's ideas, and despite all changes in emphasis or detail, there is a remarkable consistency in his views of how Spanish America should be governed—or perhaps above all, how it should not be governed. The author whom he cited most often in support of his political thinking was Montesquieu, who in his *Spirit of the Laws* had argued so forcefully for the careful adaptation of any country's laws and institutions to its immediate geographic and cultural environment. To Bolívar this meant that his compatriots should scrupulously avoid trying to create ideal types of government ("ethereal republics," he called them) and, perhaps above all, should never yield to the temptation to copy the institutions of the United States, however successful they might appear to be in North America. As he once observed to a correspondent, he would rather see "America" (by which he meant Spanish

America) adopt the Koran than adopt the system of government of the United States, even though he did not hesitate to add that it was "the best on earth."[5] It just was not "best" for his part of the hemisphere. In effect, while Anglo-America, thanks to its distinctive historical background among other factors, had become a "singular model of political and moral virtue"—as Bolívar put it in his Angostura Address—and thus fully prepared to govern itself under a set of liberal institutions, the former Spanish colonies having suffered for three centuries under "the triple yoke of tyranny, ignorance, and vice" were not prepared for anything of the sort.

Bolívar was particularly wary of the example of federalism that was contained in the United States constitution and all too often appealed to by Latin American federalists in justification of their various efforts to concentrate power at the provincial or other regional level rather than at the center, a tendency that he considered a disastrous source of weakness in the midst of a war for national independence. Of course, his own proposal for a Federation of the Andes and the occasional references (by Bolívar himself as well as others) to his projected Spanish American league as a "federation" have at times led to terminological confusion. The federalism to which Bolívar so vehemently objected was simply that which took entire captaincies-general—or other major subdivisions of the former Spanish empire—and broke them down into groups of self-governing provinces loosely joined for matters of common interest, as in the constitution of Venezuela's First Republic. He thus blamed the collapse of the First Republic in no small part on its federalist organization. But he was sure that any flirtation with federalism would remain a threat to political and social order for years to come, and he lost few opportunities to dismiss it as a noxious example of unwise infatuation with foreign models. In that regard he was guilty of exaggeration, because the vogue of federalism in Venezuela and other parts of early Latin America represented more than a copying of the United States or other ancient or modern foreign examples. It stemmed equally from the presence of real differences of interest and identity among regions of a given country and from the sometimes bitter regional rivalries which had been only partly repressed under the outward uniformity of the colonial system. Even so, Bolívar could make his argument with plausibility because of the way in which the federalists themselves kept pointing to the stability and rapid development of the United States as a reason for establishing their own federal republics.[6]

Federalism was not the only aspect of the United States model that Bolívar considered inapplicable to Spanish America; he also felt that the legislative and judicial branches enjoyed too much independence vis-à-vis the executive. Curiously, however, Bolívar could not resist citing North American precedents in justification of the provision in his draft constitution for Bolivia that authorized the life-term president to choose his successor. Bolívar pointed out that this had in fact been happening in the United States, where each of the last few presidents had been succeeded by the secretary of state whom he himself appointed (Jefferson followed by Madison, and so forth). The argument was ingenious, even if more than a little misleading—as the ex-secretary still had to win an election and could serve only a fixed term or terms.

The appointive presidential succession was a relatively late addition to Bolívar's list of concrete recommendations for Spanish America, but there were nevertheless underlying consistencies in what he proposed as well as in what he warned against. The obverse of his constant antifederalism was naturally the demand for a strictly centralized political organization, and he was no less insistent over the years on the need for a vigorous executive if ever the disparate elements of the Spanish American population were to be transformed into proper citizens of a free republic—a task bound to be difficult under the best of conditions. For another common thread running through Bolívar's thought was his pessimistic assessment of the human material that state builders in his part of America would have to work with.

Bolívar discussed the inadequacy of his fellow Spanish Americans for assuming control of their own destinies in a number of personal letters as well as in the Jamaica Letter and Angostura Address, but nowhere does he treat the problem as comprehensively as in the latter. A large part of the problem, from his viewpoint, was the legacy of the colonial regime itself, which he painted in unremittingly negative terms. Spain had given her colonial subjects no opportunity whatsoever to practice the art of government, appointment to all significant posts being denied them; in this regard, he complained, Spain in America had outdone such oriental despotisms as China and Turkey, which at least recruited agents from among their own subjects, whereas Spain used only European Spaniards to rule the colonies. Thus reduced to a purely "passive" role, the Americans were entirely unschooled in politics and administration. In this complaint Bolívar anticipated what later became a cliché of historians and others for explaining the revolutions and related ills of postindependence Latin America, and obviously he was guilty of exaggeration. While only exceptionally did colonial-born subjects become viceroys or captains-general or occupy other high offices, they inevitably occupied most local offices and filled much of the midlevel bureaucratic apparatus. Not only that, but informally and unofficially they exerted significant influence on the decisions of Spanish-born administrators, through informal negotiation and social pressures.

Yet in Bolívar's view there was more to the problem than just the political repression and exclusion associated with the colonial regime, for another obstacle difficult to overcome was the heterogeneous and indeterminate nature of the population itself. As he declared at Angostura, "Our people are not European, nor North American, but are closer to a blend of Africa and America than an emanation from Europe, for even Spain herself lacks European identity because of her African blood, her institutions, and her character. It is impossible to say with certainty to which human family we belong. ... [T]he European has mixed with the American and the African, and the African has mixed with the Indian and with the European. All born in the womb of our common Mother, our Fathers, different in origin and blood, are foreigners, and all differ visibly in the color of their skin." In this passage Bolívar obviously was not describing the Spanish American people as the end result of a melting-pot experience, nor was he looking forward to a future of multiculturalism. Instead, he was sketching a condition of latent disunity in which it was hard even to identify the disparate elements of society. Thanks in part to the "ignorance, tyranny, and vice" of the colonial system, those elements were all too often inherently unruly, a trait which wartime experiences had only magnified; hence Bolívar's somber warning, in a letter of 1820, "I fear peace more than war."[7]

The pardos were a particular cause of concern to Bolívar, who in his correspondence expressed his fear of "African hordes"[8] and repeatedly raised the specter of "pardocracy."[9] Such comments did not arise from innate racism on Bolívar's part, for he readily accepted that racial differences were nothing more than an "accident of skin,"[10] and he consistently supported the principle of legal equality for all inhabitants regardless of that or other "accidents" of birth. Instead, what he dreaded was that the pardos might join together along racial lines to seek power for themselves as pardos, in opposition to his own officially colorblind project of liberation. As he stated in the manifesto that he issued concerning the execution of the pardo general Manuel Piar, the revolution had already offered equal rights and opportunity to all; therefore, any attempt to set one race against another was an intolerable threat to patriotic unity.

Even though Bolívar never lost sight of that pressing need for unity, and for a strong central executive to somehow bring order out of chaos and lead his compatriots on the way to political and social virtue, the details of his specific recommendations varied over time. He also marshaled a variety of historical antecedents as lessons and examples; and curiously perhaps, in view of his insistence that institutions must be molded to particular local circumstances, he seldom looked to Spanish America's own heritage—either Hispanic or Native American (or much less African). When cataloging the iniquities of Spanish rule, he did not neglect to include the injustice of the Conquest itself or the subsequent oppression of the original inhabitants, but it never occurred to him to model any of the institutions he proposed on those of the preconquest civilizations or to suggest the title of Inca (as Miranda did)[11] for an independent head of state. As for the agencies and statutes of the Spanish colonial regime, they were to be excoriated rather than adapted for republican use. The Spanish liberals, of course, looked still further back, to the parliamentary institutions of medieval Spain, which they took as precedents for the Cádiz Constitution of 1812 that they hoped would serve as an enlightened basis for peacefully reuniting the Iberian provinces and overseas territories. However, the bitterness of fighting in Venezuela and the consequent revulsion against the former mother country—which comes out so clearly in Bolívar's decree of war to the death and in his 1813 "Manifesto to the Nations of the World"—not only made it unthinkable to accept the Spanish constitution but made the Venezuelan patriots and their leader disinclined to see anything worth conserving in the Spanish heritage. Only when faced with the disappointments and frustrations of the postwar period did Bolívar come to take a more positive view of that heritage. He then began rolling back innovations that he considered to have been premature and declared to José Antonio Páez at the start of his final dictatorship that he proposed to base his actions as far as possible on "the old laws, less complicated and more sure and efficacious."[12]

In his major political texts, Bolívar displayed an impressive familiarity with both ancient and modern European history, from which he derived certain general principles and numerous concrete examples. One of the former was his conclusion that laws and institutions were less important than political and civic virtue–in spite of which, of course, he always insisted with Montesquieu that institutions must be consonant with a people's particular circumstances, and he further believed that if well designed they could encourage virtuous conduct. Among the various political systems of the ancient world, Bolívar especially admired that of the Roman Republic, and the Bolivian constitution that he considered his masterpiece was duly sprinkled with Roman-sounding senators, tribunes, and censors. But it also bore a striking resemblance to the system invented by Augustus Caesar for the early Roman Empire. The Bolivian president who served for life and chose his own successor calls to mind Augustus himself, who also served for life and, having no legitimate heir, chose Tiberius to follow him in office. Not only that, but the formal powers vested in the Bolivian president, like those of the first Roman emperor, were modest. He would, however, have at his disposal a vast fund of moral authority along with the advantage of indefinite tenure.

In his own contemporary world, Bolívar reserved the highest praise for the constitutional monarchy of Great Britain, which appeared to combine executive vigor, personal freedom, and institutional stability in just the right proportions. A telling example is his proposal to the Congress of Angostura to implant a creole version of the House of Lords, in the form of a hereditary senate for Venezuela. Bolívar stopped short, however, of suggesting at any time that Spanish America embrace monarchy per se, even of the constitutional variety. In support of this stand he cited miscellaneous lessons of ancient history, but he rested his case principally once again on an argument in the vein of Montesquieu. The very depth of Spanish America's social and ethnic divisions, which apologists for monarchy insisted could only be bridged through the reverential respect owed to a crowned head (preferably of some ancient dynasty) in Bolívar's opinion made all the more essential a cult of republican equality. Only thus would it be possible to satisfy the aspirations of so many diverse castes. There is no real evidence that he changed his mind on this matter even when, in the next-to-last year of his life, his ministers launched a feasibility study of monarchy as a possible solution to the problems of Colombia, something that Bolívar was perhaps just a little slow in disavowing.

Bolívar's critics were correct in asserting that his concept of life presidency, which in fact antedated the draft of the Bolivian constitution, was little more than a form of monarchy in republican trappings. Bolívar nevertheless insisted, not without some reason, that his proposal was an eminently liberal document. By this he chiefly meant that the branches of government were balanced in such a way as to prevent the abuse of power. Individual freedoms enjoyed protection as well, to the extent that in his draft he included not only another call for the abolition of slavery but a call for the grant of religious tolerance, which was rather more daring for the Spanish America of those years. In the last analysis, however, in his political thought Bolívar was more concerned with seeing that government properly interpreted the Rousseaunian general will than with Lockian guarantees of individual rights. His rejection of doctrinaire liberal individualism comes out most clearly, perhaps, in the opening passages of his 1828 address to the Convention of Ocaña, at which point he was already fully convinced that in Colombia liberal reforms had been carried too far. Moreover, Bolívar never advocated electoral democracy in the present-day sense. For him as for Rousseau, the general will was not a simple matter of the opinions expressed by one-half plus one of the population, and he favored both a restricted right to vote—albeit not as restricted as in Venezuela's First Republic—and holding elections as infrequently as possible. He had, finally, an obvious preference to govern always with the aid of extraordinary powers, whether by delegation from the legislative body to deal with a specific emergency or in the form of outright dictatorship. Even so, he never regarded dictatorship as a long-term solution, invariably assuming that in due course limited, constitutional government (ideally in line with his recommendations) would be restored.

Bolívar's appreciation of things British extended to the area of foreign policy, where he looked for British protection for the newly independent Latin American nations. He readily accepted that in dealing with other countries the British government was guided by national interest, but he believed that British interest in Latin America revolved around peaceful trade and investment, both of which he was prepared to welcome. He was no less prepared to welcome whatever social and cultural influences came as a by-product of such economic relations. In trade policy, it is true, he had a penchant for raising tariffs, but for fiscal reasons and not out of systematic protectionism. And as for the welcoming of investment, Bolívar set a personal example through his persistent efforts to rent and ultimately sell part of his own patrimony, the Aroa copper mines in Venezuela, to British businessmen. Similarly, when in Peru, he recommended that the Peruvian government try to sell state-owned silver mines to the British.[13]

Bolívar did not display the same degree of confidence regarding the United States. He could be as effusive as anyone in praise of George Washington, but the failure to take a more active role in support of those who were fighting to win the same freedom for Spanish America was to him more reprehensible on the part of the land of Washington than on that of Great Britain. Concrete frictions that arose with North American maritime interests as a result of Venezuelan naval warfare in the Caribbean soured Bolívar's first encounter, at Angostura, with an informal U.S. representative, Baptis Irvine. Then, too, the rapid growth and development of the United States, while exciting admiration, also raised concern, and not just because of the danger that its federal institutions would prove an irresistibly attractive example. The northern republic was simply too powerful a neighbor for comfort and too potentially expansive.

Those feelings of distrust found their extreme and today best-known expression in the letter of 1829 (to the British minister in Bogotá) in which Bolívar stated that the United States appeared "destined to plague America with miseries in the name of Freedom." He wrote those words at a time when he was under bitter attack in the North American press and from some U.S. official agents as well for his supposed betrayal of republican principles, and they were thus among other things a response to what he regarded as unwarranted hostility and interference in Latin American affairs. Some years earlier, Bolívar's latent distrust of the northern neighbor can only have reinforced his decision to omit the United States from the Inter-American system (in effect, Hispanic American system) for which he had been laying plans since the earliest stage of the independence movement. However, his primary stated reason for not inviting the United States to the Congress of Panama in 1826—the meeting that he hoped would create a permanent structure of Hispanic American collaboration—was his conviction that its people, with their distinctive history and culture, were just too different from the Spanish Americans (too "heterogeneous," he said in his May 1825 letter to Santander) for true understanding and cooperation to occur.

Bolívar justified his failure to invite Haiti to the Panama Congress, despite the crucial aid he had received from the Haitian government in time of need, on exactly the same grounds of "heterogeneity," although in this case his realistic awareness of independent Haiti's pariah status in the concert of nations no doubt entered in. For that matter, neither did Bolívar invite Brazil, even if here the omission was not on grounds of cultural-historical heterogeneity but rather because of the independent Brazilian Empire's diplomatic and dynastic ties with continental European powers hostile to the Spanish American cause. When Vice President Santander and the Colombian foreign ministry in Bogotá proceeded to invite the United States and Brazil (but not Haiti) to attend the meeting anyway, Bolívar politely acquiesced, but he could hardly have been regretful when Brazil sent no delegation and when neither of the two U. S. delegates arrived for the meeting.[14] Indeed, Pan Americanism as incarnate in the current Organization of American States is something that Bolívar quite explicitly rejected. But despite his slighting of Haiti and Brazil—and despite the failure of the Panama Congress to produce the Hispanic American league he had in mind—it is not far-fetched to claim him as a precursor of Latin American integration.

The Social and Economic Agenda

Old-fashioned historians, of whom there are many still busily writing about Bolívar, tend to pay scant attention to his economic and social measures even while praising them generically as wise and beneficent. One of the few things normally mentioned has been his opposition to slavery, in which he indeed was ahead of most of his class. His limited effectiveness would be blamed, not altogether unfairly, on the narrower vision and selfish interests of his associates. Bolívar's stand in the matter had its intellectual roots in the philosophy of the Enlightenment, but his earliest official action was the Carúpano decree of 1816, which offered immediate emancipation only to slaves who took up arms to fight for independence (and to their family members). It was several years later, in connection with the military recruitment of slaves in New Granada, that Bolívar most clearly spelled out his rationale for abolitionism. In his letter of 18 April 1820 to Santander, he emphasized the need for an additional source of military manpower but cited the teaching of Montesquieu and the example of Haiti to show the incompatibility of slavery with the existence of free government and then as clinching argument pointed to the desirability of freeing blacks so that they could suffer their proportionate share of war casualties. Of course, while the demographic factor gave some urgency to slave emancipation, Bolívar's support for abolition was not limited to potential soldiers (plus respective dependents). He repeatedly urged total and immediate eradication of slavery; he simply did not take it upon himself to put it in effect by executive decree.

Bolívar's thinking about Spanish America's Indian population was more sporadic and in the end less consistent than his views on slavery (or on the rights of free pardos). No doubt a major reason for the difference was the mere fact that in Venezuela itself the Indian population, though appreciable, was chiefly located in peripheral areas, out of sight and out of mind. Thus most of his pertinent comments on the subject and measures taken date from the years when his attention was focused on New Granada, Quito, and above all Peru. On numerous occasions he deplored the misery in which the native Americans appeared to be living, but his initial prescriptions were unremarkable, adhering to the conventional liberal approach of treating the Indians as equal citizens with the same rights and obligations as anyone else, including the right to private property that necessarily entailed the distribution of communal lands to individual Indian owners. Bolívar's support of the nineteenth-century liberal objective of making all property freely transferable was likewise evident in the articles of his Bolivian constitution abolishing both entailed estates and ecclesiastical mortmain. But as far as the Indians were concerned, during his final dictatorship Bolívar reverted to the unequal, formally paternalistic, approach of colonial legislation, placing the Indians under the care of special "protectors" yet at the same time restoring the recently suppressed Indian tribute.[15] He took the latter step in large part for fiscal reasons, but like his general reordering of Indian policy it reflected his growing conviction that the "old laws" were best, if only because people were used to them and they were accordingly easier to enforce.

Apart from his opposition to slavery, the best known of Bolívar's initiatives in social policy is his 1817 bonus decree. It was, to be sure, a political-military measure, designed to strengthen republican morale at the expense of enemy partisans whose confiscated assets were slated for distribution to patriot veterans. The Venezuelan historian and spokesman for the social-democratic Acción Democrática Party, José Luis Salcedo-Bastardo, seized on this decree as a precocious example of agrarian reformism.[16] The maldistribution of landed property was not, however, a problem that Bolívar addressed in any of his major political documents. He was more concerned with holding out the promise of some tangible reward to his followers, who formed a broad cross-section of the Venezuelan populace and among whom the llaneros, redoubtable fighters of the Orinoco plains, probably cared little about landownership—only about cattle. A good many patriot officers, to whom Bolívar's decree offered a more lucrative scale of bonuses, did make good use of the opportunity to amass ex-royalist assets. Common soldiers were more likely in the end to sell their bonus certificates to speculators.[17]

For those eager to present Bolívar as a precursor of fashionable contemporary causes, a better example would perhaps be the decree that he issued during his final dictatorship for the conservation of forest resources. We can safely imagine that it remained a dead letter in practice, yet in its intent it anticipated some of the aims of modern environmentalism. The one economic matter that consistently held his intention, in any case, was government finance, unglamorous but useful, which was not an end in itself but a means to accomplish all his political and military ends. And Bolívar's approach to fiscal policy, grounded in pressing immediate needs rather than the science of economics that was still in its infancy, was inevitably somewhat heavy-handed, as witness his repeated calls for summary execution of those who defrauded the public treasury. His eagerness to maximize treasury receipts largely explains his tendency to increase tariff rates, in spite of a sincere commitment to the opening of Spanish America to foreign trade and investment (and in spite of the fact that in reality higher rates did not necessarily yield more revenue). Toward the end of his career, the same eagerness helps explain Bolívar's restoration of Indian tribute. Nor did he by any means share the interest of doctrinaire liberals in progressive tinkering with the tax code. Bolívar was hardly surprised when one of their proud achievements, the substitution of a novel direct tax for the colonial alcabala or sales tax, produced more complaints than revenue. It was therefore one of the reforms to be rolled back in the final years of Gran Colombia.[18] Indeed, in no area was his stated preference for the "old laws," as simpler and more effective, so patent as in fiscal affairs.

Of Education and Culture

Although untouched by formal higher education, Simón Bolívar stands out among the military leaders of Latin American independence for the extent of his humanistic learning. Wherever possible, he would carry a portable minilibrary with him on campaign. As one who had met and conversed with luminaries of the world of art and letters during his visits to Europe, he valued any opportunity to engage in cultivated discourse when he encountered a person of similar tastes and breadth of knowledge; one such was the French officer Louis Peru de la Croix with whom he whiled away over a month of waiting at Bucaramanga in 1828, during the Convention of Ocaña, discussing history, literature, and philosophy in the broadest sense.[19] And when the Guayaquil poet and politician José Joaquín Olmedo sent Bolívar a copy of the ode he had written in celebration of the victory of Junín, Bolívar wrote back not only to give thanks but to make some observations (in a generally sprightly vein) on aspects of poetic style that reflected his close familiarity with ancient and modern literary classics. It is hard to image either George Washington or José de San Martín doing anything of the sort.

Like other leaders of his period, Bolívar made frequent reference in his speeches and letters to the importance of education, and unlike a good many of them, he was giving more than lip service. This was, after all, one of the prime concerns of the Moral Power that he proposed to the Congress of Angostura and that later reappeared, in altered guise, in the Chamber of Censors of his Bolivian constitution. As he went about liberating provinces, he also went issuing decrees for the establishment of schools—and for girls as well as boys, although he was not prepared to contemplate other than domestic careers for the female sex, even warning his highly capable older sister María Antonia that women should not get mixed up in political affairs.[20] For lack of resources, the practical effect of his educational measures was limited, but it should be noted that in certain cases he was prepared to devote personal assets to the cause of public instruction. The best example is his allocation of a part of the bonus voted him by the Peruvian Congress to cover the expenses of bringing the English pedagogue Joseph Lancaster to Caracas. It also appears that the draft he wrote for this purpose against the promised Peruvian bonus was not honored, since the funds had not been paid as expected, and that he ended up paying Lancaster's travel expenses from his other resources.[21]

Bolívar's sponsorship of Lancaster is one indication that in the realm of education he was more open to innovative approaches than in, for example, government tax policy. Lancaster was the proponent of the novel method of "mutual instruction" or each-one-teach-one, whereby advanced pupils were assigned to help in the instruction of other classmates and thus a single professional teacher could educate a greater number of children. And Bolívar's own original thinking comes out in his instructions for the education of his nephew Fernando Bolívar, who after studying first at Germantown Academy in Philadelphia went on to the University of Virginia.[22] Of particular interest is his recommendation that history should be taught starting with recent events and work back from there. This was in line with his own approach to history as a storehouse of lessons for the solution of contemporary problems, but it does have pedagogic advantages that not all professional historians (least of all the textbook writers) are prepared to recognize.

The one other educational text in this volume is quite different in spirit, for instead of promoting innovation of any sort, its purpose was to defend Catholic orthodoxy in Colombian higher education. Adopted during Bolívar's final dictatorship, it is his decree prohibiting the use of works by the English philosopher of utilitarianism Jeremy Bentham, and it represents at first glance a striking reversal, Bolívar having been an admirer and correspondent of Bentham, whom he met personally during his London mission in 1810.[23] To Catholic traditionalists, however, Bentham was a dangerously corrupting influence because of his attempt to devise an ethical system based on quantitative rationality without regard to revealed truth. The formal prohibition of Bentham (whose works nevertheless remained in practice readily available to the young) thus served to consolidate the support of the church and of conservative laymen for Bolívar's government, and he himself, though he no doubt agreed with Bentham on many points, could scarcely sympathize with the Englishman's call for a general revamping of Spanish American law at the very time when he was preparing to roll back reforms that may have been desirable in themselves but for which in his view his countrymen were not ready.

A somewhat comparable measure was the subsequent decree, issued as part of the general reaction that followed the September 1828 attempt on Bolívar's life, for the prohibition of secret societies. This was directed primarily against Freemasonry, something that Bolívar had briefly dabbled in, while in Paris, during his second visit to Europe. He did not retain an affiliation, although many other military and political leaders of independence became strong supporters of the lodges, as did a good many of their Spanish opponents. But whether republican or royalist, the Masons had to defy assorted papal condemnations of their movement. Bolívar, to be sure, dropped out not because of anything the popes had said but, apparently, because he found Masonic rituals hard to take seriously.[24] However, papal disapproval was reason enough for conservative clerics to fulminate constantly against Freemasonry, and the fact that the lodges attracted chiefly men who were both political liberals and anticlerical in matters of religious policy increased the intensity of that opposition. Hence the prohibition of secret societies, while ostensibly a public-order measure—and directed against people who were mostly aligned with his enemies—was also one more instance of Bolívar's courting of clerical favor during the last stage of his career.

It is easy to discern Bolívar's conscious effort to forge an alliance with the church, of which the decrees just mentioned are only two examples, but harder to categorize his personal religious beliefs or lack of belief. In his public papers he was careful to show proper respect for the church as an institution and for the symbols of Roman Catholicism, even though his references to religion tended to emphasize its potential contribution to social order rather than its spiritual values. At the same time, in private correspondence and in casual remarks attributed to him by others, Bolívar was often scathing in his attitude toward members of the clergy, which would not in itself mean that he rejected whatever beliefs the clergy strove to instill yet is quite compatible with the widespread consensus that he was throughout most of his life an agnostic freethinker.[25] Certainly he respected the rights of other men and women to think freely in matters of religious faith, as he demonstrated by his eloquent call for religious toleration in his address on the Bolivian Constitution. He did not see fit to expend political capital struggling to have that recommendation actually accepted in Bolivia, or even at home in Colombia, but neither is there any indication that he had changed his mind on the issue even when otherwise appeasing the institutional church toward the end of his life. As much as anything, and regardless of the extent to which he often felt compelled to compromise his personal beliefs for the sake of some immediate good, this one stand clearly marks him as an heir of the intellectual Enlightenment.

NOTES

1. Germán Carrera Damas, *El culto a Bolívar* (Caracas, 1969), 23, 39–41, 285.

2. Felipe Larrazábal, *La vida y correspondencia general del Libertador Simón Bolívar*, 6th ed., 2 vols. (New York, 1883), I, 5.

3. Letter to Francisco de Paula Santander, Arequipa, 20 May 1825, *Obras completas del Libertador*, 3 vols. (Havana, 1950, or Caracas, 1963[?]), II, 137.

4. The measures cited are in *Decretos del Libertador*, 3 vols. (Caracas, 1961). The same decree that declared universal suffrage in the case of the military specified that for the moment only those soldiers could vote who *did* meet the specified requirements, on the ground that a truly massive voting by the soldiery in the midst of war was just not practicable.

5. Letter to Daniel F. O'Leary, 13 September 1829, *Obras*, III, 315.

6. A particularly egregious example is Miguel de Pombo, *Constitución de los Estados Unidos de América . . . precedida de las actas de independencia y federación* (Bogotá, 1811), reprinted in Javier Ocampo López, *La independencia de los Estados Unidos de América y su proyección en Hispanoamérica: el modelo norteamericano y su repercusión en la independencia de Colombia, un estudio a través de la folletería de la independencia de Colombia* (Mexico City, 1979), 87–152.

7. Letter to Pedro Gual, 24 May 1821, *Escritos*, xx, 62.

8. Letter to Santander, 8 August 1826, *Obras*, II, 455.

9. For example, letters to Santander, 7 April 1825, and to Antonio José de

Sucre, 12 May 1826, in *Selected Writings of Bolívar*, comp. Vicente Lecuna and ed. Harold A. Bierck Jr., 2 vols. (New York, 1951), II, 490, 589.

10. Proclamation of 5 August 1817, *Escritos*, x, 333–42.

11. Francisco de Miranda, *Textos sobre la independencia* (Caracas, 1959; Biblioteca de la Academia Nacional de la Historia, 13), 67–77.

12. Letter to Páez, 30 June 1828, *Obras*, II, 905.

13. Paul Verna, *Las minas del Libertador* (Caracas, 1977); letter to Santander, 21 October 1825, *Selected Writings*, II, 545.

14. Stephen J. Randall, *Colombia and the United States: Hegemony and Interdependence* (Athens, Ga., 1992), 18–22.

15. On these and certain related measures, see my article "The Last Dictatorship: Betrayal or Consummation?" *Hispanic American Historical Review* 63 (February 1983): 90–92.

16. See esp. José Luis Salcedo-Bastardo, *Visión y revisión de Bolívar*, 7th ed. (Buenos Aires, 1966), 147–52, 154–57.

17. On the priorities of the llaneros, see Germán Carrera Damas, *Boves: aspectos socieconómicos de la guerra de independencia* (Caracas, 1972), 250. The bonus question is further discussed in Bushnell, *The Santander Regime in Gran Colombia* (Newark, Del., 1954; reprint, Westport, Conn., 1970), 275–79.

18. Bushnell, *The Santander Regime in Gran Colombia*, 81–84, 342–43. This reversal of policy was actually decreed by Vice President Santander, but he made clear that he was acting at the behest of Bolívar. Unfortunately, no systematic study of Bolívar's economic and fiscal policies exists. A useful synthesis is J. León Helguera, "Bolívar: una interpretación de su política económica en la teoría y en la práctica," *Boletín Histórico* (Caracas), 17 (May 1968): 3–18.

19. Louis Peru de la Croix, *Diario de Bucaramanga*, ed. Nicolás E. Navarro (Caracas, 1935, and numerous other editions). There is no reason to assume that the diarist always recorded accurately what Bolívar had said on a given topic, but there can be no doubt as to the remarkable breadth of topics discussed.

20. For some decrees on school foundation, see *Decretos*, I, 164–65, 300–302, 323, 354, 417–18, 420. His comment to María Antonia Bolívar is in the letter of 10 July 1826, *Obras*, II, 430.

21. Darío Guevara, "Bolívar y Lancaster," *Boletín de la Academia Nacional de la Historia* (Caracas) 51:201 (January–March 1968): 81–90.

22. Jerry W. Knudson, "A Venezuelan in Virginia," *Virginia Cavalcade* (Charlottesville) 11 (Autumn 1961): 30–35.

23. Theodora L. McKenna, "Jeremy Bentham and the Colombian Liberators," *The Americas* 34 (April 1978): 460–75.

24. Masonic authors naturally tend to exaggerate the intensity and duration of Bolívar's affiliation. The most authoritative discussion is José A. Ferrer Benimeli, "Bolívar y la masonería," *Revista de Indias* (Madrid) 43 (July–December 1983): 631–87.

25. Clerical authors naturally tend to exaggerate the extent of Bolívar's religious belief at any stage of his career, and anticlericals tend to minimize or flatly deny it. Easily the best treatment of the topic is Alberto Gutiérrez, *La iglesia que entendió el Libertador Simón Bolívar* (Bogotá, 1981), which is notably balanced, whether because or in spite of its author's membership in the Jesuit order.

I

The Major Political Statements

The Cartagena Manifesto: Memorial Addressed to the Citizens of New Granada by a Citizen from Caracas

Cartagena of the Indies, 15 December 1812

My purpose in writing this memorial is to spare New Granada the fate of Venezuela and to redeem Venezuela from the affliction it now suffers.[1] Please deign, fellow citizens, to accept it with indulgence out of respect for such admirable intentions.

I am, Granadans, a son of unhappy Caracas who, miraculously escaped from amid her physical and political ruins and ever faithful to the just and liberal system proclaimed by my country, now follow the banners of independence fluttering so gloriously in these States.

Allow me, inspired by a patriotic zeal that emboldens me to address you, to sketch for you the causes that led Venezuela to her destruction, and to flatter myself that the terrible and exemplary lessons proffered by that extinct Republic will persuade America to improve her own conduct, correcting the failures of unity, strength, and vigor manifest in her several governments.

The most grievous error committed by Venezuela as she entered the political arena was undoubtedly her fatal adoption of the governing ideal of tolerance, an ideal immediately rejected as weak and ineffective by everyone of good sense, yet tenaciously maintained right up to the end with unparalleled blindness.

The first signs our government gave of its folly were manifested when it refused to acknowledge the legitimacy of the subject city of Coro and declared it insurgent and treated it as a hostile power.

Instead of subjugating that defenseless city, which was ready to surrender as soon as our maritime forces came into view, the Supreme Junta allowed it to build up its defenses and adopt an attitude of such defiance that it later managed to humble the entire federation, almost as easily as we might initially have humbled it. The operating principle of our Junta was apparently the mistaken notion of human nature that restrains any government from liberating by force any town too stupid to see the value of its rights.

The operating codes our leaders consulted weren't those they might have learned from any practical science of governance, but those formulated by certain worthy visionaries who, conceiving some ethereal republic, sought to achieve political perfection on the presumption of the perfectibility of the human species. So we ended up with philosophers for generals, philanthropy for legislation, dialectics for tactics, and sophists for soldiers. This subversion of principles and affairs shook the social order to its core, and naturally enough the State rushed with giant steps toward universal dissolution, which was not long in coming.

This led to the notion of impunity for crimes against the State committed so audaciously by malcontents, and particularly by our born, implacable enemies, the European Spaniards, who remained in our country for the malicious purpose of provoking endless unrest and fomenting as many conspiracies as our judges allowed, always pardoning them, even when their plots were of such magnitude as to threaten the health of the nation.

The doctrine behind this conduct had its origin in the philanthropic maxims of certain writers who defend the idea that no one has the right to take the life of a human being, even one who has committed the crime of treason against the State.

Shielded by this pious doctrine, each conspiracy was followed by a pardon, and each pardon by another conspiracy, subsequently pardoned, because, you know, liberal governments feel obliged to distinguish themselves by the quality of mercy. But this is a criminal mercy that contributed more than anything else to the destruction of the machine we had not yet finished building!

This was the source of the determined opposition to the practice of calling up veteran troops, disciplined and capable of appearing on the field of battle, fully trained and ready to defend freedom with success and glory. Instead, countless poorly disciplined militias were established, which had the effect not only of exhausting the national treasury with exorbitant salaries but also of destroying agriculture, tearing the farm workers away from their farms, and turning the government into an object of hatred, because it forced them to take up arms and abandon their families.

Republics, we are told by our statesmen, do not require salaried soldiers to maintain their freedom. Every citizen will become a soldier when the enemy attacks. Greece, Rome, Venice, Genoa, Switzerland, Holland, and recently North America defeated their enemies without the help of mercenary troops, who are ever ready to uphold despotism and subjugate their fellow citizens.

The simple-minded were easily taken in by these impolitic and imprecise arguments, but they did not fool the prudent, who were well aware of the immense difference existing between nations, times, and the customs of those republics and ours. It is true that they did not pay for standing armies, but that was because in antiquity there were none, and they entrusted their salvation and the glory of the State entirely to their political virtues, Spartan habits, and military character, qualities we are far from possessing. With regard to modern republics that have thrown off the yoke of their tyrants, it is no secret that they did so by maintaining a strong enough veteran contingent to guarantee their security. One exception to this rule is North America: being at peace with the rest of the world and surrounded by oceans, they saw no need in recent years to maintain an army of veteran troops to defend their borders and towns.

Venezuela learned the error of its policy the hard way: the militiamen, marching against the enemy with no training in the use of their weapons and unaccustomed to discipline and obedience, were routed at the very outset of this last campaign, despite the heroic and extraordinary efforts of the officers to spur them on to victory. This produced a mood of general discouragement in both soldiers and officers, as it is a military truism that only seasoned armies are capable of overcoming the initial setbacks in a campaign. The novice soldier thinks all is lost if he suffers a defeat, because experience has not yet shown him that courage, skill, and persistence can make up for bad fortune.

The subdivision of the Province of Caracas, which was planned, discussed, and sanctioned by the federal Congress, aroused and fomented an implacable rivalry in the smaller cities and towns against the capital, which was, according to members of Congress, anxious to gain power and influence in their districts, "the tyrant of cities and leech of the state."[2] This is how the flames of civil insurrection were fanned in Valencia and never extinguished even with the defeat of that city but, still burning secretly, spread from neighboring towns to Coro and Maracaibo where they took on greater intensity and thus facilitated the entry of the Spaniards, bringing about the fall of Venezuela.

The waste of public revenues on frivolous and harmful items and in particular, salaries for hordes of office workers, secretaries, judges, magistrates, and local and federal legislators, dealt a mortal blow to the Republic, because it was forced to turn to the dangerous expedient of printing paper money, with no guarantee other than the power and anticipated revenues of the confederation. This new money seemed to most a clear violation of the rights of property, because they imagined themselves stripped of objects of intrinsic value in exchange for others whose value was uncertain or even illusory. The paper money exacerbated the discontent of the stolid citizens of the interior, who called on the commandant of the Spanish troops to come and liberate them from a currency they regarded as more monstrous than slavery.

But what most weakened the government of Venezuela was the federalist structure it adopted, embodying the exaggerated notion of the rights of man. By stipulating that each man should rule himself, this idea undermines social pacts and constitutes nations in a state of anarchy. Such was the true state of the confederation. Each province governed itself independently, and following this example, each city claimed equal privilege, citing the practice of the provinces and the theory that all men and all peoples have the right to institute whatever form of government they choose.

The federal system, although it is the most perfect and the most suitable for guaranteeing human happiness in society, is, notwithstanding, the form most inimical to the interests of our emerging states. Generally speaking, our fellow citizens are not yet ready to take on the full and independent exercise of their rights, because they lack the political virtues marking the true citizen of a republic. Such virtues are impossible to attain in absolutist governments, where there is no training in the rights or duties of citizenship.

On the other hand, is there a country anywhere, no matter how sensible and republican it is, capable of ruling itself during times of internal unrest and external warfare by a system as complicated and weak as a federalist government? It would not be possible to maintain order during the tumult of battle and internal factionalism. The government must necessarily adjust itself, so to speak, to the context of the times, men, and circumstances in which it operates. If these are prosperous and serene, it has to be gentle and protective, but if they are calamitous and turbulent, it has to be severe and armed with a strength equal to the dangers, without regard for laws or constitutions until such time as happiness and peace are restored.

Caracas had to suffer greatly because of flaws in the confederation, which far from being helpful exhausted her revenues and military supplies. When danger threatened, it abandoned the city to her own devices, without providing even minimal military support. Moreover, it exacerbated her problems by encouraging competition between the federal and the local authority, which allowed the enemy to reach the very heart of the State and occupy a large sector of the province before there was time to resolve the question of which troops, federal or provincial, should drive them back. This fatal dispute produced a delay that had terrible consequences for our forces, which were defeated in San Carlos before the reinforcements needed for victory arrived.

I am of the opinion that until we centralize our American governments, our enemies will gain irreversible advantages. We will be inevitably embroiled in the horrors of civil dissension and ingloriously defeated by that handful of bandits infesting our territories.

The popular elections conducted by the rustic inhabitants of the countryside and by the intriguers living in the cities pose an additional obstacle to the practice of federation among us, because the former are so ignorant that they vote mechanically while the latter are so ambitious that they turn everything into factions. Therefore, we never experienced a free, correct election in Venezuela, so that the government ended up in the hands of men who were incompetent, corrupt, or uncommitted to the cause of independence. The party spirit prevailed in all matters, causing more chaos than the events themselves. Our division, not the Spanish forces, reduced us to slavery.

It is true that the earthquake of 26 March was as devastating physically as it was spiritually and can fairly be said to have been the immediate cause of Venezuela's ruin, but this catastrophe would not have produced such fatal effects if Caracas had been governed by a single authority that could have quickly and vigorously set about repairing the destruction, without the complications and conflicts that slowed down the recovery in the provinces, exacerbating the harm until it was incurable.

If instead of a languid and untenable confederation Caracas had established a simple government as required by her political and military situation, you would still exist today, Venezuela, and would be enjoying your freedom!

Following the earthquake, the ecclesiastical influence was a considerable factor in the insurrection of the smaller towns and cities and in the introduction of the enemy into the country, abusing the sanctity of its ministry most sacrilegiously in favor of those fomenting civil war. Still, in our naivete we have to confess that these treacherous priests were encouraged to commit the execrable crimes they have been accused of because impunity for crimes was absolute, a situation scandalously abetted by the Congress. This travesty of justice reached such a height that after the insurrection of the city of Valencia, whose pacification cost nearly a thousand lives, not a single rebel was made to answer to the law; all of them left with their lives intact and most of them with their property unconfiscated.

From the foregoing, it is clear that among the causes leading to the fall of Venezuela, first was the nature of her constitution, which was, I repeat, as inimical to her interests as it was favorable to those of her enemies. Second was the spirit of misanthropy that took hold of our governors. Third was the opposition to the establishment of a standing army that could have saved the Republic and warded off the blows dealt by the Spaniards. Fourth was the earthquake accompanied by the fanaticism that gave such dire interpretations to this event. Finally, there were the internal factions that were in reality the mortal poison that pushed the country into her grave.

These examples of errors and misfortunes are not void of value for the peoples of South America who aspire to freedom and independence.

New Granada has witnessed the collapse of Venezuela; in consequence it ought to avoid the reefs that destroyed her. To this end I present as an indispensable measure for the security of New Granada the reconquest of Caracas. On the surface this project will seem fruitless, costly, and perhaps impracticable, but when we examine it deeply, carefully, and with foresight, it is impossible to ignore its necessity and to neglect carrying it out, once we understand why.

The first consideration in favor of this operation is the origin of the destruction of Caracas, which was precisely the disdain with which she regarded the existence of an enemy that seemed inconsequential, but not when regarded in its true light.

Certainly, Coro could never have competed with Caracas in terms of her intrinsic power, but since in the order of human vicissitudes it is not always the greater physical mass but rather the superiority of moral force that determines political balance, the government of Venezuela should not have refrained from extirpating an enemy that despite its apparent weakness nonetheless had the advantage of support from the following sources: the province of Maracaibo, including all those subservient to the [Council of] Regency; gold and the cooperation of our eternal enemies the Europeans who live among us; the clerical party, ever addicted to its master and crony, despotism; and above all, the unwavering support of every ignorant and superstitious resident of our states. So all it took to dismantle the machinery of state was for one treasonous official to summon the enemy, after which all the exemplary and patriotic efforts performed by the defenders of Caracas could not prevent the fall of an edifice already toppling from the blow it received from a single man.

Applying the example of Venezuela to New Granada, and expressing it algebraically, we could say that Coro is to Caracas what Caracas is to all America. The danger that threatens this country is related to this formula, because given Spain's control over the territory of Venezuela, she can easily commandeer men, supplies, and munitions enabling her, under the direction of officers seasoned in battle against the masters of war, the French, to penetrate from the provinces of Barinas and Maracaibo to the very tip of South America.

Spain has a great number of general officers, ambitious and bold, accustomed to danger and privation, who would love to come here and seek an empire to replace the one she just lost.[3]

It is quite likely that with the decline of fortunes in the Peninsula there will be a prodigious emigration of men of all kinds, and in particular droves of cardinals, archbishops, bishops, canons, and revolutionary clergymen capable of subverting not only our tender and hapless states but of enmeshing the entire New World in frightful anarchy. The religious influence, the empire of civil and military power, and all the privileges and prestige they can use to seduce the human spirit will be just that many more instruments available to them in their subjugation of these territories.

Nothing can stop this emigration from Spain. It is likely that England will facilitate the exodus of a group whose departure will weaken the strength of Bonaparte in Spain and strengthen and stabilize their own power in America. France will not be able to prevent this; neither will North America; and neither will we, because since none of our countries possesses a respectable navy, our efforts will be in vain.

These fugitives will no doubt receive a warm welcome in the ports of Venezuela, since they will be coming to reinforce the oppressors of that country and to undertake the conquest of the independent States.

They will raise fifteen or twenty thousand men who will be quickly trained by the generals, officers, sergeants, corporals, and veteran soldiers. This army will be followed by an even more terrible host of ministers, ambassadors, advisors, magistrates, the entire ecclesiastical hierarchy, and the grandees of Spain, whose profession is fraud and intrigue, and these will be bedecked with ostentatious titles to dazzle the multitudes. This host, spreading like locusts, will swamp everything, pulling up the seeds and roots of the tree of freedom of Colombia.[4] The soldiers will assault us on the fields of battle, and the latter, from their offices, will wage war on us with the instruments of seduction and fanaticism.

Therefore, we have no other recourse to guard against these calamities but to quickly pacify our rebellious provinces, and then to turn our arms against the enemy and in the process prepare a body of soldiers and officers worthy of calling themselves the army of the nation.

Everything conspires to make us adopt this measure. Without mentioning the urgent necessity of bolting our doors against the enemy, there are other equally powerful reasons for taking the offensive, so that to fail to do so would be an inexcusable military and political mistake. We have been invaded and are thereby obliged to drive the enemy back across our borders. In addition, it is a principle of the art of war that defensive warfare is harmful and ruinous to the country conducting it, since it brings damage with no hope of compensation, whereas hostilities in enemy territory are always advantageous because of the good that results from harm done to the enemy. Therefore, under no circumstances should we consent to go on the defensive.

We should consider as well the current state of the enemy, which is in a very vulnerable position, since most of their creole troops have deserted just when they need to defend Caracas, Puerto Cabello, La Guaira, Barcelona, Cumaná, and Margarita, where they keep their supplies. They dare not abandon these patriot cities for fear of a general insurrection as soon as they leave. So it is not impossible that our troops could march all the way to the gates of Caracas without a battle.

Another advantage is that as soon as we show up in Venezuela, thousands of brave patriots who are anxiously awaiting our arrival to help them shake off the yoke of their tyrants will join their forces to ours in defense of freedom.

The nature of the present campaign gives us the opportunity of reaching Maracaibo through Santa Marta, and Barinas through Cúcuta.

Let us take advantage, then, of such a propitious moment; do not let the reinforcements that could arrive from Spain at any moment totally change the strategic balance; do not let us lose, perhaps forever, the happy opportunity to assure the fortune of these States.

The honor of New Granada absolutely demands that we teach these audacious invaders a lesson, pursuing them to their last strongholds. Since our own glory requires that we undertake the campaign against Venezuela, to liberate the cradle of Colombian independence, the martyrs and worthy people of Caracas, whose cries are addressed only to their beloved compatriots, the Granadans, whom they await with mortal impatience, as their redeemers, let us march forth to break the chains of those victims groaning in dungeons, still awaiting salvation from us. Do not betray their trust; do not be deaf to the pleas of our brothers. Rush forth to avenge death, to give life to the dying, succor to the oppressed, and freedom to all.

The Jamaica Letter: Response from a South American to a Gentleman from This Island

Kingston, 6 September 1815

I hasten to reply to the letter of 29 August, which you [Henry Cullen] honored me by writing and which I received with the greatest satisfaction.[5]

Duly sensitive to the concern you expressed for the fortunes of my country and your distress over the torments she has suffered from the moment of the discovery until the ravages most recently afflicted on her by the Spaniards, I am nonetheless troubled by the obligation I feel to respond to your sympathetic questions concerning the most important aspects of American politics. I find myself torn between the desire to satisfy the trust you place in me and the difficulty of doing so, as much for lack of documents and books as for my limited knowledge about such an immense, varied, and mysterious land as the New World.

In my opinion it is impossible to answer the questions you honored me by asking. Baron von Humboldt himself, with his vast theoretical and practical knowledge, could scarcely do so with exactitude, because although some statistical and historical information about America is known, I dare say that most is shrouded in darkness. Consequently, one can only offer imprecise conjectures, especially concerning future successes and the true plans of the Americans. Because of our physical geography, the vicissitudes of war, and the unpredictable effects of politics, we are susceptible to the same uncertainties marking the history of the other nations.

As I feel obliged to address the concerns of your kind and well-meaning letter, I am inspired to send these lines to you, in which you will find not the brilliant ideas you hope for but merely the candid expression of my thoughts.

"Three centuries ago," you write, "marked the beginning of the atrocities committed by the Spaniards in the vast hemisphere of Columbus." Atrocities discounted as fables by contemporary historians, simply because they seem to transcend the limits of human perversity. Modern critics would never have accepted such horrors as true had they not been verified by an endless stream of texts documenting the events. The philanthropic bishop of Chiapas, the apostle of America, [Bartolomé de] Las Casas, has bequeathed to posterity a brief account of them, extracted from the summaries of the indictments brought against the conquistadores in Seville, with testimony by every respectable person living in the New World at the time, and with the detailed records of the accusations the tyrants leveled at each other, all of this documented by the most sublime historians of the period. All impartial accounts support the integrity and passion for truth of that friend of humanity, who so fervently and forcefully denounced before his own government and contemporaries the most depraved acts of that bloodfest.

How deeply grateful I am to read the passage from your letter where you write, "May the good fortune experienced at that time by the Spanish armies now favor the armies of their enemies, the terribly oppressed South Americans!" I take this wish as a prediction, if justice has any part in the conflicts between men. Success will crown our efforts because the destiny of America is irrevocably fixed; the tie that bound her to Spain is severed, for it was nothing but an illusion binding together the two sides of that vast monarchy. What formerly united them now separates them. The hatred we feel for the Peninsula is greater than the sea separating us from it; it would be easier to bring the two continents together than to reconcile the spirits and minds of the two countries. The habit of obedience, a commerce of shared interests, knowledge, and religion; mutual goodwill; a tender concern for the birthland and glory of our ancestors; in brief, everything that constituted our hopes came to us from Spain. This was the source of a principle of adhesion that seemed eternal, even though the behavior of our rulers undermined that sympathy, or to put it more accurately, that closeness imposed on us by rule of force. Today, the opposite is true: death, dishonor, everything harmful threatens us and makes us fearful. That wicked stepmother is the source of all our suffering. The veil has been rent, and now we can see the light; now she wants to return us to darkness. The chains have been broken, we've been liberated, and now our enemies want to make us slaves. This is why America fights with such defiance, and it would be rare should such desperate intensity not bring victory in its wake.

Just because our successes have been partial and intermittent is no reason to doubt our fortune. In some places the independents win victories, while in others the tyrants seem to be gaining ground. But what is the final outcome? Is not the entire New World stirred to action and armed for defense? If we look around, we observe a simultaneous struggle throughout this hemisphere.

The warlike state of the provinces of the River Plate region has purged their own territory and extended their victories to upper Peru, frightening Arequipa and making the royalists of Lima nervous. Almost a million inhabitants are celebrating their freedom there.

The kingdom of Chile, with its 800,000 souls, is resisting the enemies who seek to dominate it; they seek in vain, because those who previously stopped the Spaniards in their tracks, the free and indomitable Araucanians, are now their neighbors and fellow patriots. Their sublime example is sufficient to prove to them that a people who love their independence will end up winning it.

The Viceroyalty of Peru, whose population exceeds a million and a half inhabitants, is without a doubt the most submissive, having been subjected to the greatest sacrifices for the royal cause; yet even though accounts concerning that portion of America have been discouraging, even there unrest prevails, and the royalists have been unable to withstand the growing threat to most of their provinces.

New Granada, which is so to speak the heart of America, now obeys a general government, excepting Quito, where Spain manages with great difficulty to contain a hostile population strongly devoted to the cause of their country, and excepting also the provinces of Panama and Santa Marta, which sorrowfully endure the tyranny of their rulers. Two and a half million inhabitants now defend that territory against the Spanish army commanded by General [Pablo] Morillo, who will in all likelihood be turned back at the impregnable fortress of Cartagena. But even if he were to capture it, he would suffer great losses and would then lack sufficient forces to subjugate the disciplined and courageous inhabitants of the interior.

As for unfortunate, heroic Venezuela, events there have been so sudden, and the devastation so extreme, that she has been reduced to utter poverty and frightful desolation, though formerly she was one of the most beautiful countries, one of the glories of America. Her tyrants rule over a desert, oppressing only a few sad survivors who, having escaped death, live a precarious existence. A few women, children, and old men are the only ones left. Most of her men perished rather than become slaves, and those who still live fight on furiously in the countryside and villages of the interior, determined to die or drive back into the sea those savages insatiable for blood and crime and who rival the first monsters who obliterated the primitive tribes of America. Nearly a million people once lived in Venezuela, and I can say without exaggeration that a fourth of them have been sacrificed by the terrain, the sword, hunger, plague, and homeless wandering. Except for the earthquake, all of this is the result of war.

Baron von Humboldt informs us, accurately it would seem, that in 1808 there were 7,800,000 people living in New Spain, if we include Guatemala.[6] Since that time, the insurrection that has swept through almost all those provinces has reduced those numbers substantially; more than a million men have died, as you will see in the report made by Mr. Walton, who describes in detail the bloody crimes committed in that wealthy empire.[7] There the struggle is perpetuated by the sacrifice of humans and every other species, for the Spaniards spare no effort to subjugate those who had the misfortune of having been born on that soil, which seems destined to be drenched with the blood of its children. Despite all this, the Mexicans will be free because they have embraced the party of the country and resolved to avenge their ancestors or follow them to the grave. Now they can say with Raynal, the time has come, at last, to repay the Spaniards torment for torment and to drown that race of exterminators in their own blood or in the sea.[8]

The islands of Puerto Rico and Cuba, which combined make up a population of between seven and eight hundred thousand souls, are the lands most tranquilly possessed by the Spaniards, because they have no contact with the independents. But are those island dwellers not Americans? Are they not abused? Do they not seek their own good?

This portrait represents a military zone of 2,000 leagues of longitude and 900 leagues of latitude at its widest extension, in which sixteen million Americans defend their rights or live oppressed by the Spanish nation which, though once the vastest empire on earth, is now reduced to remnants that can neither dominate the new hemisphere nor even maintain control of the old. And civilized Europe, merchant, lover of liberty, will she allow a decrepit serpent to devour the most beautiful part of the globe out of pure venomous rage? What? Is Europe deaf to the clamor of her own interests? Has she no eyes to see justice? Has she become inured to the suffering of others to be this insensitive? The more I think about these questions, the more bewildered I become. I almost believe that Europe would prefer for America to simply disappear. But this is impossible, because Europe isn't just Spain.

Ah, the madness of our enemy, to want to conquer America once again, without a navy, with no money in the treasury, almost without any soldiers! The few she has are scarcely enough to keep her own people in a state of forced obedience and to defend herself against her neighbors. Besides, is there any way that this nation could control the commerce of half the world without a manufacturing base, with no productivity from the land, with no art, no sciences, no clear policy? Even if such a mad project were realized, and even supposing that they managed to pacify their empire, would not the children of today's Americans, allied with the children of their European conquerors, within a single generation, feel a resurgence of the same patriotic aspirations for which they now struggle and die?

Europe could do Spain a favor by dissuading her from this reckless course; she would at the very least avoid the waste of funds and the shedding of blood, so that by focusing on her own immediate interests she could begin to rebuild her prosperity and power on foundations far more solid than these uncertain conquests, precarious commercial enterprises, and violent pillaging in lands that are remote, hostile, and powerful. Europe herself, with an eye to rational foreign relations, should have prepared and carried out the project of American independence, not only because world equilibrium demands it but because this is the legitimate and sure way to acquire overseas markets. Europe, unafflicted by the violent passions of vengeance, ambition, and greed motivating Spain, would have been fully justified by reasons of fairness and enlightenment to proceed on this course dictated by her own best interests.

There is unanimous agreement in this regard among all the writers who have treated the topic. Consequently, we were justified in expecting all civilized nations to rush to our aid, helping us achieve a goal whose advantages are mutual to both hemispheres. Never were reasonable hopes so frustrated! Not only the Europeans but even our brothers to the north stood apart as idle spectators of this struggle, which is in essence the most just and in outcome the most beautiful and important of any ever undertaken in ancient or modern times. Truly, is there any way to calculate the transcendent effects of freedom for Columbus's hemisphere?

You state that Bonaparte's "felonious seizure of Carlos IV and Fernando VII, kings of this nation which three centuries earlier treacherously imprisoned two monarchs of South America, is quite clearly an act of divine retribution, as well as proof that God supports the just cause of the Americans and will grant them their independence."

I believe you are alluding to Montezuma, the monarch of Mexico, captured and killed by Cortez according to Herrera, though Solís says the Mexican people killed him,[9] and Atahualpa, the Inca of Peru, destroyed by Francisco Pizarro and Diego de Almagro. However, there is such a difference between the fortunes of the Spanish kings and the American kings that no comparison is valid; the first were treated with dignity, allowed to live, and ultimately restored to freedom and power, while the latter suffered unimaginable torture and shameful abuse. If Cuauhtemoc, Montezuma's successor, was treated as emperor and crowned, it was out of ridicule, not respect, a way of mocking him before torturing him. Similar abuse befell Catzontzin, king of Michoacán, as well as the Zipa of Bogotá, and innumerable toquis, imas, zipas, ulmenes, caciques, and other Indian dignitaries who succumbed to Spanish power. The case of Fernando VII is comparable to what happened in Chile in 1535 to the ulmen of Copiapó, who ruled that region at that time. The Spaniard Almagro pretended, as did Bonaparte, to support the claim of the legitimate sovereign, and therefore he summoned the usurper, which was Fernando's position in Spain; pretending to restore the legitimate ruler to his estates, he ended up imprisoning and burning the poor ulmen alive, without even allowing him to speak in his own defense. This parallels the example of Fernando VII and his usurper. The European kings only suffer exile; the ulmen of Chile loses his life atrociously.[10]

"After several months," you add, "I have thought much about the situation of the Americans and their hopes for the future. I take a keen interest in what happens there, but I lack much information related to their current circumstances and regarding their aspirations. I greatly desire to know the political situation of each province, as well as the approximate population, and whether they prefer republics or monarchies and whether they will establish a great republic or a great monarchy. I will greatly appreciate any information you can provide relevant to these matters or sources I can consult."

Generous souls are ever interested in the lot of a people who strive to recover the rights with which the Creator, or nature, has endowed them, and one would have to be in the grip of error or passion to reject such a noble sentiment. You have invested serious thought and interest in my country, and this act of benevolence inspires my most vivid appreciation.

My estimate of the population is based on approximate calculation, which a thousand circumstances render erroneous and whose inexactitude is not easy to remedy, because most of the inhabitants live in rustic and sometimes impermanent dwellings, as they are farmers, shepherds, nomads, lost in the middle of vast, thick forests, solitary plains, often isolated by lakes and torrential rivers. Who could come up with complete and accurate statistical data for such regions? Moreover, the taxes demanded of the natives, the painful experiences of the slaves, the obligation of offering first fruits, tithes, and other tributes demanded of farmers, as well as other circumstances, lead many wretched Americans to avoid their homes. Not to mention the genocide that has already decimated the population and frightened even more into hiding. Thus, the difficulties are insuperable and the census will likely include only half the true count.

It is even more difficult to predict the future lot of the New World, or to make definitive statements about its politics, or to make prophecies about the form of government it will adopt. Any idea relative to the future of this land seems to me to be purely speculative. Could anyone have foreseen, when the human race was in its infancy, besieged by so much uncertainty, ignorance, and error, what particular regime it would embrace for its own survival? Who would have dared predict that one nation would be a republic or another a monarchy, that this one would be unimportant, that one great? In my opinion, this is the image of our situation. We are a small segment of the human race; we possess a world apart, surrounded by vast seas, new in almost every art and science, though to some extent old in the practices of civil society. I consider the current state of America similar to the circumstances surrounding the fall of the Roman Empire, when each breakaway province formed a political system suitable to its interests and situation or allied itself to the particular ambitions of a few leaders, families, or corporations. There is, though, this notable difference, that those dispersed members reestablished their former nations with the changes demanded by circumstances or events, while we, who preserve only the barest vestige of what we were formerly, and who are moreover neither Indians nor Europeans, but a race halfway between the legitimate owners of the land and the Spanish usurpers—in short, being Americans by birth and endowed with rights from Europe—find ourselves forced to defend these rights against the natives while maintaining our position in the land against the intrusion of the invaders. Thus, we find ourselves in the most extraordinary and complicated situation. Even though it smacks of divination to predict the outcome of the political path America is following, I venture to offer some conjectures, which of course I characterize as arbitrary guesses dictated by rational desire, not by any process of probable reasoning.

The posture of those who dwell in the American hemisphere has been over the centuries purely passive. We were at a level even lower than servitude, and by that very reason hindered from elevating ourselves to the enjoyment of freedom. Allow me to offer these considerations to place the question in context. Slave states are identified as such by virtue of their constitution or the abuse of it. People are slaves when the government, by its essence or through its vices, tramples and usurps the rights of the citizen or subject. Applying these principles, we will find that America was not only deprived of its freedom but deprived as well of the opportunity to practice its own active tyranny. Let me explain what I mean. In absolute regimes, no limits are acknowledged in the exercise of governmental powers: The will of the great sultan, khan, bey, and other despots is the supreme law, and this is executed almost arbitrarily by the lesser pashas, khans, and satraps of Turkey and Persia, who have organized a system of oppression in which subordinates participate according to the authority entrusted to them. They are in charge of the civil, military, and political administration as well as the treasury and the religion. But there is this difference: The rulers of Isfahan are, after all, Persians; the viziers of the Grand Vizier are Turks; the sultans of Tartary are Tartars. China does not seek out military commanders and judges from the country of Ghengis Khan, who conquered her, even though the present-day Chinese are direct descendants of those subjugated by the ancestors of the present-day Tartars.

How different it was in our case. From the beginning we were plagued by a practice that in addition to depriving us of the rights to which we were entitled left us in a kind of permanent infancy with respect to public affairs. If we had even been allowed to manage the domestic aspects of our internal administration, we would understand the processes and mechanisms of public affairs; then we would enjoy the personal esteem in the eyes of the public that derives from a certain automatic respect so necessary to maintain during revolutions. This is why I said that we were deprived of an active tyranny, since we were not allowed to practice those functions.

The Americans, within the Spanish system still in force, and perhaps now more than ever, occupy no other place in society than that of servants suited for work or, at best, that of simple consumers, and even this role is limited by appalling restrictions: for instance, the prohibition against the cultivation of European crops or the sale of products monopolized by the king, the restriction against the construction of factories that don't even exist on the peninsula, exclusive privileges for engaging in commerce even of items that are basic necessities, the barriers between American provinces, preventing them from establishing contact, or communicating, or doing business with one another. In short, would you like to know the extent of our destiny? Fields for the cultivation of indigo, grain, coffee, sugar cane, cacao, and cotton, empty prairies for raising cattle, wilderness for hunting ferocious beasts, the bowels of the earth for excavating gold that will never satisfy the lust of that greedy nation.

So negative was our situation that I can find no other like it in any other civilized society, no matter how much I peruse the succession of epochs and political systems of all nations. To expect that a land so abundantly endowed, so extensive, rich, and populous should remain merely passive, is this not an outrage and a violation of the rights of humanity?

We were, as I just explained, lost, or worse, absent from the universe in all things relative to the science of government and the administration of the state. We were never viceroys, never governors, except in extraordinary circumstances; hardly ever bishops or archbishops; never diplomats; soldiers, only in lower ranks; nobles, but without royal privileges. In short, we were never leaders, never financiers, hardly even merchants—all in direct contravention of our institutions.

The emperor Charles V entered into a pact with the discoverers, conquerors, and settlers of America, which is, according to Guerra,[11] our social contract. The monarchs of Spain entered into a solemn contract with them, stipulating that they performed these acts at their own expense and risk, without any cost to the royal treasury, and in turn acknowledging them to be lords of the land, authorized to organize the administration and function as appellate court, with other exemptions and privileges too numerous to mention. The king pledged never to alienate the American provinces, since he held no other jurisdiction than that of supreme dominion, granting a kind of feudal ownership to the conquerors and their descendants. At the same time, there exist express laws exclusively favoring those born of Spanish parents in the new land in matters of civil and ecclesiastical employment and regarding collection of taxes. Thus, in obvious violation of the laws and subsequent agreements, those native-born Spaniards have been stripped of the constitutional authority granted them in the code.

From all that I have related, the obvious conclusion is that America was not ready to break free from the metropolis, as happened so suddenly, because of the effects of the unlawful concessions at Bayonne, and because of the vicious war which the Regency declared against us, contrary to all right, lacking not only in justice but also in legitimacy.

Concerning the nature of the Spanish governments, their threatening and hostile decrees, and the entire course of their desperate conduct, there are articles of the greatest merit in the newspaper *El Español*, written by Mr. Blanco, and since this aspect of our history is very well covered, I will simply mention it in passing. [12]

The Americans have made their debut on the world stage suddenly and without prior knowledge or, to make matters worse, experience in public affairs, having to enact the eminent roles of legislators, magistrates, ministers of the treasury, diplomats, generals, and all the other supreme and subordinate authorities that make up the hierarchy of a well-organized state.

When the French eagles swept over the peninsula, crushing every fragile government until they were stopped at the walls of Cádiz, we were left orphaned. Previously we had been delivered up to the mercy of a foreign usurper; then, flattered by the idea of justice we thought we deserved, and with these naïve hopes ever thwarted, finally, unsure of our future destiny and threatened by anarchy for lack of a legitimate, just, and liberal government, we threw ourselves headlong into the chaos of revolution. Our first impulse was to provide for domestic security, against the enemies nestled within. Then we looked to guarantee security against foreign enemies. Authorities were established to replace those we had just deposed, charged with directing the course of our revolution and with taking advantage of the propitious circumstance that would make it possible to set up a constitutional government worthy of the present century and adequate to our situation.

All the new governments started out by establishing popular juntas. These immediately formulated procedures for the convocation of congresses that produced important changes. Venezuela set up a democratic federation based on a declaration of the rights of man, maintaining the balance of powers, and writing general laws favoring civil liberty, freedom of the press, and so forth; finally an independent government was formed. New Granada modeled itself on the political institutions and the many reforms established in Venezuela, postulating as the fundamental basis of its constitution the most exaggerated system of federalism that ever existed; recently the system has been improved with respect to the general executive power, which has been provided with all the powers proper to it. According to what I've heard, Buenos Aires and Chile have followed this same line of operations; however, since we are so far away, and the documents are so rare, and the news is so inexact, I will not presume even to offer an outline of their transactions.

The events in Mexico have been too varied, complex, rapid, and unfortunate to keep track of the course of the revolution there. We lack, moreover, the necessary instructive documents to allow us to judge them. The Mexican independents, from what we've learned, took the first step toward insurrection in September 1810, and one year later they had already centered their government in Zitácuaro and set up a national junta there, under the auspices of Fernando VII, in whose name the governmental functions were conducted. Due to the vicissitudes of war, this junta was moved from place to place, and it is likely that it continues to function today, with the modifications imposed by circumstances. They say that the junta has appointed a supreme general or dictator, the distinguished general [José María] Morelos; others insist it is the famous general [Ignacio López] Rayón. What is certain is that one of these great men, or both separately, exercise the supreme authority in that country, and recently a constitution has been drawn up for the administration of the state. In March 1812, from Zultepec, the government presented a plan for peace and war to the viceroy of Mexico, conceived with the most profound wisdom. In it the rights of the people were specified, establishing principles of unquestioned rigor. The junta proposed that war should be conducted as if it were between brothers and fellow citizens, so that it wouldn't be more ruthless than between foreign nations, and that human rights and the rules of war, inviolable even for pagans and savages, ought to be even more so for Christians, who are subject to a sovereign and to the same laws. It also proposed that prisoners of war should not be treated as criminals guilty of lèse majesté, and that those who surrendered should not be beheaded, but held as hostages for later exchange, and that peaceful villages should not be razed, or decimated, or their citizens rounded up for sacrifice. It concludes that if this plan were rejected, there would be strict reprisals. These proposals were rejected with utmost scorn: No reply at all was given to the national junta; the original documents were publicly burned by the executioner in the plaza of Mexico City, and the war of extermination was continued by the Spaniards with their usual rapacity, while the Mexicans and other American nations refrained from practicing such cruelty, not even putting Spanish prisoners to death. It should be noted that it was considered politic to maintain the appearance of submission to the king and even to the royal constitution. It seems that the national junta is absolute in the exercise of legislative, executive, and judicial functions and that the number of its members is quite limited.

The events on the [South American] mainland have demonstrated that perfectly representative institutions are not appropriate to our character, our customs, and our current level of knowledge and experience. In Caracas, party spirit had its origins in the social groups, assemblies, and popular elections, and these parties returned us to slavery. And just as Venezuela has been the American republic most advanced in her political institutions, she has also been the clearest example of the impracticality of the democratic and federalist model for our emerging states. In New Granada, the excessive power of the provincial governments and the lack of centralization in general have led that precious country to the situation it finds itself in today [1815]. For this reason, its weak enemies have managed to survive, against all probability. Until our compatriots acquire the political skills and virtues that distinguish our brothers to the north, entirely popular systems, far from being favorable to us, will, I greatly fear, lead to our ruin. Unfortunately, the acquisition of these qualities to the necessary level would seem to be very remote from us; on the contrary, we are dominated by the vices contracted under the rule of a nation like Spain, which has shown itself to excel only in pride, ambition, vengeance, and greed.

"It is harder," says Montesquieu, "to rescue a country from slavery than to enslave a free one." This truth is verified by the annals of every period in history, which show most free nations being subjected to the yoke and very few subject nations recovering their freedom. Despite this convincing evidence, the people of South America have manifested the inclination to establish liberal and even perfect institutions, an effect, no doubt, of the instinct all men share of aspiring to the highest possible degree of happiness, which is invariably achieved in civil societies founded on the principles of justice, freedom, and equality. But are we capable of maintaining in proper balance the difficult undertaking of a republic? Is it conceivable that a newly liberated people can be launched into the sphere of freedom without their wings disintegrating and hurling them into the abyss, like Icarus? Such a wonder has never been seen, is inconceivable. In consequence, there is no rational basis for such a hope.

More than anyone, I would like to see America become the greatest nation on earth, regarded not so much for its size and wealth as for its freedom and glory. Although I aspire to a perfect government for my country, I can't persuade myself that the New World is ready at this time to be governed by a grand republic. Since this is impossible, I dare not wish it, and even less do I desire a universal American monarchy, because such a project, without even being practical, is also impossible. The abuses that currently exist would not be reformed, and our regeneration would be fruitless. The American states need the stewardship of paternalistic governments to cure the wounds and ravages of despotism and war. The metropolis, for example, would be Mexico, which is the only country capable of assuming that role, because of her intrinsic power, without which there can be no metropolis. Let us imagine that the Isthmus of Panama were the metropolis, being the central point for all the extremes of this vast land. Would these not persist in their current state of lethargy and disorder? For a single government to bring to life, to animate, to marshal all the resources of public prosperity, and to correct, enlighten, and perfect the New World, it would have to have the powers of a God, or at least the enlightenment and virtues of all human beings.

The partisan spirit vexing our states would then flare up more fiercely, since the only source of power capable of quenching it would be far away. Besides, the notables of the [regional] capitals would balk at the domination of the metropolitans, whom they would regard as just so many tyrants. Their jealousy would be so intense that they would compare them to the hateful Spaniards. In short, such a monarchy would be a monstrous colossus, whose own weight would bring it down at the least convulsion.

M. de Pradt has wisely divided America into fifteen or seventeen independent states, each governed by its own monarch.[13] I concur with such a division, because America is large enough to support the creation of seventeen nations. As for his second point, although it would be quite simple to achieve, it is less practical, so I am opposed to the idea of American monarchies. Here are my reasons: Rightly understood, the interest of a republic is limited to concerns about its preservation, prosperity, and glory. Since freedom exercises no power, because it is directly opposed to it, there is nothing to motivate republicans to extend the borders of their nation, in detriment of their own resources, for the mere purpose of forcing their neighbors to participate in a liberal constitution. They acquire no new rights; they derive no advantage by defeating them, unless they follow Rome's example in reducing them to colonies, either conquered or allied. Such notions and examples are in direct opposition to the principles of justice of republican systems. I will go even further: They are in clear opposition to the interests of their citizens, because a state that is too large in itself or in conjunction with its dependent territories ultimately falls into decadence and converts its free form into tyranny. It relaxes the principles that were meant to preserve it and lapses ultimately into despotism. The unique quality of small republics is their permanence, while large ones suffer a variety of changes, always tending toward empire. Almost all small republics have been long-lasting; the only large one that lasted for several centuries was Rome, but that was because the capital was a republic while the rest of its possessions were governed by different laws and institutions.

The politics of a king is quite different, his inclination being directed constantly to the increase of his possessions, wealth, and powers—with good reason, because his authority grows with these acquisitions both in the eyes of his neighbors and in those of his own subjects, who come to fear him as a power as formidable as his empire, which is maintained through war and conquest. For these reasons I believe that Americans, desirous of peace, sciences, art, commerce, and agriculture, would prefer republics to kingdoms, and it seems to me that these desires are also in keeping with the aspirations of Europe.

Of all popular and representative systems I find the federalist system too perfect, in that it requires political virtues and skills far superior to ours. For the same reason I reject the monarchical blend of aristocracy and democracy, which has brought such fortune and splendor to England. Since the most perfected form of republic and monarchy is beyond our capacity, let us avoid falling into demagogic anarchy or monocratic tyranny. Let us seek a middle way between these opposite extremes, either of which will lead us to founder on the identical reefs of misery and dishonor. In an effort to resolve my doubts about the future lot of America, I will venture the following suggestion: Let us strive not for the best but for the most likely of attainment.

For reasons of geography, wealth, population, and character, I imagine that the Mexicans will initially attempt to establish a representative republic, granting great power to the executive, concentrating it in a single individual who, if he performs his duties properly and fairly, will almost certainly hold his authority for life. Should he, through incompetence or violent exercise of power, stir up a successful popular revolt, this same executive power may end up being conferred on an assembly. If the ruling party is military or aristocratic, it will likely demand a monarchy, which will at first be limited and constitutional but inevitably deteriorate into absolutism, for we have to concede that nothing is more difficult to maintain in the political order than a mixed monarchy and that only a people as patriotic as the English could contain the authority of a king and sustain the spirit of freedom under a scepter and a crown.

The states of the Isthmus of Panama as far north as Guatemala will perhaps form a confederation. Its magnificent strategic position between two great oceans may in time result in a universal emporium, its canals shortening the distances between worlds and reinforcing commercial ties between Europe, America, and Asia, bringing tribute to this happy region from the four quarters of the globe. Here alone, perhaps, it will be possible to establish a world capital, as Constantine aspired for Byzantium to become for the ancient world.

New Granada will unite with Venezuela if they can agree to form a central republic, whose capital might be Maracaibo. Or perhaps a new city named for the philanthropic hero, Las Casas, will be built on the border of the two countries near the magnificent port of Bahía-Honda. This site, although little known, is advantageous in all respects. It is easily accessible, yet in such a dominant position that it can be made impregnable. It has a pure, healthy climate, terrain as suitable for agriculture as for raising cattle, and an abundance of wood for construction. The natives who inhabit it would become civilized, and our possessions would grow with the acquisition of the Goajira [Peninsula]. This nation would be named Colombia in fair and grateful tribute to the creator of our hemisphere. Its government might be modeled on the English, though in place of a king there would be an executive power elected for life, never hereditary, assuming that a republic is the goal. The senate or upper legislative body would be hereditary, and during times of political turmoil it would mediate between the frustrations of the people and unpopular governmental decrees. Finally, there would be a legislative body, freely elected, as unencumbered by restrictions as the English House of Commons. This constitution would borrow elements from all political forms, though I would hope it would not partake of their vices. As this Colombia is my country, I have an inalienable right to wish for it what I believe is best. It is quite possible that New Granada, being intensely addicted to the federalist system, would not wish to subject itself to a centralized government. It might, then, form on its own a state that, if it survived, would attain great prosperity because of the abundance and variety of its resources.

We know little about the opinions prevailing in Buenos Aires, Chile, and Peru; judging by what can be surmised from appearances, in Buenos Aires there will be a centralized government dominated by the military as a consequence of internal divisions and wars abroad. This system will inevitably degenerate into an oligarchy, or a monarchy with greater or lesser restrictions, these being impossible to characterize or predict. Such an outcome would be painful to behold, because the people living there deserve a more glorious destiny.

The kingdom of Chile is destined, by the nature of its geography, by the innocent and virtuous customs of its inhabitants, by the example of its neighbors, the indomitable republicans of Arauco,[14] to enjoy the blessings conferred by the just and gentle laws of a republic. If any American republic is to endure, I am inclined to believe it will be Chile. There, the spirit of freedom has never waned; the vices of Europe and Asia will come late or never to corrupt the customs of that far corner of the world. Its territory is limited; it will always be free of contagion from other peoples; it will not alter its laws, its customs, or its habits; it will preserve its uniformity in political and religious ideas; in a word, Chile can be free.

Peru, to the contrary, is marked by two elements that are inimical to any just and liberal regime: gold and slaves. The first corrupts everything; the second is inherently corrupt. The soul of a slave rarely manages to appreciate the wholesome condition of freedom. It turns to rage during uprisings or to servility in its chains.

Although these truths could be applied to all of America, I believe they are most justified with regard to Lima, because of the concepts I have presented and because of her collusion with her Spanish masters against her own brothers, the illustrious sons of Quito, Chile, and Buenos Aires. Obviously, to win freedom, some degree of effort is required. I assume that in Lima, the rich will not tolerate democracy, nor will the slaves and free pardos tolerate aristocracy. The rich would prefer the tyranny of a single individual, so as not to suffer the violence of the mob, and also to establish a somewhat peaceful order. It will be a wonder if Peru manages to recover her independence.

From the foregoing, we can deduce certain consequences: The American provinces are involved in a struggle for emancipation, which will eventually succeed; a few will constitute themselves as conventional federal and centralized republics; almost inevitably the larger territories will establish monarchies, some so wretched that they will devour their natural and human resources in present and future revolutions, for it will be difficult to consolidate a great monarchy, impossible to maintain a great republic.

The idea of merging the entire New World into a single nation with a single unifying principle to provide coherence to the parts and to the whole is both grandiose and impractical. Because it has a common origin, a common language, similar customs, and one religion, we might conclude that it should be possible for a single government to oversee a federation of the different states eventually to emerge. However, this is not possible, because America is divided by remote climates, diverse geographies, conflicting interests, and dissimilar characteristics. How beautiful it would be if the Isthmus of Panama could be for us what Corinth was for the Greeks! I hope that someday we will have the good fortune to install there an august congress of the representatives of these republics, kingdoms, and empires for the purpose of considering and discussing the important issues of peace and war with the nations of the rest of the world. Such a corporation might conceivably emerge at some felicitous moment in our regeneration; any other thought is as impractical as the praiseworthy delirium of the Abbé de Saint-Pierre, who proposed assembling a European congress to decide the fate and interests of those nations.[15]

You go on to write: "Important and happy mutations can often be produced by individual effort." The South Americans have a tradition that when Quetzalcoatl, the Hermes or Buddha of South America, vacated his cult and abandoned his followers, he promised to return after the passage of a specified number of centuries to reestablish his cult and restore their happiness. Is not this tradition still operative? Does it not give rise to the conviction that he must return in the near future? Can you imagine the effect it would produce if an individual should appear among them manifesting the signs of Quetzalcoatl, this Buddha of the rainforest, or Mercury, who has been the object of so much discussion in other countries? Don't you imagine that this would affect each of the states? Is not unity the only thing needed to encourage them to expel the Spaniards, their brigades, and every partisan of corrupt Spain, so that they could then establish a powerful empire with a free government and benevolent laws?

I believe as you do that individual actions can produce general effects, especially during revolutions. But it isn't the hero, Quetzalcoatl, great prophet or god of Anáhuac, who would be capable of bestowing the prodigious benefits you propose. This figure is hardly known at all by the Mexican people, nor highly regarded, for such is the lot of the defeated even if they are gods. Only historians and literary scholars have dedicated themselves to carefully investigating his origins, his mission, whether true or false, his prophecies, and the termination of his cult. Questions still remain as to whether he was an apostle of Christ or a pagan. Some suggest that his name means Saint Thomas; others, the Plumed Serpent; and others say that he is the famous prophet of Yucatán, Chilan-Cambal [Kukulkán]. In a word, most Mexican writers, polemicists, and secular historians have considered to one degree or another the question about the true nature of Quetzalcoatl. The fact is, according to Acosta, that he established a religion whose rites, dogma, and mysteries had a remarkable affinity to the religion of Jesus, being perhaps the one most like it.[16] Still, many Catholic writers have attempted to dismiss the idea that this prophet was authentic, refusing to identify him with someone like Saint Thomas, as other famous authors have done. The general opinion is that Quetzalcoatl is a divine legislator among the pagan peoples of Anáhuac, and that the great Montezuma derived his authority from him as his representative. From this it can be inferred that our Mexicans would not follow the pagan Quetzalcoatl even if he were to appear in the same beneficent forms as in his original manifestation, for they profess the most intolerant and exclusive religion of all.

Fortunately, those directing Mexican independence have been able to exploit this fanaticism to great effect, proclaiming the famous Virgin of Guadalupe as queen of the patriots and invoking her name at every critical moment and raising her image on their flags. In this way, political enthusiasm has merged with religion to produce a passionate fervor for the sacred cause of freedom. The veneration of this image in Mexico is superior to the most exalted rapture that the cleverest prophet could inspire.

Undoubtedly, unity is what we need to complete our project of regeneration. However, our division is not surprising, for such is the nature of civil wars, usually fought between two factions: conservatives and reformers. Generally, the former are more numerous, because the rule of custom inclines us to obedience to established powers; the latter are always less numerous but more passionate and enlightened. In this way physical mass is balanced by moral force, so that the conflict is prolonged and the results are uncertain. Fortunately, in our case, mass has followed intelligence.

I will tell you exactly what we need to ready ourselves to expel the Spaniards and form a free government: unity, of course; however, such unity will not come to us through divine miracle but through sensible action and well-organized effort. America has come together here because it finds itself abandoned by all other nations, isolated in the world, without diplomatic relations or military support, and besieged by a Spain that wields more machinery for war than anything we can amass in secret.

When success is uncertain, when the state is weak, and when the undertaking is still remote in time and space, all men vacillate; opinions are divided, inflamed by passion and by the enemy, which seeks to win easy victory in this way. When we are at last strong, under the auspices of a liberal nation that lends us its protection, then we will cultivate in harmony the virtues and talents that lead to glory; then we will follow the majestic path toward abundant prosperity marked out by destiny for South America; then the arts and sciences that were born in the Orient and that brought enlightenment to Europe will fly to a free Colombia, which will nourish and shelter them.

Such, sir, are the observations and thoughts that I am honored to submit for your consideration and which you may correct or reject according to their merit. I implore you to understand that I have expressed myself forthrightly, not to be discourteous but because I believe I am in a position to inform you on these matters.

Yours,
Simón Bolívar

The Angostura Address

15 February 1819

Sir: Happy is the citizen who, displaying the armorial shield of his command, has the privilege of convoking the representatives of national sovereignty so that they might exercise their will, which is absolute.[17] I number myself among those most favored by Divine Providence, in that I have the honor of assembling the representatives of the people of Venezuela in this august congress, the font of legitimate authority, repository of the sovereign will, and arbiter of the destiny of the nation.

In returning to the representatives of the people the supreme power that had been entrusted to me, I fulfill my heart's wishes, those of my fellow citizens, and those of our future generations, who place all hope in your wisdom, integrity, and prudence. In complying with this pleasant obligation, I free myself of the immense authority that so overwhelmed me, as well as the unlimited responsibility that weighed so heavily on my meager resources. Only undeniable necessity, conjoined with the imperious will of the people, could have imposed on me the terrible and dangerous office of dictator and supreme chief of the republic. But I breathe freely once again as I return to you this authority I somehow managed to exercise, with such peril, difficulty, and sorrow, amid the most horrible tribulations that ever afflicted any society.

The republic over which I presided during this period was not marked by some new political tempest, or bloody war, or even an outburst of popular anarchy. It was something worse—the upheaval of all disruptive forces combined, the inundation of an infernal torrent ravaging the soil of Venezuela. One man, a man like myself, what dikes could he marshal to hold back the power of such devastation? Adrift on this sea of troubles I was but the lowly plaything of the revolutionary hurricane tossing me about like a piece of straw. I could effect neither good nor ill: irresistible forces controlled the course of events. To attribute them to me would be unfair, granting me an importance I do not merit. Would you like to know the authors of the past events and the current situation? Consult the annals of Spain, of America, of Venezuela; examine the laws of the Indies, the system of our former rulers, the influence of religion and foreign domination; observe the first acts of the republican government, the ferocity of our enemies, and the national character. Don't question me about the effects of these upheavals, always so distressing. I can scarcely be called even the simple instrument of the great forces playing themselves out in Venezuela, yet my life, my conduct, all my public and private actions are subject to the censure of the people. Representatives, it is you who must judge them! I submit the history of my command to your impartial judgment; I will add nothing to excuse it; I have already said all I have to say in my defense. If I merit your approval, I will have achieved the sublime title of good citizen, which I prefer to the title of Liberator bestowed on me by Venezuela, or Peacemaker, given me by Cundinamarca,[18] or any other title I may be given by anyone, anywhere.

Legislators! I place in your hands the supreme command of Venezuela. It is now your august duty to dedicate yourselves to the happiness of the republic: in your hands now rest the balance of our destinies, the measure of our glory; your hands will seal the decrees that will guarantee our freedom. At this moment the supreme chief of the republic is but a mere citizen, and so he wishes to remain until his death. I will, however, serve as a soldier as long as there are enemies in Venezuela. The nation has many worthy sons capable of governing her: Talents, virtues, experience, whatever is needed to rule free men, these are the patrimony of many of those assembled here to represent the people; and beyond this sovereign body we have citizens who at every stage have shown they have the courage to confront dangers, the prudence to avoid them, and last, the skill to govern themselves and to govern others. These illustrious men will undoubtedly earn the trust of the congress and be given the responsibility to govern, a charge I relinquished moments ago with all respect and sincerity.

The continuation of power in the same individual has frequently led to the demise of democratic governments. Periodic elections are essential in popular systems, because nothing is so dangerous as to leave power in the hands of a single citizen over long periods of time. The people grow accustomed to obeying him, and he grows accustomed to ruling them, whence come usurpation and tyranny. A just zeal is the guarantee of republican freedom, and our citizens should properly fear that the same ruler who has long ruled them will wish to rule them forever.

Having demonstrated through this act my devotion to the freedom of Venezuela, and aspiring thereby to the glory of being counted among her most loyal patriots, allow me, Sir, to express with the frankness of a true member of the republic my respectful thoughts on this Project for a Constitution, which I take the liberty of offering to you as proof of the sincerity and candor of my sentiments. As it deals with the well-being of everyone, I dare to presume that I have the right to be heard by the representatives of the people. I know very well that your wisdom has no need of counsel, and I know too that my project will perhaps seem ill-conceived, impracticable. Nonetheless, Sir, kindly accept this effort which is not so much the effect of a presumptuous whim as it is the tribute of my sincere submission to this congress. In addition, as it is your function to create a political body and, it could even be said, to create an entire society, beset by all the hazards inherent in this most difficult and singular circumstance, perhaps the plea of a citizen can alert you to the presence of a hidden or unanticipated danger.

Looking back over our past history, we will see what it is that constitutes the Republic of Venezuela.

When America broke free of the Spanish Monarchy, the situation was similar to the fall of the Roman Empire, when that enormous mass fell apart in the ancient world. Each fragment formed an independent nation according to its particular situation or interests, but with this difference: those fragments ended up reestablishing their former associations. We, on the other hand, do not even retain the vestiges of what things were like in earlier times; we are not Europeans, nor Indians, but a species halfway between aboriginal and Spanish. Americans by birth and Europeans by law, we find ourselves contending with the natives for titles of ownership and at the same time trying to maintain our rights in our birth country against the opposition of the invaders; thus our case is most extraordinary and complex. But there is more; our lot has always been purely passive, our political existence nonexistent, so we find ourselves all the more disadvantaged in our quest for freedom because we have always occupied a station lower than that of servants. They took away not only our freedom but even the possibility of exercising an active domestic tyranny. Allow me to explain this paradox. In an absolute regime, the authorized power acknowledges no limits. The will of the despot is the supreme law implemented arbitrarily by the subordinates who participate in the organized oppression by virtue of the authority they enjoy. They control all civil, political, military, and religious functions; but the fact is, the Satraps of Persia are Persian, the Pashas of the Grand Turk are Turks, and the Sultans of Tartary are Tartars. China does not seek out Mandarins from the birthplace of Ghengis Khan, who conquered her. To the contrary, in America, everything was received from Spain, which in a very real sense deprived her of the pleasure of exercising active tyranny, since we were given no role in our domestic affairs and internal administration. This deprivation made it impossible for us to understand the operation of public affairs; neither could we enjoy the personal consideration that the sheen of power inspires in the eyes of the multitudes and that is of such importance in great revolutions. I will say it just once: We were kept apart, in total ignorance of everything related to the science of government.

Enslaved by the triple yoke of ignorance, tyranny, and vice, we American people have never experienced knowledge, power, or virtue. As disciples of this pernicious trio of masters, the lessons we learned and the examples we followed have been purely destructive. We've been ruled more by deceit than power and corrupted more by vice than by superstition. Slavery is the daughter of darkness. An ignorant people is the blind instrument of its own destruction. Ambition and intrigue exploit the credulity and inexperience of men totally bereft of political, economic, or civil knowledge. They mistake pure illusion for reality, license for freedom, treason for patriotism, vengeance for justice. Like a robust blind man deluded by his sense of power, they march forward as confidently as the most clear-sighted, and bouncing from reef to reef, they are unable to find the way. A corrupt people can indeed attain freedom but lose it at once. We endeavor in vain to show them that happiness consists in the practice of virtue, that the rule of law is more powerful than the rule of tyrants because the former is inflexible and everything must yield to its beneficent rigor, that good habits, not force, are the columns of the law, and finally that the practice of justice is the practice of freedom. Hence, legislators, your task is all the more difficult in that you have to reform men perverted by the illusions of error and unhealthy desire. Freedom, says Rousseau, is a succulent food but hard to digest. Our weakened citizens will have to strengthen their spirits mightily before they succeed in digesting the healthful nourishment of freedom. Their arms and legs numbed by chains, their sight dimmed in dark dungeons, and stricken by the plague of servility, will they ever be capable of marching with firm steps toward the august temple of Freedom? Can they approach near enough to admire its splendid beams of light and breathe its pure air without oppression?

Think well before choosing, Legislators. Remember, you are to lay the foundation of a nascent people who can achieve the grandeur Nature envisioned if you raise its base to the height they deserve. If your actions are not ruled by the tutelary genius of Venezuela, which should guide you to an inspired choice of the nature and form of government you will adopt for the happiness of the people, I say, if you choose incorrectly, slavery will be the outcome of our transformation.

The annals of past times will present you with thousands of different governments. Focus on the nations that have cast a brilliant light on earth, and you'll conclude with great distress that almost the entire earth has been, and is still, the victim of its governments. You will observe many systems for managing men, none that does not oppress them, and if our habit of regarding the human race as being lovingly guided by shepherds of men did not lessen the horror of such a shocking spectacle, we would be appalled to watch our docile species grazing on the surface of the globe like mindless sheep being led to slaughter for the nourishment of their leaders. It is true that nature endows us at birth with the instinct for freedom, but whether through laziness or some other proclivity inherent to humankind, it is even truer that we submit serenely to the shackles that hobble us. As we contemplate this condition of willing prostitution, it is almost as if we were justified in persuading ourselves that most men are correct in accepting this humiliating maxim: It is harder to maintain the equilibrium of freedom than to endure the weight of tyranny. Would that this maxim, so contrary to the moral imperative of nature, were false! Would that this maxim were not sanctioned by the indolence of men with respect to their sacred rights!

Many ancient and modern nations have shaken off oppression, but rare are those that have succeeded in enjoying even a few precious moments of freedom; almost at once they've fallen back into their former political vices, because it is the people, not their governments, who drag tyranny in tow. The habit of domination makes them oblivious to the charms of honor and national prosperity, and they are indifferent to the glory of experiencing true freedom, under the tutelage of laws dictated by their own will. The annals of world history proclaim this appalling truth.

Only democracy, in my opinion, is conducive to absolute freedom. But was there ever a democratic government that succeeded in conjoining power, prosperity, and permanence? And on the contrary, have we not seen aristocracies and monarchies hold together grand and powerful empires that lasted for centuries and centuries? Is there any government more ancient than China's? Has there ever been a republic that endured longer than that of Sparta or Venice? Did not the Roman Empire conquer the whole world? Hasn't France had fourteen centuries of monarchy? Who is greater than England? These nations, however, were or still are aristocracies and monarchies.

Despite these cruel reflections, I feel infused with joy over the enormous strides our republic has taken at the outset of her noble destiny. Loving what is most useful, inspired by what is most just, and aspiring to perfection as she breaks free of the Spanish nation, Venezuela has regained her independence, her freedom, her equality, and her national sovereignty. Constituting herself as a democratic republic, she has outlawed monarchy, distinctions, nobility, and special rights and privileges. She has established the rights of man, the freedom to work, think, speak, and write. These eminently liberal decrees can never be too highly praised for the purity that dictated them. The first congress of Venezuela embossed in the annals of our legislation with indelible characters the majesty of the people, fittingly expressed, when it imprinted its seal on the social decree most capable of leading to the happiness of a nation. I have to summon all my energy to express with all the vehemence of which I'm capable the supreme virtue embodied in this immortal Code of our rights and laws. Yet dare I say it? Do I dare profane with my criticism the sacred tablets of our laws? There are sentiments that cannot be kept silent in the breast of one who loves his country; they brim over, driven out by their own intensity, and against the will of the person harboring them, an imperious necessity gives them voice.

I am fully convinced that the government of Venezuela must be reformed, and that although many distinguished citizens share my thought, not all of them are daring enough to profess publicly the adoption of new principles. This consideration moves me to take the initiative in a matter of the greatest seriousness and to commit the audacity of offering advice to the advisors of the people.

The more I admire the excellence of the federal constitution of Venezuela, the more convinced I am of the impossibility of its application to our nation. In my opinion, it is a miracle that its model in North America endures with such prosperity and that it does not fall apart at the first manifestation of trouble or danger. Although that country is a singular model of political and moral virtue, and though freedom was its cradle and its nursery, and though it is nourished on pure freedom—in brief, although in many respects that nation is unique in the history of the human race—it is a miracle, I repeat, that a system as weak and complex as federalism ever managed to guide it through circumstances as difficult and delicate as those of its recent past. But I should say that however successful this form of government proved for North America, it never entered my mind to compare the situation and nature of two states as diametrically different as English America and Spanish America. Would it not be difficult to apply to Spain England's political, civil, and religious Charter of Liberties? Well, it is even more difficult to adapt the laws of North America to Venezuela. Do we not read in the Spirit of the Laws that they must be suitable to the country for which they are written? That it is an astonishing coincidence for the laws of one nation to be applicable to another? That they must take into account the physical aspect of the country, its climate, the nature of its terrain, its location, size, and the way of life of its people? That they must reflect the degree of freedom that the constitution can support, the religion of the inhabitants as well as their inclinations, their standard of living, their number, their commerce, their customs, and their character? This then is the code we should consult, not the one written for Washington!

The Venezuelan constitution, despite having taken as its model the most perfect constitution ever formulated in terms of the correctness of principles and the beneficent effects of its administration, differed essentially from the North American in one cardinal point, undoubtedly the most important. The congress of Venezuela, like that of North America, shares some of the powers exercised by the executive. We go even further, subdividing this power and vesting it in a collective body, which adds the inconvenience of periodically interrupting or suspending the authority of the government whenever its members are apart. Our triumvirate lacks, so to speak, unity, continuity, and individual responsibility; it is incapable of timely action, continuous existence, real uniformity, direct responsibility. A government dispossessed of everything constituting its moral authority might as well not exist.

Although the powers of the president of the United States are limited by excessive restrictions, he alone exercises all the governmental functions vested in him by the constitution, and his administration must necessarily be more uniform, consistent, and autonomous than that of an authority diffused among numerous individuals whose composite could hardly be more monstrous.

The judicial power in Venezuela is similar to the North American; appointments have no fixed duration, but are temporary, not for life; it enjoys the full independence proper to the judiciary.

In drafting its federalist constitution, the first congress was more attentive to the spirit of the provinces than to the solid idea of forming an indivisible and centralized republic. In this, our legislators bowed to the rash insistence of those provinces that were bedazzled by the happy fortune of the people of North America, mistakenly believing that the blessings that country enjoys are due exclusively to her form of government rather than to the character and customs of her citizens. In effect, the astonishing prosperity of the United States was an example too seductive not to be followed. Who can resist the triumphant appeal of the full and absolute enjoyment of sovereignty, independence, and freedom? Who can resist the love inspired by an intelligent government that conjoins simultaneously individual and societal rights, that bases the supreme law of individual behavior on the will of society? Who can resist the rule of a benevolent government that with a single, active, and powerful hand continually and everywhere directs all of its resources toward social perfection, which is the only proper goal of human institutions?

But no matter how enticing this magnificent federalist system may seem to be, it was not conceivable for the Venezuelan people to adopt it overnight on emerging from their chains. We were not ready for such bounty; good, as well as evil, is fatal when it comes too suddenly or in extreme doses. Our moral constitution did not yet possess the necessary consistency to receive the benefit of a completely representative government, one so sublime that it might better suit a republic of saints.

Representatives of the people! You are called to consecrate or annul whatever portion of our social contract you deem worthy of preservation, reform, or omission. It falls to you to correct the works of our first legislators; I almost said, it falls to you to cover over part of the beauty contained in our political code, because not all eyes are capable of withstanding the heavenly light of perfection. The writings of the apostles, the moral wisdom of Jesus, the divine project sent us by Providence for the betterment of mankind is a thing so sublime, so holy, that it would rain fire on Constantinople and all of Asia would burst into flame if this book of peace were suddenly imposed on it as the code of religion, of laws, and of customs.

Allow me to call the attention of congress to a matter that may be of vital importance. Let us bear in mind that our people are not European, nor North American, but are closer to a blend of Africa and America than an emanation from Europe, for even Spain herself lacks European identity because of her African blood, her institutions, and her character. It is impossible to say with certainty to which human family we belong. Most of the indigenous peoples have been annihilated. The European has mixed with the American and the African, and the African has mixed with the Indian and with the European. All born in the womb of our common mother, our fathers, different in origin and blood, are foreigners, and all differ visibly in the color of their skin; this difference implies a bond and obligation of the greatest transcendence.

The citizens of Venezuela, governed by a constitution that serves to interpret Nature, all enjoy a perfect equality. While such equality may not have been a feature of Athens, France, or North America, it is important for us to consecrate it in order to correct the differences that are so apparent here. As I see it, legislators, the fundamental principle of our system demands that equality be immediately and exclusively established and put into practice in Venezuela. That all men are born with an equal right to the benefits of society is a truth sanctioned by most wise men, as is the following: All men are born equally capable of aspiring to the highest attainments. Well, all men should practice virtue, but not all do; all should be courageous, but not all are; all should have talent, but not all do. This is the source of the effective difference we observe among the individuals of even the most liberally conceived society. If the principle of political equality is generally recognized, so too is the principle of physical and moral inequality. Nature makes men unequal, in intelligence, temperament, strength, and character. The laws correct this difference because they place the individual in society so that education, industry, the arts, the services, and the virtues can give him a fictitious equality that is properly called political and social. It was an eminently beneficent inspiration to merge all classes into a single state where diversity would increase along with the propagation of the species. By this single step, cruel discord has been eradicated. How much jealousy, how much enmity, how much hatred has been thus avoided!

Having addressed the questions of justice and humanity, let us turn to politics and society, smoothing the difficulties that arise in a system so simple and natural, but so weak that the slightest adversity upsets and destroys it. The diversity of origins requires an infinitely firm and infinitely delicate touch to manage this heterogeneous society whose complex structure becomes dislocated, divided, and dissolved at the slightest alteration.

The most perfect system of government is the one that produces the greatest possible happiness, the highest level of social security, and the greatest degree of political stability. Based on the laws enacted by the first congress, we have the right to expect that happiness will be the legacy Venezuela bequeaths her citizens, and with those enacted here by this assembly we should expect that security and stability will make that happiness eternal. It is your task to resolve this problem. How, after having broken all the shackles of our former oppression, can we perform the miraculous labor of preventing the rusty vestiges of our chains from becoming weapons destructive of our freedom? The relics of Spanish domination will be with us for many years before we manage to obliterate them: The contagion of despotism pervades our atmosphere, and neither the flames of war nor the details of our wholesome laws have succeeded in purifying the air we breathe. Our hands are now free, but our hearts still suffer the pangs of servitude. Man, said Homer, when he loses his freedom, loses half his spirit.

A republican government has always been, still is, and must ever be Venezuela's choice. Its bases must be the sovereignty of the people, the division of powers, civil liberty, the proscription against slavery, the abolition of monarchy and privileged classes. There is no other way to say it: We need equality in order to reconstitute the race of men, political opinions, and public customs. Then, casting our gaze out over the vast terrain still left for us to traverse, let us fix our attention on the dangers we must avoid.

Let history serve as our guide in this journey. Athens is the first to provide us with the most brilliant example of an absolute democracy, and simultaneously, that same Athens offers us the most melancholy example of the extreme fragility of this form of government. The wisest legislator of Greece did not see his republic endure ten years, and he suffered the humiliation of acknowledging the inadequacy of absolute democracy for ruling any kind of society, even the most sophisticated, abstemious, and limited, because it only shines with lightning flashes of freedom. Let us acknowledge, then, that Solon let the world see past the illusion and taught it how difficult it is to rule men through laws alone.

The Republic of Sparta, which seemed a chimerical invention, produced more real effects than the ingenious creation of Solon. Glory, virtue, morality, and consequently national happiness were the results of the legislation of Lycurgus. Even though two kings in a single state are two monsters to devour it, Sparta had little to regret from its double throne, whereas Athens had promised itself the most splendid fortune, with absolute sovereignty, free election of magistrates, periodically replaced, and laws that were fair, enlightened, and politic. Pisistratus, usurper and tyrant, was of more use to Athens than her laws, and Pericles, another usurper, was her most useful citizen. The Republic of Thebes lasted only as long as Pelopidas and Epaminondas; sometimes it is men, not principles, who form the essence of governments. Codes, systems, and statutes, no matter how enlightened they may be, are dead letters that have little influence on societies. Virtuous men, patriotic men, erudite men constitute republics!

The Roman constitution produced greater power and fortune than that of any other nation on earth; in it, there were no provisions for an exact distribution of powers. The consuls, the senate, and the people served also as legislators, magistrates, judges; everyone partook of all powers. The executive power, consisting of two consuls, had the same flaw as that of Sparta. Despite its deformed structure, the republic did not suffer the disastrous discord we might have assumed to be inevitable from a leadership made up of two individuals equally vested with the powers of a monarch. A government whose sole inclination was conquest did not seem designed to secure the happiness of its nation. A monstrous and purely warlike government lifted Rome to the most brilliant level of virtue and glory, establishing on earth a Roman Empire to show men how much can be accomplished by political virtue and how unimportant institutions are.

Passing from ancient to modern times, we find England and France arousing the admiration of all nations and offering eloquent lessons on every aspect of government. The accomplishment of these two great peoples shines forth like a radiant meteor, inundating the world with such a profusion of political lights that today every thinking person understands the difference between man's rights and man's responsibilities and what it is that constitutes the virtues and vices of governments. Everyone can appreciate the intrinsic value of the speculative theories of modern philosophers and legislators. In short, this star, in its luminous passage, has ignited even the imagination of the apathetic Spaniards, who have also hurled themselves into the political maelstrom where, experimenting with the ephemeral manifestations of freedom, they quickly discovered their incapacity for living under the gentle dominion of laws and buried themselves once again in their age-old dungeons illumined only by autos-da-fe.

Now is the moment to repeat, Legislators, the words of the eloquent Volney from the dedication to his Ruins of Palmyra: "To the emerging countries of the Spanish Indies, to the generous leaders who guide them toward freedom: let the errors and misfortunes of the ancient world instruct the new world in wisdom and happiness."[19] Let us not forget the lessons of experience; let the schools of Greece, Rome, France, England, and America instruct us in the difficult science of creating and preserving nations with laws that are appropriate, just, legitimate, and above all practical. Never forget that the existence of a government depends not on its political theory, or its form, or its administrative mechanism, but on its appropriateness to the nature and character of the nation for which it is instituted.

Rome and Great Britain are the two outstanding nations of ancient and modern times; both were born to rule and be free; both were formed not with brilliant modes of freedom but on solid foundations. Therefore, Representatives, I suggest that you study the British constitution, which is the one that seems destined to bring the greatest good to the peoples who adopt it. However, for all its perfection, I am far from recommending servile imitation of it. When I speak of the British government, I refer only to its republican features. In fact, how can we use the term *monarchy* to describe a system that recognizes popular sovereignty, the division and balance of powers, civil liberty, freedom of conscience, freedom of the press, and all that is sublime in politics? Can there be greater freedom in any other form of republic? Can we expect more of any social order? I recommend this popular constitution to you, its division and balance of powers, its civil liberties, as the worthiest model for anyone aspiring to the enjoyment of the rights of man and to all the political happiness compatible with our fragile nature.

It would require no alteration in our basic laws to adopt a legislature similar to the British parliament. Like the North Americans, we have divided the national congress into two chambers: the chamber of representatives and the senate. The first is very wisely structured: it enjoys all the powers appropriate to it and is not in need of reform, since the constitution conferred on it the origin, form, and functions demanded by the people to ensure that their wishes would be legitimately and effectively represented. If the senate were hereditary instead of elective, it would, I think, be the base, the bond, and the soul of our republic. During political upheavals, this body would deflect lightning away from the government and repulse the waves of popular unrest. Loyal to the government out of a vested interest in its own preservation, it would always resist any attempted incursions by the people against the jurisdiction and authority of their magistrates. We should acknowledge it: Most men are unaware of their true interests and constantly strive to undermine them in the hands of those who hold them in trust; the individual struggles against the masses, and the masses against the authorities. Because of this, it is necessary that in all governments there exist a neutral body to take the side of the offended, disarming the offender. In order for this neutral body to maintain its neutrality, it must not owe its existence to the government or to the people, but should enjoy a complete independence that neither fears nor expects anything from these two sources of authority. The hereditary senate, being part of the people, shares their interests, their feelings, and their spirit. Thus it should not be presumed that a hereditary senate will be detached from the popular will or that it will neglect its legislative duties. The senators in Rome, the lords in London, have been the solidest of pillars supporting the edifice of political and civil liberties.

These senators will be elected originally by congress. Those who succeed them in the senate are of the highest priority to the government, which should educate them in a school specifically designed to instruct them as leaders, as the future legislators of the nation. They would learn the arts, the sciences, and the knowledge needed to adorn the mind of a public servant, from childhood they would know the career to which they are destined by Providence, and from an early age they would prepare their spirits for the dignity that awaits them.

The creation of a hereditary senate would in no way violate the principle of political equality; it is not my wish to establish a noble class: to do that, as a famous republican has said, would be to destroy equality and freedom simultaneously. I wish, rather, to point out that it is a profession demanding great knowledge and the means adequate to obtain such instruction. We should not leave everything to chance and to the results of elections: The people are more gullible than nature perfected by art, and although it is true that these senators would have no monopoly on virtue, it is also true that they would have the advantage of an enlightened education. Moreover, the Liberators of Venezuela are worthy of occupying forever an exalted rank in the republic that owes them its existence. I believe that posterity would look with regret on the obliteration of the illustrious names of our first benefactors. I will go even further: It is in the public interest, it is Venezuela's debt of gratitude, it is crucial to our national honor, to preserve with glory throughout posterity this race of virtuous, prudent, bold men who, overcoming all obstacles, have laid the foundation of the republic at the cost of the most heroic sacrifices. If the people of Venezuela fail to applaud this elevation of their benefactors, they are unworthy of being free and never will be.

I repeat: A hereditary senate will be the foundation of the legislative power and therefore the basis of all government. Equally, it will serve as counterweight for both government and the people, a mediating force to buffer the barbs these eternal rivals are forever hurling at one another. In all struggles, the calming influence of a third party functions as an organ of reconciliation, so the Venezuelan senate will be the stabilizing center of this edifice that is so delicate and susceptible to violent tremors; it will be the mediator that will calm the storms and maintain harmony between the members and the head of this political body.

It will be impossible to corrupt a legislative body vested with the highest honors, dependent only on itself and fearing nothing from the people, expecting nothing from the government—a body whose only purpose is to restrain evil and promote good in all their manifestations—and which is intensely interested in the existence of a society whose failures and successes affect it vitally. It has been said that the British House of Lords is invaluable to the nation because it provides a bulwark for freedom; I would add that the Venezuelan senate would be not only a bulwark for freedom but a nucleus to perpetuate the republic.

The British executive power is vested with all appropriate sovereign authority, but is also fenced in by a triple line of dikes, barriers, and walls. The executive is head of government, but his ministers and subordinates are more dependent on the laws than on his authority, because they are charged with personal responsibility from which not even the imperatives of royal authority exempt them. The executive is supreme commander of the army and navy; he makes peace and declares war, but it is parliament that determines the annual budget for paying these military forces. Though the courts and judges depend on him, the laws emanate from the parliament, which enacts them. For the purpose of neutralizing his power, the person of the king is held sacred and inviolable, but while his head is spared, his hands are bound to prevent him from taking action. The sovereign of England has three formidable rivals: his cabinet, which must answer both to parliament and to the people; the House of Lords, which defends the interests of the people as the representative of the nobility comprising it; and the House of Commons, which serves as organ and tribune for the British people. Moreover, since the judges are held responsible for the enforcement of the laws, they do not depart from them, and the administrators of the treasury, being subject to prosecution not only for their own infractions but even for those committed by the government, are careful not to misappropriate public funds. However much we examine the nature of the executive power in England, we find nothing to make us revise our opinion that it is the most perfect model, either for a monarchy, for an aristocracy, or for a democracy. If we apply this executive power to Venezuela in the person of a president, chosen by the people or their representatives, we will have taken a great step toward national happiness.

Whoever is chosen to carry out these functions will find himself much benefited by the constitution: Authorized to do good, he will be restrained from doing evil, because as long as he follows the laws, his ministers will cooperate with him, whereas if he tries to get around them, his own ministers will leave him standing alone before the republic, and they will even bring charges against him before the senate. When ministers are held responsible for any transgressions committed, it is they who govern, since it is they who pay the price. One of the greatest advantages of this system is that it lays a heavy obligation on those closest to the president to take an active and vested interest in the deliberations of the government, and to regard their respective department as their own. It may well be that the president will not be a man of great talent, or great virtue, yet despite the lack of these essential qualities, he will carry out his duties in a satisfactory manner, because in such cases the ministry functioning on its own will take responsibility for the state.

No matter how exorbitant the authority of the executive power in England may seem, it may not be excessive in Venezuela. Here, congress has bound the hands and even the heads of those in power. This deliberative body has assumed part of the executive functions, going against Montesquieu's maxim that discourages representative bodies from making active resolutions, limiting their role to that of enacting laws and then waiting to see if they are enforced. Nothing is as contrary to harmony between the powers as this erosion of boundaries. Nothing is as dangerous with respect to the people as weakness in the executive power. If in a monarchy it has been judged necessary to concede him so many powers, in a republic these are infinitely more indispensable.

If we turn our attention to this difference, we will discover that the balance of powers ought to be distributed quite differently in these two cases. In a republic, the executive should be the strongest power, because everything conspires against him; in a monarchy, however, the legislature should be the strongest, because everything conspires in favor of the monarch. The veneration professed by the people for their monarch is a prestige that works powerfully to augment the superstitious respect given to that authority. The splendor of the throne, the crown, and the purple; the formidable support provided by the nobility; the immense wealth accumulated in a single dynasty over generations; the fraternal protection that all kings provide to each other—these are enormous advantages that militate in favor of royal authority, making it almost limitless. These very advantages, consequently, confirm the necessity of giving greater authority to a republican president than to a constitutional monarch.

A republican president is an individual isolated within society, yet charged with restraining the impetus of the people toward rampant license and the proclivity of judges and administrators toward abuse of the laws. He is directly responsible to the legislative body, the senate, and the people—one man all alone weathering the combined force of divergent opinions, interests, and passions of society, who according to Carnot does little more than struggle constantly against the desire to control and the desire to resist control.[20] He is, in short, a single athlete striving against a multitude of athletes.

This weakness can only be corrected by an unyielding and strategically employed resistance to the opposition inevitably marshaled by the legislature, the judiciary, and the people of a republic. If the executive does not command all the means properly vested in him by the constitution, he will inevitably fall into insignificance or be tempted to abuse his power. If that happens, we have the demise of government, followed by anarchy, usurpation, and tyranny. It is natural and just to seek to curtail and limit executive authority, but we should take care that the bonds used to restrain be strong but not tight.

Let the entire system of government be strengthened and permanent balance be established, lest its own fragility be the cause of its decadence. Precisely because no other form of government is as weak as democracy, its structure should be all the more solid and its institutions continually tested for stability. If we fail in this, we can be sure the result will be an experiment in government rather than a permanent system, an ungovernable, tumultuous, and anarchic society rather than a social institution in which happiness, peace, and justice rule.

Let us be modest, not presumptuous, in our ambitions, Legislators. It is unlikely that we can achieve what the human race never achieved, what even the greatest, wisest nations never accomplished. Untrammeled freedom, absolute democracy, these are the reefs on which republican hopes have ever shattered. Take a cursory look at ancient republics, modern republics, and those newly formed; almost all sought to establish themselves as absolute democracies, and almost all have been frustrated in their noble aspirations. Men who desire legitimate institutions and social perfection are certainly laudable, but who ever led them to believe that they possess the necessary wisdom or practice the requisite virtue needed to conjoin power with justice? Only the angels, never men, can exist in a state of freedom, tranquility, and happiness while exercising supreme power!

The people of Venezuela already enjoy the rights they can legitimately and easily expect to possess, so let us head off the momentum of excessive ambitions that might well lead to the formation of a government unsuited to them. Let us abandon inappropriate federalist structures as well as the tripartite executive power: concentrating all that power in a president, let us entrust him with sufficient authority to carry on the struggle against the difficulties inherent in our current situation, the state of war weighing on us and the kind of external and domestic enemies against whom we must wage a protracted struggle. Let the legislative power relinquish the functions belonging to the executive, all the while acquiring new coherence and new influence in the balance of powers. Let the courts be strengthened by the stability and independence of the judges and by the establishment of juries and civil and criminal codes that aren't dictated by the past or by conquering kings but by the voice of nature, the cry for justice, and the spirit of wisdom.

My desire is that all branches of government and administration acquire the degree of vigor that alone can maintain balance, not only between the constituent parts of government but among the different factions forming our society. It would be of no importance for a political system to lose its resilience if that weakness did not drag the social body down with it and disaffect the members. The cries of the human race on battlefields or in angry demonstrations rail against insensitive or blind legislators who mistakenly believed they could try out whimsical institutions with impunity. Every country on earth has sought freedom, some by force of arms, others by laws, moving from anarchy to despotism or from despotism to anarchy; only a few were willing to temper their ambitions, establishing a mode of government appropriate to their means, their spirit, and their circumstances.

Let us not aspire to the impossible, lest in reaching for the ring of freedom we fall into the abyss of tyranny. From absolute freedom, nations always plunge into absolute power, and the mean between these two extremes is supreme social freedom. The pernicious idea of unlimited freedom is a product of abstract theories. Let us keep public power within the limits prescribed by reason and interest, and conform our national will to the possibilities allowed by the fair distribution of power. And let our civil and criminal legislation rule imperiously over the judiciary, as stipulated in the constitution; then there will be balance, not a series of shocks hobbling the progress of the State; society will be unified, not choked with complexity.

The formation of a stable government requires a national resolve aimed equally and consistently at two goals: the moderation of the general will and the curtailment of public authority. The polarities fixing these two points theoretically are difficult to locate precisely, but the rule establishing them can, I believe, be described most accurately as mutual restriction and concentration, intended to minimize the friction between the will of the people and legitimate authority. This science is acquired unconsciously through practice and study: the greater the knowledge, the greater the practical skill, and knowledge grows through spiritual integrity.

Love of country, love of the law, love of leaders—these noble passions must occupy the soul of a republican to the exclusion of other concerns. Venezuelans love their country, but they do not love their laws, for the latter have been noxious and productive of evil; neither do they love their leaders, because those of the past have been iniquitous, while those newly elected have yet to prove themselves. If country, law, and the authorities are not held as sacred, society is a morass, an abyss, hand-to-hand combat between individuals and groups.

To extricate our nascent republic from this chaos, not even the full weight of our moral faculties will suffice unless we can unify our country: its governmental structure, its legislative body, and its national spirit. Unity, unity, unity—that must be our motto. If the blood of our citizens is diverse, let us make it one. If our constitution has divided the powers, let us unify them. If our laws are moribund relics of every ancient and modern despotism, let us tear down this monstrous edifice and, obliterating even its ruins, build a temple of justice in whose sacred precincts we can dictate a Venezuelan code of law. If we need to consult monuments and models of legislation, Great Britain, France, and North America will offer us theirs.

Popular education should be the highest concern of paternal love for our congress. Morality and enlightenment are the poles of a republic, so morality and enlightenment are our first necessities. From Athens let us borrow her Areopagus and the guardians of customs and laws; from Rome, her censors and domestic tribunals; and, using these moral institutions to form a holy alliance, let us renew in the world the idea of a people not content with merely being free and strong, but aspiring also to be virtuous. From Sparta, we will borrow her austere institutions, and constructing from these three vital springs a fountain of virtue, let us endow our republic with a fourth power whose dominion is childhood and the hearts of men, public spirit, wholesome customs, and republican morality. Let us so constitute this Areopagus that it will keep vigil over the education of our children, over our national system of education, and purify the corrupted aspects of our republic, denouncing ingratitude, selfishness, coldness of affection for the country, idleness and negligence on the part of citizens, and condemn the causes of corruption and pernicious examples, correcting our customs with moral castigation, not only against those who violate them but also those who mock them, not only against those who attack them but also those who undermine them, not only against whatever violates the constitution but also whatever violates public respect. The jurisdiction of this truly sacred tribunal should be absolute with regard to education and instruction, merely advisory with regard to penalties and punishments. Its annals, however, or the registers where its acts and deliberations, its moral judgments, and the actions of citizens are recorded, will be our guidebooks of virtue and vice. The people will consult them for their elections, our leaders for their resolutions, and our judges for their verdicts. An institution such as this, however chimerical it may seem, is infinitely more practicable than others which ancient and modern legislators have established of far less utility for the human race.

Legislators! Regarding the constitutional project that I have reverently submitted for your judicious consideration, you will observe the spirit that has dictated it. Upon proposing to you the division of citizens into active and passive,[21] it has been my intention to incite national prosperity by means of the two great levers of industry: work and knowledge. By stimulating these two great springs of society, we achieve what is most difficult among men, making them honorable and happy. By placing fair and prudent restrictions on the Primary and Electoral Assemblies, we raise the first dam against popular license, avoiding the sort of blind, tumultuous convention that has in all periods ratified error in elections and consequently spread that contagion to our leaders and to the processes of government. For this primordial act will either generate a people's freedom or its slavery.

In augmenting the importance of congress in the balance of powers by increasing the number of its legislators and by making the senate hereditary, I have tried to provide a solid base to this first body of the nation and to invest it with the gravity necessary to the fulfillment of its supreme functions.

In setting firm boundaries between the executive and judicial branches, it has not been my intention to divide but to bind with the harmonious bonds born of independence these two supreme powers whose prolonged collision has never failed to bring down one branch or the other. In seeking to vest the executive with a range of attributes greater than those it formerly enjoyed, it has not been my desire to authorize a despot to tyrannize the republic, but to prevent congressional despotism from being the direct cause of a circle of despotic vicissitudes in which anarchy is replaced by oligarchy and oligarchy by monocracy. In requesting stability for the judges, the creation of juries, and a new code of laws, I am simply asking congress to guarantee civil liberty, which is the most precious, the most just, the most necessary, and in a word the only freedom, since in its absence all others are void. I have requested the correction of the most lamentable abuses afflicting our judiciary because of its origin in that bottomless pit of Spanish legislation, which like time itself swallows all epochs and all men, the works of madness as well as those of genius, projects that are sensible and those that are extravagant, monuments to brilliance as well as those to whimsy. This judiciary encyclopedia, a ten-headed monster that until now has been the scourge of the Hispanic nations, is the most refined instrument of torture that Heaven's wrath ever allowed to be loosed against this hapless empire.

Reflecting on the best way to regenerate the character and customs imposed on us by tyranny and war, I came up with the audacious invention of a Moral Power, drawn from the darkest depths of antiquity and from those forgotten laws that managed over long periods to preserve virtue among the Greeks and Romans. It may well be regarded as the product of a naïve delirium, yet perhaps I flatter myself that you will not reject out of hand an idea which, improved by experience and enlightened consideration, may turn out to be very effective.

Appalled by the conflict that has prevailed and must always prevail among us because of the insidious spirit marking federalist government, I have been persuaded against my will to beg you to adopt centralism and the consolidation of all the states of Venezuela into a single, indivisible republic. This measure, which is in my opinion urgent, vital, and potentially redeeming, is of such moment that without it the fruit of our regeneration will be our death.

It is my duty, legislators, to present you with a true and detailed account of my political, civil, and military administration, but to do so at this moment would exhaust your important attention and deprive you of a time of respite as precious as it is urgent. Consequently, the secretaries of state will provide congress with separate reports of their different departments, including the documents and archives needed to illustrate a precise account of the true and positive state of the republic.

I would not burden you with an account of the most noteworthy acts of my regime if it were not of crucial importance to most Venezuelans. It is a matter, Sir, of the most important resolutions of this last period.

Atrocious, wicked slavery shrouded the land of Venezuela in its black veil, and storm clouds darkened the sky, threatening a rain of fire. I implored the protection of the God of humanity, and then redemption dissipated the storm. Slavery threw off its chains, and Venezuela found herself regenerated with new and grateful children who converted the instruments of their captivity into freedom's weapons. Those who were slaves are now free; those who were previously enemies of a stepmother are now the defenders of their country. It is unnecessary for me to persuade you of the fairness, necessity, and positive effects of this measure, for you know the history of the helots, of Spartacus, and of Haiti; you also know that one cannot be simultaneously free and enslaved except by violating at one and the same time the natural law, the political laws, and the civil laws. I leave to your supreme judgment the reform or amendment of all my statutes and decrees, but I beg the confirmation of absolute freedom for the slaves, just as I would beg for my life and the life of the republic.

To portray for you the military history of Venezuela would be to remind you of the history of republican heroism among the ancients; it would be to tell you that Venezuela has taken her place in the great mural depicting the sacrifices made on the altar of freedom. Nothing could fill the noble hearts of our generous warriors except the sublime honors that are reserved for the benefactors of the human race. Fighting not for power, or fortune, or even for glory, but only for liberty, the title of Liberators of the Republic is their just reward. To this end, establishing a sacred society comprising these illustrious men, I have instituted the order of the Liberators of Venezuela. Legislators! As the function of granting honors and medals falls to you, it is your obligation to carry out this august act of national gratitude.

Men who have sacrificed all the pleasures and wealth they formerly possessed as a result of their virtues and talents; men who have experienced the depths of cruelty in a terrible war, suffering the most painful deprivations and the most bitter torments; men who deserve so much from their country demand the attention of the government. Therefore I have arranged for them to be compensated by the nation. If I have merited even the least degree of respect from the people, I implore their representatives to hear my appeal in consideration of my meager service. Let the congress legally confirm the distribution of the nation's property that in the name of the republic I caused to be conferred on those who served in the Venezuelan army.

Driven to despair at seeing us crush their armies time and time again, the Spanish court has had the audacity to issue a vain appeal for help from the generous sovereigns who recently eradicated usurpation and tyranny from Europe, and who by that same token should be the protectors of the legitimacy and justice of the American cause. Unable to bring us to our knees by force of arms, Spain reverts to this insidious policy. If she cannot defeat us, she resorts to the tactic of fear and suspicion: Fernando has humbled himself, confessing that he needs foreign protection to return us to his ignominious yoke, a yoke that no power on earth will ever impose on us again! Convinced that she is strong enough to repel our oppressors, Venezuela has used the official channels of government to issue her ultimatum: She will fight to the death to defend her political existence, not only against Spain but against all men, should it happen that all men are sufficiently depraved to come to the aid of a voracious government whose only weapons are the flames of the Inquisition and the will to exterminate—a government that no longer seeks colonies or cities or slaves but deserts, ruins, and tombs. The Declaration of [Independence of] the Republic of Venezuela is the most glorious, the most heroic act, the one most worthy of a free people; I now have the honor to offer to the congress an act already sanctioned by the unanimous expression of the people of Venezuela.

Since the second period of the republic, our army has lacked military supplies; it has always lacked weapons; it has always lacked munitions and been poorly equipped. Now, however, the warriors and defenders of our Independence are armed not only with justice but also with full military strength. Our troops compare favorably with the most select forces of Europe, since there is no longer an imbalance in destructive power. We owe these enormous advantages to the unlimited generosity of certain magnanimous foreign citizens who have seen humanity suffer and the cause of reason languish, not as passive spectators but actively, rushing to provide us with whatever the republic needed to further its philanthropic purpose. These friends of humanity are the guardian angels of America, and we owe them an eternal debt of gratitude, or more—a religious commitment to the sacred obligations we have incurred with them. This national debt, legislators, is the full store of good faith, honor, and gratitude of Venezuela. Honor it as the sacred ark in which not only the rights of our benefactors are stored, but also the glory of our loyalty. Let us perish rather than break a pledge that brought salvation to our country and life to her sons.

The union of New Granada and Venezuela into a single great state has been the constant wish of the peoples and governments of these republics. The fortunes of war have authenticated this union so desired by all Colombians; we are in fact now united. These fraternal peoples have entrusted their interests, their rights, and their destinies to you. On contemplating the unification of this immense region, my soul soars to the heights demanded by such a colossal vista, such an astonishing scene. Flying from age to age, my imagination reflects on the centuries to come, and as I look down from such a vantage point, amazed at the prosperity, splendor, and vitality of this vast region, I feel a kind of rapture, as if this land stood at the very heart of the universe, spread out from coast to coast between oceans separated by nature and which it is our task to reunite with long, broad canals. I see her as unifier, center, emporium for the human family, sending out to the entire earth the treasures of silver and gold hidden in her mountains, extracting health and vitality from her lush vegetation for the suffering men of the old world, communicating her precious secrets to the wise men still unaware of the vast stores of knowledge and wealth so bountifully provided by nature. I see her seated on the throne of liberty, grasping the scepter of justice, crowned by glory, and revealing to the old world the majesty of the modern world.

Be so kind, Legislators, as to accept indulgently this profession of my political vision, the final wishes of my heart, and the fervent prayers that I dare address to you in the name of the people. Grant to Venezuela an eminently popular government, eminently just, eminently moral, that will fetter oppression, anarchy, and rancor, a government where innocence, humanity, and peace will reign and where equality and freedom will triumph under the rule of law.

Gentlemen, begin your work; mine is done.

Simón Bolívar

The Bolivian Constitution

1. Address to the Constituent Congress

Lima, 25 May 1826

Legislators! As I offer you this draft of a constitution for Bolivia, I am overwhelmed by confusion and trepidation, knowing that I have no talent for making laws.[22] When I consider that the wisdom of all the ages is insufficient to compose a fundamental code of law that is perfect, and that the most enlightened legislator can be the direct cause of human wretchedness and the parody, so to speak, of his own divine ministry, what can I say of the soldier, born among slaves and entombed in the deserts of his country, whose political experience is limited to the sight of captives in chains and their fellow soldiers taking up arms to set them free? I, a legislator? It would be hard to say which is more foolish, your delusion or my acquiescence. I don't know who will suffer more in this horrible conflict: you, for the harm you should fear concerning the laws you requested of me, or I, for the opprobrium to which your trust condemns me.

I have summoned all my resources to convey to you my opinion concerning the best way to deal with free men, based on the principles adopted among civilized peoples, though the lessons of experience point only to long periods of disaster, interrupted by brief flashes of good fortune. What guides shall we follow in the shadow of such gloomy examples?

Legislators! Your duty calls you to resist the blows of two monstrous foes that do battle with each other reciprocally, both of which will attack you simultaneously: tyranny and anarchy form a vast ocean of oppression surrounding a tiny island of freedom that is perpetually pounded by the violence of the waves and hurricanes that seek unremittingly to sink her.

Behold the sea you hope to traverse in a fragile boat, its pilot utterly unskilled.

This draft of a constitution for Bolivia proposes four Political Powers, one having been added, without thereby complicating the classical division of all previous constitutions. The Electoral Power has been given powers not encompassed in other governments considered among the most liberal. These powers approach those commonly featured in a federal system. It has seemed to me to be not only convenient and practical but also easy to grant to the immediate representatives of the people the privileges most sought by the citizens of that particular department, province, or canton. There is no higher priority for a citizen than the election of his legislators, magistrates, judges, and pastors. The electoral colleges of each province represent their specific needs and interests and serve to expose infractions of the laws and the abuses of magistrates. I dare say, with some conviction, that this system of representation features the rights enjoyed by local governments in confederations. In this way, new weight has been added to the balance against the Executive, and the government has acquired additional guarantees, renewed popular support, and new justifications for being regarded as preeminent among the most democratic of governments.

Each ten citizens appoint an elector, so that the nation is represented by a tenth of its citizens. All that is required is ability, nor is it necessary to own property to exercise the august function of sovereign, but the electors must know how to write down their votes, sign their names, and read the laws. They must practice a trade or a craft that will guarantee an honest living. The only disqualifying factors are crime, idleness, and total ignorance. Knowledge and honesty, not money, are the requirements for exercising public authority.

The Legislative Body is constituted so as to guarantee harmony among its parts; it will not stand forever divided for lack of a judge to provide arbitration, as happens where they are only two chambers. Since there are three branches, conflict between two is resolved by the third, the question being argued by two contending sides, with an impartial third side deciding the issue. In this way, no useful law will be rejected, or at least it will have been tested once, twice, and a third time before this happens. In all negotiations between two adversaries, a third is appointed to settle disputes. Would it not be absurd, in matters so crucial to society, to dispense with this provision dictated by imperious necessity? The chambers will thus observe toward one another the mutual respect necessary to preserve the unity of the entire body, which must conduct its deliberations calmly, wisely, and with restrained passion. You will tell me that in modern times congresses have been composed of two houses. This is because in England, which has served as the model, the nobility and the common people had to be represented in two chambers. And if the same procedure was followed in North America, where there was no nobility, it is likely that the habit of being under English rule inspired that imitation. The fact is that two deliberating bodies will inevitably lead to perpetual conflict, and for this reason Sieyès preferred only one.[23] An absurd classicist.

The first chamber consists of tribunes and has the power to initiate laws related to finance, peace, and war. It will conduct direct supervision of the departments administered by the executive, with minimal intervention by the legislature.

The senators will write the law codes and ecclesiastical regulations and supervise the courts and the practice of religion. It will be the responsibility of the senate to appoint the prefects, district judges, governors, corregidores, and all the lesser officials of the Justice Department. It will also offer in nomination to the Chamber of Censors candidates to the Supreme Court and to the ecclesiastical offices of archbishop, bishop, prelate, and canon. Everything pertaining to religion and the laws falls under the jurisdiction of the senate.

The censors exercise a political and moral authority similar to that of the Areopagus of Athens and the censors of Rome. They will have prosecutorial authority over the government to ensure that the constitution and public contracts are rigorously observed. I have placed under their aegis the National Judicature, which is charged with determining whether the executive is administering the laws properly.

It is the censors who protect morality, the sciences, the arts, education, and the press. Their power is both terrible and august. They condemn to eternal opprobrium those who usurp the sovereign authority or commit other high crimes. They grant public honors for the services and virtues of illustrious citizens. The compass of national glory has been placed in their hands, so their integrity must be unquestioned, their conduct exemplary. If they stray, they will be prosecuted for the slightest offense. It is to these priests of the law that I have entrusted the preservation of our sacred commandments, because it is they who must cry out against those who profane them.

Under our constitution, the president of the republic is like the Sun, immovable at the center of the universe, radiating life. This supreme authority should be permanent, because in systems without hierarchies, a fixed point around which magistrates and citizens and men and events revolve is more necessary than in other systems. Give me a fixed point, said an ancient, and I will move the earth. For Bolivia, this point is a president for life. In him, all order originates, even though he lacks the power to act. He has been beheaded so that no one will fear his intentions, and his hands have been tied so that he can harm no one.

The president of Bolivia is endowed with powers similar to those of the American executive, but with restrictions beneficial to the people. His term of office is the same as that of the presidents of Haiti. I have chosen as the model for Bolivia the executive of the most democratic republic in the world.

The island of Haiti (forgive my digression) found herself in a state of constant insurrection. After having tried every type of government known to man—empire, monarchy, republic—and a few never seen before, she had to resort to the distinguished [Alexandre] Pétion to save her. The people put their trust in him, and the destiny of Haiti has not wavered since. Once Pétion had been named president for life with the power to choose his successor, neither the death of this great man nor the succession of the new president brought the least danger to the state: everything went forward under the worthy [Jean-Pierre] Boyer, as in the tranquility of a legitimate kingdom. This is triumphant proof that a president for life, with the power to choose his successor, is the most sublime innovation in the republican system.

The president of Bolivia will be even less a threat than the president of Haiti, since the mode of succession offers surer prospects for the health of the state. Moreover, the president of Bolivia is denied all influence: he does not appoint magistrates, judges, or ecclesiastical dignitaries at any level. This reduction in executive power has never been tried in any duly constituted government. It adds restriction after restriction to the authority of a leader who will find the entire state run by those who exercise the most important functions of society. The priests will rule in matters of conscience, the judges in questions of property, honor, and life, and the elected officials in all public acts. As the latter will be indebted only to the people for their titles, their glory, and their fortune, the president cannot aspire to involve them in his ambitious designs. If we add to this other factors that will emerge inevitably from the general opposition that a democratic government faces in every act of its administration, it seems that we are correct in assuming that the usurpation of public power is less likely to occur under this system of government than under any other.

Legislators! From this day forward, freedom will be indestructible in America. Consider the wildness of this continent, which by its very nature expels monarchical rule: the very deserts invite independence. Here there are no grand nobles or prelates. Our wealth was insignificant in the past, even more so in the present. Although the Church enjoys a certain prestige, it is far from aspiring to domination, content to maintain the power it has. Without these supports, tyrants cannot survive, and if certain ambitious men insist on establishing empires, [Jean-Jacques] Dessalines, Cristóbal [Henri Christophe], and [Agustín de] Iturbide can tell them what awaits them. There is no power more difficult to maintain than that of a new prince. Bonaparte, vanquisher of every army he encountered, was unable to transcend this principle, which is stronger than empires. And if the great Napoleon could not prevail against the combined forces of republicans and aristocrats, who will ever be able to found a monarchy in America, a land on fire with the brilliant flames of freedom that devour the planks used to build daises for kings? No, Legislators, you need not fear pretenders to a crown that will hang over their heads like the sword of Damocles. The fledgling princes who delude themselves to the point of erecting thrones over the rubble of freedom will be erecting tombs for their ashes, which will proclaim to future generations how they preferred vain ambition to freedom and glory.

The constitutional restrictions on the president of Bolivia are the severest ever known: his meager powers only allow him to appoint the ministers of the departments of the treasury, peace, and war, and to command the army. That is the extent of his power.

All administrative functions are performed by the Cabinet, which is responsible to the censors and subject to the zealous vigilance of every legislator, public official, judge, and citizen. The revenue officers and soldiers, who are the only agents of this ministry, are in truth ill suited to engage the passions of the people, so their influence is insignificant.

There has never existed a public functionary as limited in his authority as the vice president. He is subservient to both the legislative and the executive branches of a republican government. From the former he is given laws, from the latter commands, and between these two sentinels he must march down a narrow path flanked by precipices. Despite so many impediments, it is preferable to govern in this way than with absolute power. These constitutional restrictions broaden political awareness and offer firm hope of finding the light to guide the State among the reefs that surround it. They serve to moderate the impulses of our passions, which are focused on selfish interests.

In the government of the United States, the practice of appointing the secretary of state to succeed the president has been observed in recent years. Nothing is as beneficial, in a republic, as this procedure. It has the advantage of placing at the head of government a person who is experienced in managing the state. From the moment he enters office he is prepared, and he is endowed with the aura of popular approval and consummate experience. I have borrowed this idea and established it as law.

The president of the republic appoints the vice president to administer the state and be his successor. This provision avoids elections, which produce the scourge of republics, anarchy. Anarchy is the instrument of tyranny and the most immediate and terrible of dangers in popular governments. Compare the orderly succession of rulers occurring in legitimate monarchies with the terrible crises provoked by these events in a republic.

The vice president must be the purest of men. This is crucial, because if the president does not appoint a righteous citizen, he must fear him as enemy incarnate and suspect even his most hidden ambitions. This vice president must strive to win through his good services the credibility he needs to exercise the highest functions and to merit the greatest award given by the nation—the supreme power. The legislative body and the people will demand high skills and abilities of this official, as well as blind obedience to the laws of freedom.

Heredity being the principle perpetuating monarchical regimes, and this is so throughout the world, how much more useful would the method I propose be for determining the succession of the vice president? What if hereditary princes were chosen by merit, and not randomly, and instead of squandering their lives in idleness and ignorance, they were placed at the head of the administration? They would without a doubt be more enlightened monarchs and bring prosperity to their people. Yes, Legislators, the monarchies that govern the earth have been validated by the principle of heredity that makes them stable and by the unity that makes them strong. Thus, even though a sovereign prince may have been spoiled as a child, cloistered in his palace, educated by flattery, and driven by every passion, this prince, whom I would make so bold as to call the travesty of a man, has authority over human beings because he preserves the order of things and the subservience of his subjects through the uninterrupted exercise of power and consistent action. Then consider, Legislators, that these great advantages are embodied in the *president for life and in the hereditary succession by the vice president.*[24]

The Judicial Power that I propose enjoys absolute independence: nowhere else does it enjoy as much. The people present the candidates, and the legislature chooses the individuals who will make up the courts. If the Judicial Power does not come into being in this manner, it cannot possibly maintain its integrity, which is the safeguard of individual rights. These rights, Legislators, constitute the freedom, equality, and security that are guaranteed in the social contract. The truly liberal constitution rests in the civil and criminal codes, and the most terrible tyranny is that exercised by the courts through the all-powerful instrument of the law. In normal times, the executive is no more than the administrator of public matters, but the courts are the arbiters of private matters—things pertaining to individuals. The Judicial Power controls the measure of good or evil in the lives of citizens, and if there is freedom, if there is justice in the republic, they are dispensed by this power. The political organization is of little importance as long as the civil organization is perfect, that is, as long as the laws are rigorously applied and thought to be as inexorable as fate.

It was to be expected, according to the sentiments of modern times, that we would prohibit the use of torture to attain confessions and that we would reduce the time allowed for motions in the intricate labyrinth of the appellate courts.

The territory of the republic is governed by prefects, governors, corregidores, justices of the peace, and alcaldes. Even though I have not been able to examine the inner workings and powers of these jurisdictions, it is my duty to recommend to congress the rules concerning the administration of departments and provinces. Bear in mind, Legislators, that nations are made up of cities and villages, and that the happiness of the state depends on their well-being. You can never give too much attention to the efficient administration of the departments. This is a matter of highest priority in the science of legislation, yet too often it is neglected.

I have divided the armed forces into four parts: regular army, fleet, military police, and military reserve. The primary duty of the armed forces is to guard the border. God forbid that they ever turn their weapons on the citizens. The military police is sufficient for the maintenance of domestic order. Bolivia has no coasts, so the navy serves no purpose.[25] We should, however, aspire to have both someday. A military reserve is preferable in all respects to a civil guard, which is not so much superfluous as it is immoral. Therefore, it is in the best interest of the republic to secure its borders with regular army troops and to use soldiers from the military reserve against contraband and tax evasion.

I have come to the conclusion that the constitution of Bolivia should undergo gradual reform according to the demands of a changing moral climate. The procedures for reform are indicated in terms I deem appropriate to the circumstances.

The responsibility of government officials is written into the Bolivian constitution in the most explicit language. Without responsibility, without some coercion, the state is chaos. I will be so bold as to ardently urge the legislators to enact strong, definitive laws concerning this important matter. Everyone speaks of responsibility, but it goes no further than the lips. There is no responsibility, Legislators. The magistrates, judges, and other officials abuse their powers because there is no rigorous procedure for controlling the agents of the administration. Meanwhile, it is the citizens who are the victims of this abuse. I would recommend a law prescribing a strict and formal annual accounting of the actions of each official.

The most perfect guarantees have been written into this draft: *Civil liberty* is the only true freedom; the others are nominal or of little importance insofar as they affect the citizens. The *security of the individual* has been guaranteed, this being the purpose of society and the source of all other guarantees. As for *property rights*, these will depend on the civil code that in your wisdom you will compose with all dispatch for the happiness of your fellow citizens. I have left intact the law of all laws—*equality*. Without this, all guarantees, all rights perish. To ensure equality, we must make every sacrifice, beginning with infamous slavery, which I have laid at her feet, covered with shame.

Legislators! Slavery is the violation of every law. The law that would seek to preserve it would be a sacrilege. What possible justification can there be for its perpetuation? From whatever perspective you consider this crime, I cannot persuade myself that any Bolivian could be depraved enough to want to legitimize this most abominable violation of human dignity. One man owned by another! A man regarded as property! One of God's images hitched to the yoke like a beast! Let someone tell us, where do these usurpers of men file their titles of ownership? They were not sent to us by Guinea, because Africa, devastated by fratricide, can only export crime. The remnants of those warring African tribes having been transplanted here, what law or authority would be capable of sanctioning ownership of these victims? To transmit, prolong, or perpetuate a crime exacerbated by torture would be the most appalling outrage. To base ownership on savage crime would be inconceivable without the total distortion of the law and the absolute perversion of the idea of human obligation. The sacred doctrine of equality must never be violated. Can there be slavery where equality reigns? Such a contradiction would demean not so much our sense of justice as our sense of reason; our notoriety would be based on insanity, not usurpation.

If there were no God to protect innocence and freedom, I would prefer the lot of the noble lion, lord of desert and jungle, to that of a slave risking Heaven's wrath by serving as partner in crime to a tyrant. But no, God has destined man to be free; he protects him so that he can exercise the divine faculty of free will.

Legislators! I will now make reference to a matter my conscience forbade me to include. In a political system there should be no preference for one religion over another, because according to the wisest doctrines, the fundamental laws are guarantees of political and civil rights. And since religion has no relevance to these rights, it is inherently indefinable in the social order, belonging rather to the moral and intellectual order. Religion governs man in his house, in his private space, in his heart. Religion alone has the right to examine his conscience. The laws, on the other hand, observe the surface of things; they have jurisdiction only outside the citizen's home. Applying these considerations, is there any way the state can govern the conscience of its subjects, enforce the observation of religious laws, and offer reward or punishment, when the courts are in Heaven, when God is judge? Only the Inquisition could stand in for them in this world. Do we want to see a return of the Inquisition and the auto-da-fe?

Religion is the law of conscience. Any law imposed on it annuls it, because when we enforce duty, we remove merit from faith, which is the basis of religion. The precepts and sacred dogmas of religion are useful, luminous proofs of transcendence; we should all profess them, but this obligation is moral, not political.

On the other hand, what are man's rights on earth with regard to religion? They reside in Heaven; there, merit is rewarded by the tribunal which metes out justice according to the code dictated by the Great Legislator. As all of this falls under divine jurisdiction, my instinct tells me it is sacrilegious and profane to mix our laws with the commandments of the Lord. Thus, it is not the task of the legislature to prescribe religion, since it would have to levy penalties against infractions of the laws, lest they be seen as mere recommendations. Without temporal punishments, nor any judges to dispense them, the law ceases to be law.

The moral development of man is the first intent of the legislator. Once this development is achieved, man builds his morality on a base of revealed truths and in fact comes to profess a religion, which is all the more effective to the extent that he has acquired it through his own investigation. Beyond this, parents cannot neglect the religious obligation toward their children. The spiritual pastors are obliged to teach the science of heaven. The example of the true disciples of Jesus is the most eloquent teacher of his divine morality, but morality cannot be imposed, nor is the one who imposes it a teacher, nor should force be used in offering counsel. God and his ministers are the authorities on religion, which operates exclusively through spiritual means and bodies, never through the legislative body of the nation, which focuses public authority on purely temporal objects.

Legislators! As you look upon the newly founded Bolivian nation, to what generous and sublime meditations must your souls be uplifted! The entry of a new state into the community of nations is cause for rejoicing by the human race, because the great family of peoples is augmented. How great, then, must be that of its founders, and mine, to see myself compared with the most famous of the ancients, the father of the Eternal City! This glory rightly belongs to the founders of nations who, being their original benefactors, have earned immortal rewards; but mine, besides being immortal, has the bonus of being gratuitous because it is undeserved. Where is the republic, where is the city that I have founded? Your munificence, in naming this nation for me, far surpasses all my services and is infinitely superior to any treasure men can offer us.

My despair grows as I behold the immensity of your prize, because even if I had exhausted the talent, virtue, and genius of the greatest of heroes, I would still be unworthy of the name you have chosen to take for your own and which is mine! Why speak of gratitude, when it cannot begin to express the emotions stirred in me by your goodness, which like God's surpasses all understanding? Yes, only God had the power to name this land Bolivia. What does Bolivia mean? A love for freedom so boundless that when it came, you were swept away on apprehending its unequaled value. And as your rapture could find no adequate way to express the vehemence of your emotions, it stole away your name and imposed mine on all your future generations. This act, unparalleled in the history of the ages, is even more so in the history of sublime selflessness. This quality will demonstrate to ages not yet imagined in the mind of the Eternal the ardor with which you craved possession of your rights, that is, the right to practice political virtue, to acquire luminous capacities for self-government, and to enjoy being fully human. This quality, I repeat, will prove that you were entitled to the greatest of Heaven's blessings—popular sovereignty—the sole legitimate authority of nations.

Legislators! Happy are you who preside over the destinies of a republic that came into the world crowned with the laurels of Ayacucho, and which is to perpetuate its happy existence under the laws dictated by your wisdom, in the tranquility that follows the tempest of war.

Bolívar

11. Draft of a Constitution for Bolivia

In the name of God, the General Constituent Congress of the Bolivian Republic, named by the people to form the constitution of the state, decrees the following:

Title 1   Of the Nation

Chapter 1   Of the Bolivian Nation

Article 1. The Bolivian nation is the union of all Bolivians.

Article 2. Bolivia is and will be forever independent of all foreign domination and cannot be the patrimony of any person or family.

Chapter 2   Of the Territory

Article 3. The territory of the Bolivian Republic comprises the departments of Potosí, Chuquisaca, La Paz, Santa Cruz, Cochabamba, and Oruro.

Article 4. It is divided into departments, provinces, and cantons.

Article 5. One law shall be legislated to make the division more convenient, another to establish boundaries, with the consent of adjacent states.[26]

Title 2   Of the Government

Chapter 1   Form of the Government

Article 6. The government of Bolivia is a representative democracy.

Article 7. Sovereignty emanates from the people, and its exercise is vested in the powers that this Constitution establishes.

Article 8. The Supreme Power is divided for its exercise into four sections: Electoral, Legislative, Executive, and Judicial.

Article 9. Each section shall exercise the powers stipulated for it in this Constitution, without exceeding its respective limits.

Chapter 2   Of the Bolivians

Article 10. Bolivians include:

1. All those born in the territory of the Republic.
2. The children of a Bolivian father or mother, including those born outside the territory if they manifest legally their wish to reside in Bolivia.
3. The liberators of the Republic, identified as such by the law of 11 August 1825.[27]
4. Foreigners who obtain a letter of naturalization or who have three years of residence in the territory of the Republic.
5. All those who have until now been slaves and who are liberated as a consequence of the publication of this Constitution; a special law shall be enacted to determine the amount of compensation to be paid to their former owners.[28]

Article 11. All Bolivians have the following obligations:

1. To live according to the Constitution and the laws.
2. To respect and obey the constituted authorities.
3. To contribute to the public revenue.
4. To sacrifice their property and even their lives, when the well-being of the Republic so requires.
5. To be vigilant in the preservation of public freedoms.

Article 12. Bolivians who are denied the right to vote shall enjoy all the civil rights granted to citizens.

Article 13. To be a citizen, it is necessary:

1. To be a Bolivian.
2. To be married, or older than twenty-one years of age.
3. To know how to read and write.[29]
4. To have some employment or trade, or to profess some science or art, without subjection to another person as a domestic servant.

Article 14. The following are citizens:

1. The liberators of the Republic (Article 10, item 3).
2. Foreigners who obtain a letter of citizenship.
3. Foreign men who are married to a Bolivian woman and who satisfy the conditions of items 3 and 4 of Article 13.
4. Unmarried foreign men who have four years of residence in the Republic, subject to the same conditions.

Article 15. The citizens of the nations of America formerly ruled by Spain shall enjoy the rights of citizenship in Bolivia, according to the terms of any treaties entered into by those nations.

Article 16. Only those who are active citizens can obtain public employment and offices.

Article 17. The exercise of citizenship is suspended:

1. For insanity.
2. For the crime of debt fraud.
3. For those under criminal indictment.
4. For being a notorious drunkard, gambler, or beggar.
5. For buying or selling votes in elections or for interfering with the electoral process.

Article 18. The rights of citizenship are forfeited:

1. For treason to the public cause.
2. For taking citizenship in a foreign country.
3. For having been convicted of an infamous or serious crime by a court.

Title 3   *Of the Electoral Power*
Chapter 1   Of the Elections

Article 19. The Electoral Power is exercised directly by the citizens, one elector being appointed for each ten citizens.[30]

Article 20. The exercise of Electoral Power can never be suspended, and the civil administrators must convoke the people to vote at the exact time specified by the law, without awaiting orders from the Executive.

Article 21. A special law shall stipulate election procedures.

Chapter 2   Of the Electoral Body

Article 22. The Electoral Body consists of the electors appointed by the vote of the people.[31]

Article 23. When the electors have assembled in the provincial capital, they shall elect from the membership, by a plurality of votes, a president, two examiners, and a secretary; these shall hold these offices for the duration of the Body.

Article 24. Each Electoral Body shall have a term of four years, after which it shall be dissolved and replaced by its successor.

Article 25. The electors shall convene each year on the second, third, fourth, fifth, and sixth days of January to exercise the following duties:

1. To qualify the citizens who present themselves to exercise their rights and to suspend those falling under the provisions of Articles 17 and 18.
2. To elect and propose a slate of candidates: first, to the respective Chambers for membership or to fill vacancies; second, to the Executive Power, candidates for the prefecture of their department, for the governor of their province, and for corregidores of the cantons and towns; third, to the Department Prefect, the alcaldes and justices of the peace to be appointed; fourth, to the Senate, the members of the courts in the judicial district to which they belong and the primary court judges; fifth, to the Executive Power, the priests and vicars for vacancies in their respective province.[32]
3. To receive the results of the popular elections, to examine the identities of those newly elected, and to certify their election constitutionally.
4. To petition the Chambers for whatever they deem favorable to the well-being of the citizens and to forward complaints they receive from duly constituted authorities concerning grievances and injustices.

Title 4   Of the Legislative Power
Chapter 1   Of the Division, Attributes, and Restrictions of This Power

Article 26. The Legislative Power emanates directly from the electoral bodies appointed by the people; its exercise is vested in three Chambers: first, the Tribunes; second, the Senators; third, the Censors.

Article 27. Each Chamber shall consist of thirty members during the first twenty years.

Article 28. The _____ day of the month of _____ of each year, the Legislative Body shall meet on its own initiative, without awaiting convocation.

Article 29. The specific powers of each Chamber shall be enumerated in the chapter dedicated to it. General powers:

1. To appoint the president of the Republic on the first occasion and to confirm his successors.
2. To approve the vice president proposed by the president.
3. To choose the place of residence of the government, and to move that residence to another place when threatening circumstances make it necessary and a two-thirds majority of the members composing the three Chambers so resolve.
4. To determine, acting as a National Tribunal, if there is cause to impeach the members of the Chambers, the vice president, and the secretaries of state.
5. To vest, in times of war or extreme danger, the president of the Republic with the powers deemed necessary for the survival of the state.
6. To elect from among the candidates nominated by the Electoral Bodies the members who shall fill the vacancies in each Chamber.
7. To conduct internal policies and procedures by regulations and to punish their members for infractions of these regulations.

Article 30. The members of the Legislative Body can be appointed vice presidents of the Republic or secretaries of state when they step down from their Chamber.

Article 31. No individual of the Legislative Body can be incarcerated during his term, except by order of his respective Chamber, unless he be apprehended in flagrante committing a capital crime.

Article 32. The members of the Legislative Body shall be immune from prosecution for the opinions they express in their Chambers in the exercise of their duties.

Article 33. Each Legislature shall have a four-year term, and each annual session shall be two months in length. These sessions shall be convened and adjourned simultaneously by the three Chambers.

Article 34. The sessions shall be called to order each year with the president of the Republic, the vice president, and the secretaries of state in attendance.

Article 35. The sessions shall be public, and only state business requiring secrecy shall be conducted in closed session.

Article 36. In each Chamber, business shall be resolved by an absolute majority of votes of the members present.

Article 37. The employees who are appointed as deputies to the Legislative Body shall be temporarily replaced by other individuals in the exercise of their duties.

Article 38. The following restrictions apply to the Legislative Body:

1. No session shall be held in any of the Chambers unless half of the members of that Chamber plus one are present, and those who are absent should be compelled to attend to perform their duties.
2. None of the Chambers shall be permitted to initiate legislation relative to matters that the Constitution commits to a different Chamber, but a Chamber may invite the other Chambers to give consideration to the motions it consigns to them.
3. No member of the Chambers shall be allowed to obtain for himself, during his term, any except a one-step promotion in his career.

Article 39. The Chambers shall meet together:

1. When their sessions are opened and adjourned.
2. To examine the conduct of the Ministry when brought under indictment by the Chamber of Censors.
3. To review the laws returned by the Executive Power.
4. When any of the Chambers requests it with good cause, as in the case of Article 29, item 3.
5. To confirm the transfer of power from the president to the vice president.

Article 40. When the three Chambers convene together, one of their presidents, in turn, shall preside.

Chapter 2   Of the Chamber of Tribunes

Article 41. To be a Tribune, one must:

1. Be an active citizen.
2. Be twenty-five years of age.
3. Never have been convicted in criminal court.

Article 42. The Tribuneship has the initiative:

1. In the establishment of the territorial division of the Republic.
2. In annual contributions and public expenses.
3. In authorizing the Executive Power to negotiate loans and to issue bonds to pay off the public debt.
4. In the value, type, law, weight, and denomination of currency, and in the establishment of weights and measures.
5. In opening every type of port.
6. In the construction of roads, highways, bridges, and public buildings and in the improvement of the police force and the branches of government.
7. In the salaries of state employees.
8. In reforms considered necessary in the areas of finance and war.
9. In making war or peace, on the recommendation of the government.
10. In alliances.
11. In granting passage to foreign troops.
12. In determining the size of the navy and army for the year, on the recommendation of the government.
13. In issuing ordinances for the navy, the army, and the military police, on the recommendation of the government.
14. In foreign affairs.
15. In granting letters of naturalization and citizenship.
16. In granting general amnesties.

Article 43. Half of the Chamber of Tribunes shall be renewed every two years, and terms shall be for four years.

Article 44. The Tribunes may be reelected.

Chapter 3   Of the Chamber of Senators

Article 45. To be a senator, one must:

1. Have the qualifications required for elector.
2. Be thirty-five years of age.
3. Never have been convicted in criminal court.

Article 46. The attributes of the Senate are:

1. To formulate the civil, criminal, procedural, and commercial codes and the ecclesiastical regulations.

2. To initiate all laws relative to reforms in judicial matters.
3. To be vigilant in the prompt administration of civil and criminal justice.
4. To initiate laws to discourage infractions of the Constitution and the laws by magistrates, judges, and ecclesiastics.
5. To exact responsibility of the superior tribunals of justice, the prefects, and the subordinate magistrates and judges.
6. To nominate three candidates, to the Chamber of Censors, for each position on the Supreme Tribunal of Justice and as archbishop, bishop, dignitary, canon, and prebendary of the cathedrals.
7. To approve or reject the prefects, governors, and corregidores whom the government presents to it from the nominations made by the electoral bodies.
8. To elect, from the nominees presented by the electoral bodies, the district judges and all the subordinate officials of the Department of Justice.
9. To regulate the exercise of the patronage and propose laws on all ecclesiastical matters that concern the government.
10. To examine conciliar decisions, papal bulls, rescripts, and briefs in order to approve them or not.

Article 47. The term of office for members of the Senate shall be eight years, half of the members to be replaced after four years, these being chosen in the first legislature by random lot.

Article 48. The members of the Senate may be reelected.

Chapter 4   Of the Chamber of Censors

Article 49. To be a Censor, one must:

1. Have the qualifications required for a senator.
2. Be forty years of age.
3. Never have been convicted of any crime, however slight.

Article 50. The attributes of the Chamber of Censors:

1. To see that the government fulfills and enforces the Constitution, laws, and public treaties.
2. To make accusation before the Senate for any infractions committed by the Executive against the Constitution, laws, and public treaties.

3. To petition the Senate for the removal of the vice president and secretaries of state if the health of the Republic urgently demands it.

Article 51. It is the exclusive duty of the Chamber of Censors to bring accusations against the vice president and secretaries of state before the Senate in cases of treason, arbitrary or fraudulent seizure, or manifest violation of the fundamental laws of the state.

Article 52. Should the Senate find the accusation made by the Chamber of Censors to be justified, a National Hearing of Impeachment shall be held, and if, on the contrary, the Senate should not so find, it shall forward the accusation to the Chamber of Tribunes.

Article 53. Should two of the Chambers agree, the National Hearing shall be initiated.

Article 54. Then the three Chambers shall convene together, and in consideration of the documents presented by the Chamber of Censors, a determination based on an absolute plurality of votes shall be made as to whether the vice president or the secretaries of state are to stand trial.

Article 55. Should it be decreed in the National Hearing that the vice president or secretaries of state are to stand trial, they shall be suspended from their duties immediately, and the Chambers shall forward all evidentiary documents to the Supreme Tribunal of Justice, which shall have exclusive jurisdiction over the proceedings, and the verdict that it pronounces shall be executed without appeal.

Article 56. Once the Chambers declare that there is cause to bring to trial the vice president and secretaries of state, the president of the Republic shall present to the combined Chambers a candidate for the interim vice presidency and shall appoint interim secretaries of state. If the first candidate should be rejected by absolute plurality of the Legislative Body, the president shall present a second candidate, and should he be rejected, he shall present a third candidate, and if he should be rejected as well, then the Chambers shall elect by absolute plurality, within twenty-four hours, one of the three candidates proposed by the president.

Article 57. The interim vice president shall exercise his duties from the moment of his election until a verdict has been handed down against the incumbent.

Article 58. The provisions of a law to be originated in the Chamber of Censors shall decide in which cases the vice president and the secretaries are mutually or personally responsible.

Article 59. Further attributes corresponding to the Chamber of Censors are:

1. To choose from among the nominees presented by the Senate the individuals who are to form the Supreme Tribunal of Justice.
2. All laws on printing, the economy, and the curriculum and method to be used in public education.
3. To protect the freedom of the press and to name the judges who are to see press cases in final appeal.
4. To propose regulations for the encouragement of the arts and sciences.
5. To grant prizes and national rewards to those who merit them for their services to the Republic.
6. To decree public honors to the memory of great men and to the virtues and services of citizens.
7. To condemn to eternal opprobrium the usurpers of public authority, infamous traitors, and notorious criminals.

Article 60. The Censors shall serve for life.

Chapter 5   Of the Formation and Promulgation of Laws

Article 61. The government may present to the Chambers proposals for laws it deems suitable.

Article 62. The vice president and the secretaries of state may attend the sessions and discuss the laws and other matters but may not vote or be present during voting.

Article 63. When the Chamber of Tribunes adopts a proposal for legislation, it shall remit it to the Senate with the following formula:

The Chamber of Tribunes remits to the Chamber of Senators the attached proposal for legislation, which it deems appropriate.

Article 64. If the Chamber of Senators approves the proposed legislation, it shall return it to the Chamber of Tribunes with the following formula:

The Senate returns to the Chamber of Tribunes the proposed legislation (amended or not), and believes that it should be forwarded to the Executive for its implementation.

Article 65. All the Chambers shall observe the same formula in similar cases.

Article 66. Should one of the Chambers decline to approve the reforms or amendments of another, and the recommending Chamber continues to deem the proposed legislation, exactly as proposed, to be advantageous, it shall be permitted to suggest, by a delegation of three members, a meeting of the two chambers to discuss the proposal, or the reform or rejection to which it has been subjected. This meeting of Chambers shall have no other purpose than to reach an accord, and each Chamber shall adopt anew the deliberations it considers convenient.

Article 67. When the legislation has been proposed by two Chambers, two copies signed by the president and secretaries of the Chamber under whose jurisdiction the law falls shall be forwarded to the president of the Republic with the following formula:

> *The Chamber of _____ with the approval of the Chamber of _____ submits the law on _____ to the Executive Power for its promulgation.*

Article 68. Should the Chamber of Senators decline to adopt the legislation proposed by the Chamber of Tribunes, it shall submit it to the Chamber of Censors with the following formula:

> *The Chamber of Senators remits the attached proposal to the Chamber of Censors, considering it inappropriate.*

Then the decision of the Chamber of Censors shall be final.

Article 69. Should the president of the Republic consider the law to be inappropriate, he shall within ten days return it to the originating Chamber with his observations, using the following formula:

> *The Executive believes that it should be considered anew.*

Article 70. Any legislation passed during the final ten days of the session may be held for consideration by the Executive Power until the next session, at which time it must return it with observations.

Article 71. When the Executive Power returns the laws with observations to the Chambers, the latter shall meet, and what they decide by plurality shall be carried out without further discussion.

Article 72. Should the Executive Power have no observations to make regarding the laws, it shall order them published with this formula:

> *To be promulgated.*

Article 73. The laws shall be promulgated with this formula:

> _____, *President of the Bolivian Republic. Be it known to all Bolivians: that*

the Legislative Body has decreed and we do publish the following law. [Insert here the text of the law.] We do therefore ordain to all authorities of the Republic that they shall fulfill and enforce it.

The vice president shall have it printed, published, and circulated to those to whom it pertains.

And it shall be signed by the president with the vice president and the respective secretary of state.

Article 74. Any proposed legislation originating in the Senate shall be forwarded to the Chamber of Censors, and should it be approved there, it shall have the force of law. If the Censors should decline to approve it, it shall be forwarded to the Chamber of Tribunes, and their decision shall be carried out, as has been said, with respect to the Chamber of Tribunes.

Article 75. Proposed legislation originating in the Chamber of Censors shall be forwarded to the Senate. Approval by the Senate shall confer on it force of law. But should the Senate decline to recommend the legislation, it shall be forwarded to the Chamber of Tribunes, which shall sanction or decline to sanction it, as in the case of the preceding article.

Title 5   Of the Executive Power

Article 76. The exercise of the Executive Power is vested in a president who serves for life, a vice president, and three secretaries of state.

Chapter 1   Of the President

Article 77. The president of the Republic shall be named the first time by absolute plurality of the Legislative Body.

Article 78. To be named president of the Republic, one must:

1. Be an active citizen and native of Bolivia.[33]
2. Be thirty years of age.
3. Have rendered important services to the Republic.
4. Have known talents in the administration of the state.
5. Never have been convicted of a criminal offense, however slight.

Article 79. The president of the Republic is the chief of the administration of the state, without responsibility for the acts of said administration.

Article 80. By resignation, death, sickness, or absence of the president of the Republic, the vice president will succeed him immediately.

Article 81. In the absence of the president and vice president of the Republic, the three secretaries of state shall assume provisional charge of the administration, the one with seniority presiding until the Legislative Body convenes.

Article 82. The attributes of the president of the Republic are:

1. To open the sessions of the Chambers and present them a message on the state of the Republic.
2. To nominate the vice president to the Chambers and to name by himself alone the cabinet secretaries.
3. To remove by himself alone the vice president and the cabinet secretaries, whenever he sees fit.
4. To order the laws to be published, circulated, and kept.
5. To authorize regulations and orders for the better fulfillment of the Constitution, laws, and public treaties.
6. To order and cause to be carried out the sentences of the tribunals of justice.
7. To petition the Legislative Body to extend their ordinary sessions for as many as thirty days.
8. To convoke the Legislative Body for extraordinary sessions when it becomes absolutely necessary.
9. To dispose of the permanent forces of sea and land for the external defense of the Republic.
10. To command the armies of the Republic in person, in peace and war.[34] When the president is absent from the capital, the vice president shall be left in charge of the Republic.
11. When the president directs the war in person, he shall be permitted to reside in any territory occupied by the national forces.
12. To dispose of the military police for internal security within the limits of their departments and outside of them, with the consent of the Legislative Body.
13. To name all the employees of the army and navy.
14. To establish military schools and nautical schools.
15. To order the establishment of military hospitals and homes for invalids.
16. To approve leaves of absence and retirements, grant pensions to the military and their families, and regulate all other matters pertaining to the military, in accordance with the laws.

17. To declare war in the name of the Republic, following the decree of the Legislative Body.
18. To grant patents of privateering.
19. To attend to the collection and investment of taxes, in conformity with the laws.
20. To name financial employees.
21. To direct diplomatic negotiations and enter into treaties of peace, friendship, federation, alliance, truces, armed neutrality, commerce, and of any other kind, always with the approval of the Legislative Body.
22. To name the ministers, consuls, and subordinates of the Department of Foreign Relations.
23. To receive foreign ministers.
24. To grant approval to or suspend conciliar decisions, pontifical bulls, briefs, and rescripts with the consent of the power concerned.
25. To nominate to the Senate, for its approval, one of the three candidates proposed by the electoral body for prefects, governors, and corregidores.
26. To nominate to the ecclesiastical authority one of the three candidates proposed by the electoral body for priests and vicars of the provinces.
27. To suspend employees for up to three months, whenever there is cause to do so.
28. To commute capital sentences imposed on criminals by the tribunals.
29. To issue the titles or appointments of all employees in the name of the Republic.

Article 83. Restrictions on the President of the Republic are:

1. The President may not deprive any Bolivian of his freedom, nor impose any penalty by himself.
2. When the security of the Republic demands the arrest of one or more citizens, he must, within forty-eight hours, place the accused at the disposal of the competent tribunal or judge.
3. He may not deprive any individual of his property unless the public interest urgently demands it, but just compensation to the owner must first be made.

4. He may not prevent the elections or other functions that by law correspond to the powers of the Republic.

5. He may not absent himself from the territory of the Republic, nor from the capital, without permission of the Legislative Body.[35]

Chapter 2 *Of the Vice President*

Article 84. The vice president is named by the president of the Republic and approved by the Legislative Body, as stipulated in Article 56.

Article 85. The mode of succession shall be determined by a special law, covering all the cases that might occur.

Article 86. To be vice president, the same qualities are required as for president.

Article 87. The vice president of the Republic is the chief of the ministry.

Article 88. He shall be responsible, with the cabinet secretary of the respective department, for the administration of the state.

Article 89. He shall dispatch and sign, in the name of the Republic and the president, all the business of the administration, with the secretary of state of the respective department.

Article 90. He may not absent himself from the territory of the Republic, nor from the capital, without permission of the Legislative Body.

Chapter 3 *Of the Secretaries of State*

Article 91. There shall be three cabinet secretaries: one to administer the Departments of Government and Foreign Relations, another for the Department of Finance, and another for War and the Navy.

Article 92. These three secretaries shall serve under the direct orders of the vice president.

Article 93. No tribunal or public person shall carry out orders of the Executive that are not signed by the vice president and cabinet secretary of the respective department.

Article 94. The cabinet secretaries shall be responsible with the vice president for all the orders that they authorize against the Constitution, laws, or public treaties.

Article 95. They shall form the annual budgets of expenditures that must be made in their respective branches and will render account of those that have been made in the previous year.

Article 96. To be secretary of state, one must:

1. Be an active citizen.
2. Be thirty years of age.
3. Never have been convicted in a criminal case.

Title 6   *Of the Judicial Power*

Chapter 1   Attributes of This Power

Article 97. The tribunals and courts exercise no other functions than that of applying existent laws.[36]

Article 98. The magistrates and judges shall remain in office as long as their good behavior warrants.

Article 99. The magistrates and judges may not be suspended from their positions except in cases determined by the laws, which are to be applied by the Chamber of the Senate and the district courts with regard to magistrates, and with regard to judges, only after previous notification of the government.

Article 100. Every grave fault of the magistrates and judges in the performance of their respective offices produces popular action, which may be undertaken within the course of one year through the electoral body.[37]

Article 101. Justice shall be administered in the name of the nation, and verdicts and provisions of the tribunals shall be prefaced by the same formula.

Chapter 2   Of the Supreme Court

Article 102. The primary judicial magistracy of the state shall be vested in the Supreme Court of Justice.

Article 103. This shall consist of a president, six justices, and a prosecutor, assigned to the appropriate chambers.

Article 104. To be a member of the Supreme Tribunal of Justice, one must:

1. Be thirty-five years of age.
2. Be an active citizen.
3. Have been a member of one of the district courts of justice, and until such time as these are established, attorneys who have practiced with distinction for eight years shall be eligible.

Article 105. The attributes of the Supreme Tribunal of Justice are:

1. To hear the criminal charges against the vice president of the Republic, the secretaries of state, and members of the Chambers when the Legislative Body determines that there are grounds for indictment.
2. To hear all litigation against the national patronage.
3. To examine the bulls, briefs, and rescripts when they affect civil matters.
4. To hear litigation against ambassadors, resident ministers, consuls, and diplomatic agents.
5. To hear cases of suspension of district court magistrates and departmental prefects.
6. To resolve jurisdictional disputes between Courts of Justice and between the Courts and other authorities.
7. To hear, in the final instance, the review of conduct of all public employees.
8. To hear concerns of the lower courts as to the interpretation of a law, and to confer with the Executive in order to seek clarification from the Chambers.
9. To hear appeals for annulment of verdicts given in final instance by the Courts of Justice.
10. To examine, through means established by law, the status and progress of civil and criminal cases pending in the district courts.
11. To exercise supreme administrative, economic, and correctional authority over the tribunals and courts of the nation.

Chapter 3   Of the District Courts of Justice

Article 106. To serve as judge in these courts, one must:

1. Be thirty years of age.
2. Be an active citizen.
3. Have been a justice of the peace or practiced law with distinction for five years.

Article 107. The attributes of the district courts of justice are:

1. To hear in second and third instance all the civil cases in common jurisdiction, public finance, commerce, mining, seizures and attachments, with an individual from one of these professions also serving as associate judge.

2. To rule in jurisdictional disputes between subordinate judges of their judicial district.
3. To hear appeals from the ecclesiastical tribunals and authorities of their territory.

Chapter 4 *Judicial Divisions*

Article 108. Proportionately equal judicial divisions shall be established in the provinces, and in each division capital there will be a justice of the peace assigned to the court to be determined by the laws.

Article 109. The powers of these judges are limited to litigation, and they can render verdicts in civil cases up to 200 pesos, without possibility of appeal.

Article 110. To be a justice of the peace, one must:

1. Be twenty-eight years of age.
2. Be an active citizen.
3. Be a lawyer recognized in any tribunal in the Republic.
4. Have practiced the profession with distinction for four years.

Article 111. The justices of the peace are personally responsible for their conduct before the district courts of justice, just as the members of these courts are personally responsible before the Supreme Tribunal of Justice.

Chapter 5 *Of the Administration of Justice*

Article 112. There shall be justices of the peace in each town for conciliation of disputes, no civil or criminal petitions for damages being allowed without first seeking this remedy.

Article 113. The function of conciliators is limited to hearing petitions from both parties, instructing them of their rights, and seeking to achieve a prudent compromise between them.

Article 114. Fiscal prosecutions are not subject to conciliation.

Article 115. There are only three instances in legal suits.

Article 116. The recurso de injusticia notoria is abolished.[38]

Article 117. No Bolivian may be arrested without previous information of the act for which he merits a corporal penalty and a written order of the judge before whom he is to appear, with the exception of the cases covered in Articles 83 (restriction #2), 123, and 133.

Article 118. In the same act, whenever possible, he shall give his declaration without oath, this being delayed in no case for longer than forty-eight hours.

Article 119. Every criminal may be arrested in flagrante by any person and brought to the presence of the judge.

Article 120. In criminal cases, judgment shall be public, the facts determined and declared by juries (when they are established), and the law applied by judges.

Article 121. Torture shall never be used, nor shall confession be coerced.

Article 122. All confiscation of property and any kind of cruel punishment and hereditary infamy are abolished. The criminal code shall limit, so far as possible, the application of capital punishment.

Article 123. If in extraordinary circumstances the security of the republic should demand the suspension of any of the formalities prescribed in this chapter, the Chambers may decree it. And if the latter should not be in session, the Executive may perform this same function, as a provisional measure, and shall provide full information of his act in the next session of the Chambers, assuming responsibility for any abuses he may have committed.

Title 7   Of the Internal Organization of the Republic

Article 124. The superior government of each department shall be vested in a prefect.

Article 125. That of each province, in a governor.

Article 126. That of the cantons, in a corregidor.

Article 127. In each town and its surrounding district with a population greater than 100, there shall be a justice of the peace.

Article 128. Where the inhabitants in the town or in its district exceed 1000, there shall be (in addition to one justice of the peace for every 200) an alcalde; and where the number of inhabitants exceeds 1000, there shall be for every 500 a justice of the peace and for every 2000 an alcalde.[39]

Article 129. The positions of alcaldes and justices of the peace are obligatory, and no citizen, without just cause, may be excused from performing them.

Article 130. The prefects, governors, and corregidores shall hold their positions for a term of four years, but they may be reelected.

Article 131. The alcaldes and justices of the peace shall be renewed every two years, but they may be reelected.

Article 132. The attributes of the prefects, governors, corregidores, and alcaldes shall be determined by law in order to maintain order and public security, with due subordination to the supreme government.

Article 133. All judicial action is forbidden to them, but if public tranquility requires the arrest of an individual and the circumstances do not allow the respective judge to be informed of the matter, they shall be allowed to order the arrest, provided that they notify the competent court within forty-eight hours. Any abuse that these magistrates commit, relative to the security of an individual or his domicile, produces popular action.

Title 8   Of the Armed Forces

Article 134. There shall be in the Republic a permanent armed force.

Article 135. The armed force shall be composed of an army of the line and a squadron.

Article 136. There shall be, in each province, bodies of national militia composed of the inhabitants of each one of them.

Article 137. There shall also be a military police, whose principal function shall be to prevent all clandestine trade.

Title 9   Observance of the Constitution

Chapter 1   Reform of the Constitution

Article 138. If after ____ years following its adoption it becomes apparent that certain of the articles of the Constitution are in need of reform, the proposed amendment shall be submitted in writing, signed by no fewer than ten members of the Chamber of Tribunes and supported by two-thirds of the members present in the Chamber.[40]

Article 139. The proposed amendment shall be read three times with an interval of six days between one reading and the next, and after the third the Chamber of Tribunes shall deliberate whether the amendment shall or shall not be introduced for debate, adhering in all other respects to the procedures for enacting legislation.

Article 140. Once the proposed amendment is admitted for debate and the Chambers are convinced of the need to reform the Constitution, a law shall be issued instructing the electoral bodies to confer on the deputies of the three Chambers special powers to alter or reform the Constitution, indicating the grounds justifying such reform.

Article 141. In the first session of the Legislature following that in which the motion was made to alter or reform the Constitution, that motion shall be proposed and debated, and whatever the Chambers resolve shall be fulfilled, the Executive Power being consulted as to the need for the reform.

Chapter 2   Appointment and Responsibilities of Employees

Article 142. Any proposed appointment of an employee shall be presented along with two alternates to the Executive Power, which shall choose one and present it for confirmation to the appropriate Chamber. Should that Chamber not approve it, a second shall be presented. Should that one also be rejected, a third shall be presented, and should the Chamber then deny approval, it must accept one of the three that have been proposed by the Executive.

Article 143. Public employees are strictly responsible for the abuses they commit in the exercise of their functions.

Title 10   Of Guarantees

Article 144. Civil liberty, individual security, property, and equality before the law are guaranteed to the citizens by the Constitution.

Article 145. All may communicate their thoughts by word or in writing, and publish them by means of the press, without prior censorship, but under the responsibility that the law determines.

Article 146. Every Bolivian may remain in or leave the territory of the Republic, as he sees fit, taking his property with him but observing police regulations and provided that the right of third parties is always respected.

Article 147. Every home of a Bolivian is an inviolable asylum. By night no one may enter it, except with his consent; by day entrance shall be allowed only in the cases and the manner that the law determines.

Article 148. Taxes shall be distributed proportionately without any exception or privilege.

Article 149. Hereditary offices and privileges and entails are abolished, and all properties are alienable, even though they belong to pious works, religious communities, or other objectives.

Article 150. No type of work, industry, or commerce may be prohibited, unless it is opposed to public customs or to the security and health of Bolivians.

Article 151. Every inventor shall have ownership of his discovery and of his productions. The law shall ensure him a temporary exclusive privilege or indemnification for the loss he suffers in case of its being made public.

Article 152. The constitutional powers may not suspend the Constitution, nor the rights enjoyed by Bolivians, except in the cases and circumstances expressed in the Constitution itself, indicating without fail the period that the suspension is to last.

Message to the Convention of Ocaña

Bogotá, 29 February 1828

To the Representatives of the People in the National Convention

Fellow Citizens:

I congratulate you on the honor extended to you by the nation in entrusting its high destinies to your care.[41] As the representatives of Colombian sovereignty, you are endowed with the most sublime powers. I, too, experience the greatest good fortune as I restore to you the authority that had been deposited in my weary hands. The supreme authority, the supreme rights, belong to those chosen by the people, to you delegates of the august, omnipotent people whom I serve as subject and soldier. To what more eminent power could I surrender the president's staff, the general's sword? Dispose freely of these symbols of power and glory on behalf of the people, oblivious to personal considerations that might hinder a perfect reform.

Required by duty to reveal to you the state of the Republic, I must offer you, sadly, the portrait of its afflictions. Don't imagine that the colors I use have been inflamed by exaggeration or that they have emerged from the gloomy mansion of mystery. I painted them by scandal-light. The rendering may seem illusory to you, but if it were, would Colombia be calling you?

The afflictions of the country have, of course, begun to be remedied, since those assigned to diagnose them have gathered here. Your undertaking, truly, is as difficult as it is glorious, and if the difficulties have been eased by the good fortune that you stand before a Colombia united and eager to hear you speak, I should tell you that this invaluable advantage comes to us only by virtue of the hopes taking wing in this convention, hopes that reveal to you the burden of trust soon to encumber you.

It should suffice you to review our history to discover the causes of our decline. Colombia, which managed to spring to life, lies lifeless. Identifying itself at first with the will of the people, it no longer regards duty as the sole condition of health. The very ones who during the struggle were content with their poverty, and who had not incurred a foreign debt of even three million, now, in order to keep the peace, have had to burden themselves with shameful debts in consequence. Colombia, which breathed an atmosphere of honor and virtue in the face of oppressive forces, now gasps for air as if it were unaware of its national dishonor. Colombia, which once thought only of painful sacrifices and distinguished service, now thinks only of its rights, not its duties. The nation would have perished if some remnant of public spirit had not driven it to cry out for remedy and drawn it up short at the edge of the grave. Only some horrible danger could have led us to alter the fundamental laws; only this danger could have proven superior to the devotion we professed for the legitimate institutions we ourselves had conceived and whose foundations had won us the desired emancipation.

I would add nothing to this dismal outline if the position I hold did not require me to give an account to the nation of the flawed nature of her laws. I know that I cannot do this without exposing myself to sinister interpretations and that ambitious aspirations will be read into my words. But since I have never refused to dedicate my life and my reputation to Colombia, I feel obliged to make this last sacrifice.

I have to say it: Our government is essentially poorly constituted. Without considering that we have barely thrown off our yoke, we let ourselves be dazzled by exaggerated aspirations that universal history shows to be incompatible with human nature. At times, we proceed unwisely and attribute poor outcomes to having failed to follow closely enough the deceptive guidebook leading us astray, ignoring those who try to proceed rationally—weighing the various parts of our constitution one against the other, and with it the limits of our education, our customs, and our inexperience—so as not to fling ourselves into a stormy sea. Our diverse powers are not distributed according to the needs of the social structure and the well-being of the citizens. We have transformed the legislature into the sovereign body, whereas it should be no more than a constituent part. We have subjected the executive branch to the legislative, granting the latter far more power in the general administration than legitimate interest allows. Worst of all, all power has been inscribed in what is presumed to be the will of the people, all weakness in the official proceedings of the social order.

The right to propose legislation has been left exclusively to the legislature, which by nature is purely theoretical and far from knowing the reality of government. The power of veto conceded to the executive is all the more ineffective because the vanity of the congress views its use as a rebuff. The congress can successfully override with as little as a fifth of the vote or even less than a fifth of its members, which leaves no room to avert harmful effects.[42]

With free access to our chambers denied to cabinet secretaries for the purpose of explaining or giving an account of the intentions of the administration, not even this recourse can be adopted to enlighten the legislature in cases where some decision needs to be vetoed. Harm could have been avoided by requiring a specific lapse of time or a considerably larger proportional number of votes to override executive veto.

Be it noted that our bulky code, instead of leading to felicitous outcomes, presents obstacles to any progress. Our laws seem fashioned arbitrarily; they lack consistency, method, classification, legal diction. They contradict each other, appearing confused, often unnecessary, and even contrary to their intent. There are cases where it has been unavoidable to use strict measures to curb widespread destructive behavior, for the laws, drafted for specific cases, have turned out to be far less effective than those they replaced, indirectly encouraging the vices they were meant to discourage.

Striving for perfection, we adopted as a base of representation a ratio exceeding our capacity. By electing too many to this august function, it has lost its prestige and ended up seeming, in some provinces, unimportant and scarcely honorable to represent the people. This is the source of the discredit into which legislation has fallen, and what benefit can come from discredited laws?

In Colombia, the executive branch is not equal to the legislative, nor even to the judicial; it has become a weak arm of the supreme power, unable to exercise fully the powers invested in it, because congress encroaches on its natural jurisdiction over the judiciary, the church, and the military. The government, which ought to be the source and engine of public power, has to seek power beyond its proper jurisdiction, depending on others that ought to be subservient to it. In essence, it is the role of government to be the hub and mansion of power, though its authority comes from without. Stripped of its proper nature, it succumbs to lethargy, doing great harm to the citizens and dragging the institutions down with it.

This does not exhaust the list of flaws in the constitution with respect to the executive power. Equally harmful is the lack of responsibility of the cabinet. When all responsibility falls on the head of the administration, the force of the constitution is diminished, rendering impossible any harmonious and systematic interaction between administrative branches and diminishing equally the guarantees for observance of the law. We will see more zeal in the application and execution of the law when the ministers are invested with and accept the burden of moral responsibility for upholding it. This will create powerful incentives for them to work for the public good. If they fail, unfortunately, to meet their responsibility, their punishment will not be the seed of greater evil, will not lead to violent upheavals or revolutions. The responsibility of the chosen agent of the people will always be illusory unless it is voluntarily accepted or unless, less likely, no way can be found to get around the law. On the other hand, such responsibility can never be effective unless we clearly stipulate and define its exercise and the penalties for failure to exercise it.

We are appalled by the contrast manifested in the executive, endowed with a superabundance of power, yet afflicted with extreme weakness. It is unable to ward off invasions from without or subversion from within except by assuming dictatorial authority. The constitution itself, as if convinced of its own inadequacy, goes to excess in granting powers it had initially been loathe to provide. As a result, the government of Colombia is a meager fountain of health or a torrent of devastation.

Nowhere have we seen the faculty of judging so enthroned as in Colombia. Considering the way in which we have constituted the powers, it is inaccurate to say that the functions of the body politic of the nation can be understood as determining the popular will and then carrying it out. A third supreme power was expanded, as if deciding which laws apply to specific cases were not the primary responsibility of the executive. To keep the judges from being too much influenced in their decisions, they were kept totally separated from the executive branch, of which they are inherently an integral part; moreover, though it was the function of the executive to monitor continuously the prompt and thorough administration of justice, that function was impaired since no means were provided to determine when any necessary intervention might be opportune, nor even how far such intervention might extend. Even the executive's power to choose qualified judges has been usurped.

Not satisfied even with this exaltation, in subsequent legislation we have given civil courts absolute supremacy in military cases, against the standard practice of centuries, a circumstance undercutting the authority the constitution confers on the president and harmful to the discipline crucial to a standing militia. These new laws related to the judiciary have extended judicial authority over the military beyond all reason. As a consequence of the law of procedure, litigation has been complicated. Everywhere, new judgeships and regional courts have been established, prompting calls for reform by the unfortunate villages, which are forced to conspire and sacrifice to satisfy the judges. Superior courts, consisting almost entirely of lay members, have had to rule repeatedly on the good or bad application of the law. The executive has heard pitiful complaints against the scheming and prevarication of the judges, but has had no recourse to punish them. It has seen the public treasury drained by the ignorance and malice of the courts, but could not remedy the abuse.

The accumulation of all the administrative functions by its agents in the departments only augments the impotence of the executive; for instance, the intendant, head of civil order and internal security, has the additional obligation to administer the national revenues, whose care demands the attention of many individuals, if only to prevent waste. However convenient such accumulation may seem, it is not so, except with respect to the military authority, which in the maritime departments ought to be merged with the civil authority, and the civil authority should be kept separate from that of revenues so that each branch can serve the people and the government satisfactorily.

The municipalities, which could be useful in advising the governors of the provinces, have scarcely fulfilled their own proper functions. Some of them have had the audacity to claim the sovereignty belonging to the nation, while others have fomented sedition. Almost all the new municipalities have undermined rather than improved the general welfare, the appearance, and the health of their towns. These corporate bodies are not serving the function they were designed to serve. They have ended up making themselves hated because of the fines they levy and the bothersome workload imposed on those serving on them, and because in many towns there aren't even qualified persons to replace the membership. The most harmful aspect of these bodies is the obligation they impose on the citizens to perform a yearlong judicial function, which costs time and money in addition to compromising their reputation as responsible, honorable persons. It often happens that individuals simply abandon their homes and property just to avoid being forced to accept this unpleasant obligation. *If I may be so bold as to voice the common opinion, no decree would be as popular as the one eliminating the municipalities.*

Since no general law exists concerning public order, this scarcely exists. As a result, the country is in a state of confusion or, more precisely, is a mystery for the subordinates of the executive, who must deal with people individually. Such a situation is unmanageable without diligent and effective policing to provide each citizen with a direct connection with the agents of the government. This causes a number of problems for the intendants in trying to enforce the laws and regulations in every area of their jurisdiction.

Denied all security and peace of mind, which are a people's primary aspiration, it has been impossible for the agricultural sector even to maintain the deplorable condition in which it previously operated. Its decline has negatively affected other sectors of industry, demoralized the rural environment, and undermined the purchasing power of people there. Everything has sunk into a state of desolation, and in some districts the citizens have reassumed their condition of primitive independence, because once all benefits and amenities are lost to them, there is nothing to bind them to society and they even become hostile to it. Foreign trade has gone the way of domestic industry, so that you could say that not even our basic needs are being met. To make things worse, financial fraud encouraged by the laws and by the judges, leading to numerous bankruptcies, has undermined the trust of a profession entirely dependent on credit and good faith. And how can commerce thrive without trade and profits?

Our army was once the model for all America, the glory of liberty. Its loyalty to the law, to the legal system, and to the general recalled the heroic times of republican virtue. Lacking uniforms, soldiers bedecked themselves in weapons; dying of hunger, they lived off the spoils of victory over the enemy; lacking all ambition, they lived only for love of country. These generous virtues have been eclipsed, ironically, by new laws meant to provide the army with order and security. The soldier has been shaken by the same ills afflicting the rest of society, and he retains only his devotion to the cause that redeemed him and a healthy respect for his own scars. I have mentioned the sinister effect it must have had on him to find himself subjected to civil courts, whose doctrines and dispositions are fatal to the severe discipline, passive submission, and blind obedience crucial to military power, which is the guarantor of the entire social structure. The law that allows the soldier to marry without governmental permission has done considerable harm to the mobility, strength, and morale of the army. It was reasonable to prohibit the recruitment of heads of family; contravening this regulation, we have turned soldiers into fathers. Scurrilous attacks on officers by soldiers in the press have done much to weaken discipline. When one declares corrective discipline a form of arbitrary detention, human rights are converted into military ordinance, and anarchy is spread among the soldiers, whose cruelty and savagery are limitless once they become demagogues. Such writings and the resulting debates in congress provoke dangerous hostilities between civilians and military officers, who are suddenly seen to be executioners of liberty rather than liberators of the nation. Was this the reward reserved for our heroes? The scandal has even reached the point of arousing hatred and rancor between soldiers from different provinces, so that no trace of unity or strength can survive.

I would rather not mention the practice of granting clemency to military crimes during this ominous period. Our legislators are fully aware of the gravity of this scandalous indulgence. How can any future army fulfill its duty of defending our sacred rights if crime is rewarded, not punished, if glory is no longer a function of loyalty, nor valor a function of obedience?

Since the year 1821, when we began the reform of the treasury, the result has been a series of failed efforts, each one leaving us more disillusioned than those preceding it. The lack of commitment by the administration, in each and every one of its sectors, the general reluctance to pay taxes, the notorious corruption and carelessness on the part of the tax collectors, the creation of unnecessary positions, at substandard salaries, and even the laws themselves, have contributed to erode the treasury. From time to time efforts have been made to overcome this pattern of resistance by recourse to the courts, but the courts, posing as champions of innocence, have acquitted both the reluctant taxpayer and the indicted tax collector, while the slow pace and resulting log-jam of court cases have kept congress from passing new laws to further weaken the government's action. To date, congress has failed to reform the offices that handle the largest revenues. To date, congress has failed to examine, even once, the investment of funds of which the government is merely the trustee.

The extended stay in Europe of the person who by orders issued in 1823 is responsible for the millions of pesos owed for the loan he contracted and ratified in London,[43] the expulsion of our former diplomatic agent in Peru whom we had sent to negotiate the collection of debts for aid given to that republic, and finally the distribution and consumption of our national property have forced us to enter numerous debits in the book of national debt, debits which those individuals could have satisfied. The treasury of Colombia, therefore, has succumbed to the crisis of not being able to redeem our national honor in the eyes of the generous foreigners who have loaned us their money, trusting in our good faith. The army receives less than half the money it is owed in salaries, and with the exception of the employees of the treasury, the rest suffer the saddest penury. I am embarrassed to tell you that the nation is bankrupt and that the republic is being besieged by a formidable assemblage of creditors.

In describing the chaos afflicting us, it has seemed to me to be almost superfluous to speak to you of our relations with the other countries of the world. They prospered in direct proportion to the exaltation of our military glory and the prudence of our fellow citizens, thus inspiring confidence that our civil organization and our social prosperity would attain the heights reserved for us by Providence. Progress in foreign relations has always depended on the wisdom of the government and the harmony of the people. No nation ever won favorable regard except through the practice of these advantages; no nation ever won respect without the strength that comes from unity. And Colombia, in a state of total discord, scorning her own laws, her credit ruined, what incentives can she offer new allies? Or what guarantees even to keep those she already has? Moving backward, not forward, in her civil orbit, she inspires only disdain. Recently she has found herself provoked, vilified by an ally that would never have existed without our generosity.[44] Your deliberations will determine whether our allies, regretful of having acknowledged our existence, will erase us from among the nations composing humankind.

Legislators! Arduous and vast is the task with which the national will has charged you. Satisfy the obligation our fellow citizens have imposed upon you; do so by saving Colombia. Peer deep into the secret hearts of your constituents. There you will read the protracted anguish afflicting them. They yearn for security and peace. A firm, strong, just government is what your country cries out for. Look how she stands over the ruins bequeathed by despotism; look how, pale with fear, she weeps for the 500,000 heroes who died for her,[45] their blood sown in the fields, giving birth to her rights. Yes, Legislators, both the living and the dead, sepulchers and ruins, cry out for guarantees. Now, as I take my seat by my hearth as a simple citizen, one among many, I reclaim my voice and my right, being the last to insist on the true purpose of society. As one who has consecrated a veritable religious cult to my country and to freedom, I must not be silent on such a solemn occasion. Give us a government where the law is obeyed, where the judge is respected, where the people are free, a government that forbids any transgression against the popular will, against the mandate of the people.

Consider, Legislators, that strength in the forces of order is the safeguard for the weakness of the individual, the threat that makes aggressors tremble, and the hope of society. Consider that the corruption of a nation is born of the indulgence of the courts and impunity for crimes. Consider, without strength there is no virtue, and without virtue the republic perishes. Consider, finally, that anarchy destroys freedom, and that unity preserves order.

Legislators! In the name of Colombia I beg you with a thousand prayers that you give us, in the image of the Providence you represent, as arbiters of our destiny, for the people, for the army, for the judge, and for the president, . . . inexorable laws!

Simón Bolívar

A Glance at Spanish America

(1829)

We shall begin this outline with the Argentine Republic, not because it stands in the vanguard of our revolution, as her own citizens have claimed in their excess of vanity, but because it is the farthest south while at the same time presenting the clearest perspectives regarding every kind of anarchic revolution.[46]

On 15 May 1810,[47] the city of Buenos Aires began her political career. Her example did not spread to the rest of the provinces, so it became necessary to use force to oblige them to embrace the revolutionary cause. In their march through the provinces, the troops from Buenos Aires took the first step in what was to become a harsh and merciless campaign by shooting down Viceroy [Santiago] Liniers, who had previously liberated that country from the English forces.[48] At the same time the persecution of the pastors of the Church was initiated in the person of a bishop whose only crime was his faithfulness to his vows.

Continuing their operations, within six months the troops commanded by the people's representative, a man named [Juan José] Castelli, reached the Desaguadero River. Such auspicious beginnings seemed to herald most prosperous fortune for the Argentine Republic. However, due either to the inexperience of that revolutionary commander or to the absolute ignorance of military and political tactics on the part of the people and the army, what did happen is that very quickly the expeditionary philosopher was routed with all his troops near the Desaguadero River and the stragglers were pursued all the way to Córdoba. That rout initiated a gradual and uninterrupted series of disasters.[49]

The Río de la Plata has produced only one man capable of serving his country with integrity and genius. [Cornelio] Saavedra demonstrated from the beginning his worthiness to preside over the destiny of that Republic, but very soon death robbed his country of its only hope.[50] From that day forward, there has been no order, no harmony, in Argentine affairs. The federal government took control of the land, which was to become its victim. All the provinces recovered the local sovereignty God gives each man over his own fate, but that sovereignty was then tacitly relinquished to society, which then undertook to guarantee the safety of the individual. Nothing is as dangerous as the incompatibility between natural law and a political system. Each province ruled itself, and every military expedition suffered humiliating defeat. The towns took up arms against each other as if they were enemies. Blood, death, and every crime were the patrimony resulting from a federation combined with the rampant appetite of a people who have broken their chains and have no understanding of the notions of duty and law and who cannot cease being slaves except to become tyrants.

Every election is plagued with confusion and intrigue. Frequently, armed soldiers show up to vote in formation, something unheard of even in primitive Rome, even on the island of Haiti. Everything is decided by force, faction, or bribery. And to what end? To rule for a moment amid alarming confusion, fighting in the streets, and sacrifice. Public officials are routinely replaced by blood-stained conquerors and suffer the most horrendous of fates, being forced into exile or prison or assassinated. It is rare for an election to proceed without some frightful calamity, even rarer for an incumbent to leave his post at the end of his lawful term, replaced by a constitutionally elected successor.

We scarcely remember [Martín] Rodríguez, the governor of Buenos Aires who preceded [Bernardino] Rivadavia.[51] And how did the former come to power? By force of arms, plunder, assassination. Rivadavia was unable to remain in his post for even half the legal term. He resigned, almost forced to do so by the discredit into which his administration had fallen and by the opposition party. Despite this, his intrigues have hardly allowed his successor, [Manuel] Dorrego, to breathe, following [Vicente] López's brief term as president.

When all the provinces, and even Buenos Aires, were clamoring for Dorrego to accept the general directorship of the Republic, he was in the midst of conducting a brilliant and tenacious war against the emperor of Brazil. When he accepted the presidency, the public cause was in a state of neglect, as the government lacked resources, men qualified for public office, and military forces. These were the circumstances that led Rivadavia to renounce his post, and not content with committing this cowardly act, he provoked new disputes when the time came for peace with Brazil. Then he had the audacity to summon General [Juan] Lavalle, a reckless, immoral man, a soldier worthy of Catiline, whose career has followed the steps that lead a criminal to the gallows.[52]

As a soldier, he was insubordinate; as an officer, rebellious. Later he became an assassin and a sacker of villages, as Ica sadly attests. Finally, he emerged as the treasonous assassin of the leader of his country. He usurped the supreme authority, doubtless in the hope that his action would be spuriously legitimized by the corrupt delegates of the people, who might well be capable of consecrating the abominable conduct of such a depraved man, as happened in Mexico.

However, let us be fair regarding the Río de la Plata. What we have just related is not peculiar to this country; its history is the history of Spanish America. We will observe the same principles at work, the same processes, the same consequences in all the republics, with no difference from one country to another except in details altered by circumstances, events, and geography.

We will observe throughout America a single impetus in public affairs, identical stages of development according to the times and circumstances, analogous to other stages and circumstances in each newly emerging state.

Nowhere do we find legal elections. Nowhere do we see a normal transfer of elective power based on law. If Buenos Aires manages to abort a Lavalle, the rest of America finds itself overrun by Lavalles. If Dorrego is assassinated, assassinations are rife in Mexico, Bolivia, and Colombia: 25 September is all too recent for us to forget. If [Juan Martín de] Pueyrredón[53] robs the public treasury, there is always someone in Colombia ready to do the same. If Córdoba and Paraguay are oppressed by bloodthirsty hypocrites, Peru has its General [José] La Mar decked out in a donkey skin, sporting tiger claws instead of fingers, licking his lips in anticipation of American blood. If anarchist movements spring up in every Argentine province, Chile and Guatemala are in such a state of tumult that there is scarcely any hope of peace. There [i.e., in Argentina, Manuel de] Sarratea, Rodríguez, and [Carlos María de] Alvear oblige their country to welcome bandits into the capital under the name of Liberators. In Chile, the Carrera regime and its thugs commit acts that are in every way similar.[54] [Ramón] Freire, serving as director, destroys his own administration and, lacking the capacity to govern, constitutes anarchy, and to bring this about, he collaborates with the congress in acts of extreme violence. [Pedro Alcántara] Urriola takes over the legislature, having first defeated the government troops along with the director who had led them with such distinction. And is there any coup that Guatemala hasn't attempted? The legitimate authorities are overthrown, the provinces rebel against the capital, brothers wage war on brothers (an atrocity that even the Spaniards had not inflicted), and it's war to the death. Towns attack towns, cities attack cities, each one claiming its own government, each street declaring itself a nation. In Central America, nothing but bloodshed and terror!

Although it is true that in Buenos Aires public officials seldom last three days, it is also true that Bolivia has recently chosen to follow this atrocious example. The illustrious Sucre had scarcely departed from that unfortunate country when the perfidious [Pedro] Blanco hatched a plot to seize power, which by right should have gone to General [Andrés] Santa Cruz. After only five days of rule, Blanco was captured and killed by a faction, only to be succeeded by a legitimate leader, [José Miguel de] Velasco, who was succeeded once again by Santa Cruz. So in less than two weeks, poor Bolivia was ruled by four leaders. Only the Inferno could offer such a monstrous spectacle, to the shame of the human race.

We note with amazement the almost infinite subdivision of the Argentine territory, which up to a certain point reminds us of the regime of the ancient barons, this federation standing in the same relation to a free society as the feudal system under the monarchy. Those feudal lords imposed taxes, built castles, and governed as they pleased, in total disregard of the sovereign, even waging war against him. Buenos Aires, Chile, and Guatemala imitate and surpass the practices and doctrines of those feudal lords, driven to the same extremes by the same motives of personal ambition.

But what just happened in Mexico seems to us far worse than everything we have related so sorrowfully with regard to Río de la Plata and the rest of America. Buenos Aires, then, must cede to opulent Mexico, a city now afflicted with leprosy. Yes, the most criminal atrocities inundate that beautiful land. A new class of barefoot poor, or rather shirtless poor, now occupies the seat of power and possesses everything in sight. The casual law of usurpation and pillage has been enthroned in the capital as king and in the provinces of the federation as well. A barbarian from the southern coasts, the vile miscarriage of a savage Indian woman and a ferocious African,[55] has climbed to power on the backs of 2000 corpses and at the cost of twenty million pesos of stolen property. This new Dessalines [Vicente Guerrero] spares no one. He violates everything; he strips the country of its freedom, the citizen of his, the innocent of his life, and the women of their honor. All the wickedness committed there is by his command or in his cause. Unable to ascend to power by way of the laws and public suffrage, he collaborates with General Santana [meaning Antonio López de Santa Anna], that most corrupt of all mortals. First, they destroy the empire and put the emperor to death, since they were unable to occupy the throne.[56] Then they establish the federation in collaboration with other demagogues who are as immoral as they themselves, in order to take over the provinces and even the capital. They join the Masons with an eye to winning converts to their cause. The latter harass General [Nicolás] Bravo, a rival worthy of competing with honorable men, and because his virtue makes them look bad, they exile him from his country along with hundreds of competent officials, alleging discord which they themselves provoked in order to destroy him.

A fierce soldier [Guerrero], illiterate like Pizarro, is rejected in the general elections. With Bravo out of the way, the vast majority of the people cast their vote for General [Manuel Gómez] Pedraza, in accordance with the constitution and the hopes of all the people. The ambitious Guerrero has no compunction about resorting to crime. In collaboration with [Guadalupe] Victoria, a president who brings shame to his office,[57] he steeps the capital in blood and, unleashing the rabble on the landowners, inundates the most beautiful city in America in everything loathsome. These nauseating lepers,[58] led by generals of the same ilk— Guerrero, [José María] Lobato, and Santana—take over the country, and like the soldiers of Attila in Rome, they ravage and annihilate their own freedom, their own government, their own wealth. What kind of men, or devils, are they? From one end to the other, the New World is a vast abyss of abomination, and if anything were lacking to round out this frightful chaos, Peru would fill it to the brim. In collusion with her tyrants during the war of independence, scarcely has she won her freedom when she begins to savage her own bosom during the first days of her existence. The splendid General San Martín, leading the Chileans and the Argentines, drives out the Spaniards from Trujillo to Ica. For Lima, Peru cannot exist without freedom, and almost immediately some soldiers break ranks with San Martín, whose services they need more than ever. This act of ingratitude destroys Peru's political career, and from there things go downhill as far as Girón, where the most despicable event takes place.[59]. . . But let us continue with our survey.

[Francisco Javier] Luna Pizarro (appropriately named on both counts), despising [José de la] Riva-Agüero and [the marquis of] Torre-Tagle, conspires with both of them to force San Martín out. This accomplished, the Triumvirate is not content with dividing up the empire of the Incas among themselves; rather, each of them wants to possess it entirely, but without fighting for it or doing anything to deserve it. Luna Pizarro sets La Mar on the others, easily vanquishing two rivals less treacherous than he, but more immoral, more discredited. Under the sway of his puppet-master, La Mar loses San Martín's army in Torata and Moquegua because of his reliance on Alvarado.[60] This opens the gates of the country to the Spaniards. Then General Santa Cruz, colluding with Riva-Agüero, deposes the traitor La Mar, driving him into exile. These new leaders ask Colombia to send them the auxiliary forces that La Mar had maliciously sent back to their own country to prevent them from interfering with his treasonous designs. So the Colombians return to Peru to liberate the country from its enemies. Then President Riva-Agüero, deposed and impeached by the Congress, offers to sell his country to the Spaniards. The Congress names Torre-Tagle president, and would you believe it? He, too, sends for the Spaniards: he gives them Lima and El Callao![61] Behold, the most treasonous Triumvirate the world has ever known! Never, absolutely never before in history, have three successive leaders of a single nation been known to deliver up their country to the most brutal enemies of their own independence and political existence.

The Liberator returns to Colombia, leaving Peru headless. Almost immediately he learns of the insurrection of the auxiliary forces in Lima. And what does the government of Peru do in these circumstances? It decides, without hesitation, to send these traitors back to their country so they can seize a large part of its territory and sell it for a price offered by the infamous [José] Bustamante.[62] General La Mar, a subject of Peru, lends powerful support to this revolutionary movement, and before long he manages to take possession of Guayaquil and have himself named chief of that department by his friends and relatives.

To reward this unimaginable perfidy, the Peruvian congress—in other words, Luna Pizarro—names him president of the republic. This wretched Colombian[63] wastes no time. Marshalling all his forces, he invades Bolivia without provocation and engages in atrocious political machinations enabling him to wage even greater war against his own country. Finally he declares war, desolating the soil where he was born, and orders the sacking of the city where he first saw the light of day. He carries hostilities to levels never conceived by the most savage barbarians. But his assaults are no less ruinous to Peru.

As cowardly as he is treacherous, he flees Guayaquil in frenzied stupefaction; he flees from a boy leading a handful of soldiers; in Saraguro he and his entire reserve army flee from twenty men from Yaguachi; in Portete he flees in panic from this same batallion, terrified of its commander, [Juan Eligio] Alzuru. He reaches Girón, realizes he is lost, and signs a treaty which he then violates once it has served the purpose of saving him from Colombian vengeance. Then, to reward our generosity, he renews his war to the death against us.

In America there is no good faith, not even between nations. Our treaties are scraps of paper, our constitutions empty texts, our elections pitched battles, our freedom mere anarchy, and our lives pure torture.

Such, Americans, is our deplorable condition. If we cannot change it, we would be better off dead. Nothing is worse than this endless conflict, whose indignity seems to grow in violence with each new faction and with the passage of time. Let us not be deluded: The evil proliferates moment by moment, threatening us with total destruction. Popular unrest, armed uprisings—these will ultimately oblige us to detest the very principles constituting our political life. We have lost all guarantees of individual freedom and security, which were the very goals for which we had sacrificed our blood, and the possessions we treasured most before the war. And if we look back on those times, who can deny that our rights were more respected then? Never before have we been as unfortunate as we are at this moment. Then, we possessed certain positive benefits, tangible benefits, whereas now our hopes are sustained only by fantasies of a better future. The bitter reality of the present leaves us in a state of constant torment, constant disillusionment. Let us have done, then, with twenty agonizing, painful, fatal years. We long for a stable government, reflective of our current situation, worthy of the character of our people, a government that will rescue us from the ferocious hydra of discordant anarchy, a bloodthirsty monster that feeds on the most exquisite marrow of the Republic, and whose inconceivable nature reduces men to such a state of frenzy that it simultaneously fills everyone with an insatiable lust for absolute power and an implacable hatred of legal process.

The true portrait of this chimera is the revolution from which we have just emerged but which still lies in wait if we fail to support with all our vigor the social body tottering on the edge of the abyss. The country is waiting for congress to convene so it can impose on us the task of saving her. Then she will say:

"Colombians! You have suffered greatly, sacrificed greatly and in vain, because you strayed from the healing path. You became infatuated with freedom, dazzled by her powerful allure; but because freedom is as dangerous as beauty in women, whom all seek to seduce out of love, or vanity, you failed to preserve her in her natural innocence and purity, just as she descended from heaven. Power, the visceral enemy of our rights, has stirred the private ambitions of each sector of our state. The second magistrate of our republic assassinated the first; the third division invaded the South.[64] Pasto rebelled against the republic, Peru laid waste the territory of her benefactors, and there is scarcely a province anywhere that has not abused its power or its privileges. This entire period has been rife with misfortune, blood, confusion, and ruin. Now your only hope is to bring all your moral energy to the task of constituting a government that can prevail over ambition and protect freedom. Otherwise, you will be the laughing-stock of the world and the victim of your own devices."

Public officials, citizens, provinces, armies—heed the cries of your country, so that by creating a social body impervious to factional violence, we can gird our national representatives with the virtue, the strength, and the natural enlightenment of Colombia.

Address to the "Congreso Admirable": Message to the Constituent Congress of the Republic of Colombia

Bogotá, 20 January 1830

Fellow Citizens!

Allow me to congratulate you for this meeting of Congress, which now undertakes the sublime duties of lawgiver for the nation.[65]

This is a grand and arduous project, to constitute as a nation a people recently emerged from oppression via anarchy and civil war, and who are ill prepared to receive the healthy reforms to which they have aspired. But the lessons of history, the examples of both the old and the new world, and the experience of twenty years of revolution must serve you as so many beacons placed to guide you through the darkness of the future. I flatter myself that your wisdom will rise to the task of controlling with a firm hand the passions of the few and the ignorance of the multitudes, consulting when need be the enlightened judgment of sensible men whose good wishes are a precious resource for resolving questions of high policy. Beyond this, you will also discover important guides to action in the very nature of our country, which includes the lofty regions of the Andes and the burning shores of the Orinoco. Study them closely, and you will learn there, in that infallible teacher of men, what Congress should decree for the happiness of the people of Colombia. Our history will teach you much, our needs will teach you more; but you will find even more persuasive the clamor of our sorrow over the lack of tranquility and secure freedom.

Members of Congress, if you can proffer to Colombia the enjoyment of these supreme benefits, you will be most fortunate, deserving of our heartfelt blessing!

Congress having convened to create the fundamental code that will rule the republic and to appoint the high officials who will administer it, it is now the obligation of the government to provide the information available to the various ministries regarding the current state of the union, so that you can legislate statutes in keeping with the circumstances. It is the duty of the presidents of the Council of State and Council of Ministries to give you an account of their labors during the last eighteen months; if they have not lived up to our highest hopes, they will at least have overcome the two obstacles blocking the progress of the administration, the turbulent circumstances of wars abroad and domestic discord, ills which, thanks to Divine Providence, have receded as clemency and peace gained ground.

Fix your full attention on the origin and evolution of these disturbances.

The troubles that occurred so unfortunately in 1826 necessitated my return from Peru, even though I was determined not to accept the position as first constitutional magistrat, to which I had been reelected during my absence. Urgently entreated to restore order and avoid civil war, I could not deny my services to my country which had offered me that new honor and that unequivocal demonstration of trust.

The representatives of the nation launched an investigation into the causes of the discord plaguing people's spirits, and convinced that they were substantial, and that radical measures had to be adopted, they resigned themselves to the need to move up the timetable for the meeting of the Great Convention. This body convened at the height of partisan animosity, which led to its adjournment with no agreement among the members as to the reforms under consideration. Seeing the republic threatened with total disarray, I was forced to step forward again at this critical juncture. Had there not been a sudden resurgence of the national will to self-preservation, the republic would have been torn apart by the hands of its own citizens. It chose to honor me with its trust, a trust I was obliged to respect as the most sacred law. With the country on the verge of perishing, could I hesitate?

Repeatedly violated by armed conflicts and public uprisings, the laws could not be enforced. Acknowledging the crisis, the legislature had already decreed that there should be a meeting of the assembly for constitutional reform, and the convention had at last made a unanimous declaration of the urgent need for such reform. This solemn declaration, and the events leading up to it, constituted a formal verdict annulling

Colombia's political pact. In the view of public opinion, and in fact, the constitution of year eleven ceased to exist.

The plight of the country was appalling, and mine even worse, because it subjected me to judgment and suspicion. I was not deterred, however, by the assault on a reputation acquired through a long series of public services during which such sacrifices had been frequently required.

The organic decree that I issued on 27 August 1828[66] should have convinced everyone that my most ardent desire was to lay down the unbearable burden of an unlimited authority and that the republic should reconstitute itself through its representatives. But scarcely had I begun to exercise the functions of supreme leader when the opposing forces responded with violent passion and criminal ferocity. An attempt was made against my life; civil war broke out; the government of Peru, encouraged by these events, invaded our southern provinces, seeking to conquer and usurp. Citizens, I am not speaking from conjecture. The facts and the documents verifying them are authentic. War became inevitable. In Tarqui our forces won a most glorious and splendid victory against the army of General La Mar; their lives were spared by the generosity of the victors. Despite the magnanimity of the Colombians, General La Mar started up a new war in violation of the treaties, opening hostilities to which I responded by inviting him to make peace once again, but he slandered us with outrageous insolence. The department of Guayaquil was the victim of his wild ambition.

Having no navy, beset by winter floods and other obstacles, we had to wait for good weather to retake the plaza. During this interval, a national verdict, in the words of the Supreme Chief of Peru, vindicated our conduct and rid our enemies of General La Mar.[67]

This transformation in the political scene of the Republic of Peru facilitated negotiations, and we recovered Guayaquil through an armistice. Finally, on 22 September, the peace treaty was concluded, ending a war in which Colombia defended her rights and her dignity.

I congratulate myself before Congress and the nation for the satisfactory results of the negotiations in the South, both for concluding the war and for the unequivocal demonstrations of goodwill we have received from the Peruvian government, nobly admitting that we were provoked into that war by depraved intentions. Never did a government so thoroughly satisfy another as the Peruvian government did ours, for which generosity it has earned our fullest respect.

Fellow citizens! If we have achieved this peace with the moderation one expects between brother nations, which should never open fire on one another with weapons devoted to freedom and mutual preservation, we have also been merciful with the unfortunate peoples of the South who allowed themselves to be dragged into civil war or to be seduced by our enemies. I am delighted to inform you that in bringing domestic dissension to an end, not a single drop of blood has stained the vindication of our laws, and though a brave general and his followers have fallen on the field of battle, their punishment came to them from the hand of the Almighty, whereas from our hand they would have received the clemency with which we have treated the survivors.[68] They all enjoy their freedom despite their depraved actions.

The country has suffered too much from these upheavals, which we will always remember with sorrow. If anything can assuage our affliction, it is our consolation in knowing that we were blameless in these events and that we behaved with generosity toward our adversaries when they were at our mercy. We are of course saddened by the sacrifice of a few delinquents on the altar of justice, and even though patricide deserves no mercy, I spared many of them, perhaps the most cruel.

Let us learn from this grim picture, which it has been my misfortune to paint for you. May it be a lesson for the future, like those formidable blows Providence sometimes deals us in the course of life for our instruction. It is Congress that must pluck sweet fruit from this bitter tree, or at least draw back from its venomous shadow.

Had I not been the one honored to summon you to represent the rights of the people so that you could create or improve our institutions according to their wishes, this would be the moment for me to offer you advice based on twenty years devoted to the service of the country. But I must refrain from asking what all citizens have the right to ask of you. All can, all are obligated to submit their opinions, their fears, their desires to those whom we have appointed to cure a society sick with dissension and weakness. I alone am forbidden to exercise this civic duty. Because it was I who called you together and designated your powers, I am not permitted to influence your deliberations in any way. Besides, it would be presumptuous of me to repeat to those chosen by the people what Colombia has written in characters of blood. My single duty consists of subjecting myself without reservation to the law and the leaders you give us, and my single hope is that the will of the people be echoed, respected, and carried out by their delegates.

With this intent, I made provision that all the people should have the right to express their opinions with absolute freedom and safety, the only restrictions being those needed to guarantee order and moderation. This has been done, and you will find in the petitions that will be submitted for your consideration the pure expression of popular desire. All of the provinces await your resolutions; everywhere, the meetings held for this purpose have been ruled by civility and respect for the authority of the government and the constituent congress. Only in Caracas do the excesses of the junta give us cause for regret.[69] Your prudence and wisdom must render a judgment there.

I have good reason to fear that my sincerity will be called into question when I express my opinion concerning the magistrate who is to preside over the republic. But the Congress must understand that its honor militates against my being considered for this post, as does mine against accepting it. Would you be so unwise as to return the mantle of this precious authority to the one who renounced it? Could you concede your votes to me without tarnishing your reputation? Would this not mean I had appointed myself? Far be it from you or me to commit such an ignoble act.

Obligated as you are to constitute the government of the republic, you will find distinguished citizens both within and without this chamber fully capable of carrying out the duties of the presidency of the state with glory and skill. All, all of my fellow citizens enjoy the invaluable fortune of appearing to be above suspicion, while I alone am considered tainted with aspirations to tyranny.

Spare me, I beg you, the affront that awaits me if I continue to live out a destiny that can never be free of the vituperation of ambition. Believe me: A new leader is indispensable to the republic at this time. The people want to know if I will ever cease to rule them. The American states regard me with a certain anxiety that may one day bring to Colombia new miseries like the war with Peru. Even in Europe there are those who fear my conduct may discredit the beautiful cause of freedom. Ah, think how many conspiracies and wars we have endured whose only purpose was to undermine my authority and my person! Those assaults have brought suffering to the people, a sacrifice that could have been avoided if from the beginning the legislators of Colombia had not forced me to shoulder a burden of responsibility harder than war with all its whiplashes.

Fellow citizens, show that you are worthy of representing a free people, casting aside any notion that I am indispensable to the republic. If a single man were necessary to sustain a state, that state should not exist, and in the end would not.

The leader you choose will undoubtedly be a harbinger of domestic harmony, a bond between brothers, a consolation for the defeated factions. All Colombians will come together around this lucky mortal. He will embrace them in friendship, turning them into a family of citizens. I will obey this legitimate ruler with the most cordial respect, follow him as if he were the angel of peace, and support him with my sword and all my energies. Everything will add power, respect, and obedience to the man you select. I swear it, Legislators. I promise this in the name of the people and the Colombian army. The republic will be happy if when you accept my resignation you appoint as president a citizen beloved of the nation; it will fall if you insist that I rule it. Hear my pleas. Save the republic. Save my glory, which belongs to Colombia.

Dispose of the presidency that I respectfully abdicate into your hands. From this day forth, I am but a citizen armed to defend the country and obey the government. My public functions have ceased forever. In all solemnity and formality, I hand over to you the supreme power conferred on me in the national elections.

You belong to every province; you are their most distinguished citizens; you have served in every public office; you know the needs of your province and the nation; you will lack nothing to regenerate this languishing Republic in all branches of administration.

Let my final act be to urge you to protect the holy faith we profess, which is the abundant source of heaven's blessings. The national treasury demands your attention, especially in the matter of revenue collection. The public debt, which is Colombia's cancer, cries out for you to honor its sacred obligations. The army, entitled to the gratitude of the nation a thousand times over, is in need of radical reorganization. Justice demands laws capable of defending the rights and the innocence of free men. Everything must be created anew, and you must lay the foundation for our prosperity by establishing the basis for our political organization.

Fellow citizens! I blush to say this: Independence is the only benefit we have acquired, to the detriment of all the rest. But independence opens the door for us to win back the others under your sovereign authority, in all the splendor of glory and freedom.

Simón Bolívar

II

Lesser Bolivarian Texts

I. POLITICAL AND MILITARY

Oath Taken in Rome

15 August 1805

So then, this is the nation of Romulus and Numa, of the Gracchi and the Horaces, of Augustus and Nero, of Caesar and Brutus, of Tiberius and Trajan?[1] Here every manner of grandeur has had its type, all miseries their cradle. Octavian masks himself in the cloak of public piety to conceal his untrusting character and his bloody outbursts; Brutus thrusts his dagger into the heart of his patron so as to replace Caesar's tyranny with his own; Antony renounces his claim to glory to set sail on the galleys of a whore; with no projects of reform, Sulla beheads his fellow countrymen, and Tiberius, dark as night and depraved as crime itself, divides his time between lust and slaughter. For every Cincinnatus there were a hundred Caracallas, a hundred Caligulas for every Trajan, a hundred Claudiuses for every Vespasian. This nation has examples for everything: severity for former times, austerity for republics, depravity for emperors, catacombs for Christians, courage for conquering the entire world, ambition for turning every nation on earth into a fertile field for tribute; women capable of driving the sacrilegious wheels of their carriages over the decapitated bodies of their parents; orators, like Cicero capable of stirring crowds to action; poets, like Vergil, for seducing with their song; satirists, like Juvenal and Lucretius; weak-minded philosophers, like Seneca; complete citizens, like Cato. This nation has examples for everything, except for the cause of humanity: corrupt Messalinas, gutless Agrippas, great historians, distinguished naturalists, heroic warriors, rapacious consuls, unrestrained sybarites, golden virtues, and foul crimes; but for the emancipation of the spirit, the elimination of cares, the exaltation of man, and the final perfectibility of reason, little or nothing. The civilization blowing in from the East has shown all its faces here, all its parts. But the resolution of the great problem of man set free seems to have been something inconceivable, a mystery that would only be made clear in the New World.

I swear before you, I swear by the God of my fathers, I swear on their graves, I swear by my Country that I will not rest body or soul until I have broken the chains binding us to the will of Spanish might!

Simón Bolívar

Decree of War to the Death

Trujillo General Headquarters, 15 June 1813

Simón Bolívar, Brigadier General of the Union, Commander-in-Chief of the Army of the North, Liberator of Venezuela

Venezuelans:

An army of brothers, sent by the Supreme Congress of New Granada, has come to liberate you, and it now stands among you, after having expelled the oppressors from the provinces of Mérida and Trujillo.[2]

We are sent to destroy the Spaniards, to protect Americans, and to reestablish the republican governments that formed the Federation of Venezuela. The states protected by our arms are once again ruled by their former constitutions and leaders, in the full enjoyment of their freedom and independence, because our sole mission is to break the chains of servitude that still oppress some of our people, not to make laws or seize power, as the rules of war might authorize us to do.

Moved by your misfortunes, we could not witness with indifference the afflictions visited upon you by the savage Spaniards, who have annihilated and destroyed you with pillage and death, who have violated the sanctity of human rights, rendered null the most solemn articles of surrender and treaty, and committed every imaginable crime, reducing Venezuela to the most horrific desolation. Thus, justice demands retribution, and necessity obliges us to take it. Let the monsters who have infested Colombian soil, covering it with blood, vanish forever; let their punishment be equal to the enormity of their perfidy, thus washing away the stain of our ignominy and demonstrating to the nations of the world that one cannot offend the sons of America with impunity.

Despite our just resentment against the foul Spaniards, our generous hearts still see fit one last time to open the way to reconciliation and friendship; we invite them once again to live peacefully among us under the condition that, renouncing their crimes and acting henceforth in good faith, they cooperate with us in the destruction of the Spanish government of occupation and in the reestablishment of the Venezuelan Republic.

Any Spaniard who does not join our fight against tyranny to further this just cause, actively and effectively, will be regarded as an enemy and punished as a traitor to the country and consequently put to death without appeal. On the other hand, a general and absolute pardon is hereby granted to those who come over to our armies, with or without their weapons, and who lend their support to the good citizens who are struggling to shake off the yoke of tyranny. Military officers and civil leaders who join us in proclaiming the government of Venezuela will keep their rank and offices; in a word, Spaniards who render distinguished service to the state will be regarded and treated as Americans.

And you Americans who have been led from the path of justice by error or perfidy, be sure that your brothers forgive you and sincerely lament your offenses, convinced in our hearts that you cannot be to blame, and that only the blindness and ignorance in which you have been held hitherto by the instigators of your crimes could have led you to commit them. Do not fear the sword that comes to avenge you and to sever the ignominious bonds that bind you to the fate of your executioners. You may count on absolute immunity regarding your honor, your lives, and your property: the mere title of Americans will be your guarantee and your safeguard. Our weapons are here to protect you and will never be turned against a single one of our brothers.

This amnesty extends even to the traitors who have most recently committed acts of felony, and it will be so religiously fulfilled that no reason, cause, or pretext will be sufficient to cause us to break our promise, no matter how grievous and extraordinary the motives you give us to arouse our loathing.

Spaniards and Canarians, even if you profess neutrality, know that you will die unless you work actively to bring about the freedom of America. Americans, know that you will live, even if you are guilty.

Simón Bolívar

Manifesto to the Nations of the World

General Headquarters of Valencia, 20 September 1813

Simón Bolívar, Brigadier General of the Union, and Commander-in-Chief of the Army of the North, Liberator of Venezuela, etc.

To the Nations of the World:

The people of these provinces, after having proclaimed their independence and freedom, were subjugated by an adventurer who—seizing power through usurpation and taking advantage of the consternation caused by an earthquake rendered frightening more through the ignorance and superstition of its victims than through the devastation it produced—invaded the territory, shedding American blood, robbing its inhabitants, and committing horrific atrocities that will appall and move you to sympathy once they have been sufficiently documented and presented for your consideration.[3]

Meanwhile, for the purpose of avoiding calumny by our enemies, it is urgent and obligatory to provide you with a preliminary account, succinctly expressed since there is no other way of proceeding given the current situation to explain our present conduct, in the expectation that it will persuade you to condemn and abhor the conduct of our oppressors and to turn on them as enemies of the human species, authors of the most vicious crimes against justice and human rights, perpetrated shamelessly, and whose wickedness has yet to be punished by the nation in whose name they have shed our blood, savaged our citizens, and desolated our state.

Entering the province against the express orders of his superior, [Captain-General Fernando] Miyares, [Domingo de] Monteverde reached the outskirts of the city of Caracas, which had recently been destroyed by the terrible earthquake of 26 March 1812, subjugating a people confused and uncertain of his intentions. The only troops opposing him were unfortunately led by an officer who, motivated by ambition and violent passions, either failed to understand the risks or chose to sacrifice the freedom of his country to those personal motives, conducting himself arbitrarily and despotically to the extreme, upsetting not only his troops but also the personnel in the offices of public administration, and rendering the province or what was left of it null and void.[4]

Monteverde, aided by several ignorant and corrupt clergymen who saw in our independence and freedom the destruction of their own empire, spared no resource in his effort to complete the seduction of the majority and to render the minority defenseless, the city destroyed, its population dispersed in the countryside, the people dying of hunger and misery, all of them terrorized by the assassinations carried out by [Eusebio] Antoñanzas, [José Tomás] Boves, and other subordinates whom he had stationed throughout the province, murdering ruthlessly, in cold blood and without due process, anyone considered a patriot, leaving the soldiers without direction or leaders, and the people uncertain as to their fate . . . .

Such was the hapless condition of Caracas when the revolt of blacks, both slaves and freed, erupted in the eastern valleys and seacoast, incited, abetted, and sustained by the emissaries of Monteverde. This inhuman and savage mob, thirsty for blood and for the property of the patriots that had been mapped out and detailed in lists for them in Curiepe and Caucagua, marched against the population of Caracas, perpetrating in those valleys, and especially in the town of Guatire, the most horrific acts of murder, plunder, violence, and devastation. Those conquered—peaceful farmers, distinguished citizens, the innocent—were cut down with pistols and swords or were whipped barbarously after the armistice had been signed. Blood ran everywhere, and corpses were hung as ornaments in the streets and public squares of Guatire, Calabozo, San Juan de los Morros, and other towns inhabited by peaceful working people who, far from taking up arms, fled to the woods as the soldiers approached and who were rounded up, tied, and executed without any more formality, hearing, or trial than being forced to kneel down. Any officer or soldier was authorized to put to death anyone regarded as a patriot or whom they wanted to rob.

In this conflict Caracas—assaulted from the east by the blacks incited by the European Spaniards occupying the town of Guarenas, thirty miles from the city, and from the west by Monteverde, who was encouraged by his victory in Puerto Cabello, the only troops opposing him being those quartered in the town of La Victoria, weakened and demoralized by the arbitrary and violent actions of a hated leader—made an effort to surrender and in fact, after several attempts at negotiation, did sign articles of capitulation, by virtue of which her citizens surrendered their arms, supplies, and munitions to Monteverde, who marched unopposed into the city and took control.

The main article of capitulation, signed in San Mateo on 25 July 1812, stipulated that the lives and properties of the citizens would not be taken, that no one would be tried for political opinions expressed prior to the surrender, that no one would be harassed, and that there would be a general amnesty concerning past events. This treaty, entered into with a leader of the forces of a civilized European nation ever boastful of acting in good faith, eased the fears of even the most untrusting and timid, and everyone was resting from their recent exhaustion, not exactly content with the fate Providence had assigned them, but at least at peace and trusting in the guarantees offered in the armistice. They had fought enthusiastically to maintain their freedom, and even if they had failed in that effort, they took some consolation and satisfaction in having used all the means available to them.

On 29 July Monteverde entered Caracas at night and met with the Europeans and with distinguished groups and individuals, proffering to all of them the assurances which the surrender must have inspired, knowing full well that the perturbation, nervousness, and uncertainty manifested by the province were a consequence of desperation occasioned by acts of injustice and excess committed by the government of Spain and by the atrocious conduct of the officials Spain had assigned to administer and govern it. He must surely have known that people are never unhappy when treated fairly and governed equitably, and that the way to heal wounds is to follow the letter of the law. Violating these principles and the terms of the surrender, Monteverde set about arresting the most respected citizens, humiliating them publicly by placing them in stocks and, in order to mask his violation of law, spreading the word that those arrests and abuses were in retaliation for acts committed subsequent to the armistice. To make these charges seem credible, he issued a proclamation dated 3 August in which he swore that his promises were sacred, that his word was inviolable, and that these public proceedings were punishment for later infractions.

So the people, not daring to doubt this or even to conceive that Monteverde could be so hypocritical, malicious, and shameless, responded with uncertainty and timidity when, on 14 August, bands of Canary Islanders, Catalans, and other Europeans stationed throughout the city and countryside, issuing orders to subordinates in the interior of the province, began rounding up and arresting the Americans. The most decorated men from the period of the Republic were torn from the arms of their wives, children, and families in the dead of night; tied to the tails of the horses of shopkeepers, wine merchants, and other low-brow people; dragged off ignominiously to jail, some shoved along on foot, others trussed hand and foot to a yoke for oxen, hauled off to the dungeons of La Guaira and Puerto Cabello; locked up there in arm and leg irons; and subjected to the inhuman vigilance of savage men, some of whom had been themselves persecuted during the time of the revolution; and worst of all, this was all done under the pretext that these wretched captives were the instigators of a revolutionary conspiracy against the terms of the surrender. In this way uncertainty was perpetuated, and everyone held back, until the slanderous felony was accepted as fact; then they fled into the woods to seek safety among the wild animals, leaving the cities and towns deserted, so that the only people to be seen in their streets and public roads were the Europeans and Canary Islanders armed with pistols, swords, and blunderbusses, menacing everyone and spewing forth acts of revenge, perpetrating atrocities against women as well as men, and committing the most shameless acts of plunder, so that there was not a single one of Monteverde's officers not wearing a shirt, or a cassock, or the trousers of some American whom he had stripped. Even some officers who served as garrison commanders participated in such abuse, as for instance in the public square of La Guaira, where the atrocious [Francisco Javier] Cervériz burst into the dungeons of that port to heap insults on the very victims in whose garments he was dressed from head to foot.

These men took possession of everything. They camped in the haciendas and homes of the villagers, and they destroyed or rendered useless whatever they couldn't take. Given the brevity demanded by the circumstances, it is impossible to depict the condition of that province. The most honorable men, heads of families, fourteen-year-old boys, priests who modeled their lives on the Gospels and true maxims of Jesus Christ, eighty-year-old men, innumerable men who had no part, who could not have had a part in the revolution, were locked in dark, hot, humid dungeons, burdened with chains and leg irons, utterly miserable. Some suffocated right in their cells. Others could not endure the grief and martyrdom and gave up their lives without medical or spiritual aid, which were ruthlessly denied them, or provided only when the dying man was too weak to move or speak. In the streets the only sounds were the cries of unhappy women calling to their husbands, mothers crying for their sons, brothers for their brothers, relatives for relatives. The house of the Tyrant echoed with the howls and weeping of countless wretched women, and he took pleasure in this homage which grew in proportion to the smoke rising from the victims, while his subordinates, especially his countrymen from the Canaries, far from being moved to pity, insulted the women with barbarous expressions and leers whereby they demonstrated how much pleasure they derived from the humiliation of the people of that land.

Amid the confusion of the widespread imprisonment, only five or six persons managed to secure passports from Monteverde allowing them to leave the province. In his stupidity the tyrant, whose decrees were purely arbitrary or issued to please some favorite, made the mistake of issuing me one. Passport in hand and wasting no time, I accompanied my compatriots to the island of Curaçao and from there to Cartagena where, relating what was happening in Caracas, I aroused the just indignation of that generous people. Its leaders took upon themselves the grievances of the Caracans, supported our claims before the Congress of New Granada and in the city of Santafé, and then we were witness to the concern Americans take for other Americans. The public response of the Granadans was unanimous in its expression of righteous indignation toward our oppressors, and the representatives of the provinces communicated their outrage to their delegates, urging them to furnish every possible aid to their oppressed brothers. The general enthusiasm matched the fire that burned inside me to liberate my country, and by virtue of my urging and my praiseworthy and holy fervor I found myself in command of a contingent of troops small in number but inspired by the virtuous desire to liberate their brothers from the unbearable yoke of tyranny, injustice, and violence. I entered the province, defeating the tyrant's armies wherever they showed their faces. They could not stand up against the might of free men, generous, brave, and determined, who had vowed to exterminate the enemies of the freedom to which the people of America so rightfully aspire. This enthusiasm grew and was kindled to even greater intensity by the discovery, upon our entry into the province, of the horrible ravages caused by the Spaniards and Canarians. Then we saw with our own eyes the devastation of the haciendas, the destruction of property, the atrocities against some and the murder of others. We wept over the ruins, and joining our tears to those of so many widows and orphans standing beside the remains of their husbands, fathers, and brothers, whose bodies were still tied to the posts where they were shot or scattered about the fields, we repeated our vow to liberate our brothers from the cells, dungeons, and jails where they lay as if buried, and from the cruel, infamous yoke of such fiendish oppressors.

Until that moment, our state of mind and our conduct in the waging of war had been concordant with the practice of civilized nations, but on discovering that the enemy routinely took the lives of prisoners whose only crime was the defense of liberty, falsely branding them as insurgents, as happened to those executed by Don Antonio Tízcar, commander of Monteverde's troops in Barinas, the prisoners being found guilty by a jury composed of judges without jurisdiction and in violation of the most basic formalities demanded by nature and by the universal code of law, civilized or not, the sentence being ordered and then carried out by a person lacking all legal authority, we resolved to wage a war to the death, sparing only the Americans, for otherwise our enemies' advantage was insuperable, they being in the habit of killing our prisoners under the pretext that they were rebels, while we treated ours with the decency proper to our character and with every consideration demanded by humanity.

The results have validated and demonstrated the justice and necessity of our conduct, because once the Spaniards and Canarians were deprived of the advantage with which they had previously fought and now realized that their lot was equal to ours, they ceased to regard themselves as our masters and began to fear us as men. Then it became palpably clear what great cowards evil men are and how unwarranted our fear of tyrants is; all one need do is stand up to despots to send them running shamelessly away. We have seen how these brave men, who earlier behaved like wild beasts as they assaulted defenseless citizens, running them through and hacking them to pieces with their swords, turned and fled from a handful of our soldiers who charged their ranks, though they greatly outnumbered us. Between Cúcuta and Caracas they only showed their faces seven times, each time being routed immediately, and their terror was so great that the famous Monteverde, who had formerly swaggered around Caracas in imitation of the despots of Asia in manner, style and conduct, abandoned Valencia, leaving behind an enormous battery of artillery, to take hasty refuge in Puerto Cabello, with no recourse but to surrender. Even so, as we approached Caracas several emissaries from the governor came to us, offering to surrender, and although they were utterly defenseless and had no means to oppose us, we granted them their lives and property and a total amnesty. But you should know that this mission was a scheme to gain time so they could embark at La

Guaira, taking their weapons and ammunition with them and jamming the artillery. These scoundrels left with as many men as they could prior to the formal surrender, leaving the Spaniards and Canarians to face our just wrath.

It is not possible to convey the pusillanimity of the coward [Manuel del] Fierro, or the state of chaos and anarchy in which he left the city of Caracas when he so shamelessly escaped. That we did not encounter a bloodbath on our entry into the capital is evidence of an enormous generosity of spirit, a quality ever manifest among the Americans. We did discover shops and stores broken into and looted by the very people who had previously been robbed by Monteverde and his henchmen, but even though the Europeans and Canarians were at the mercy of an angry population, they were treated with moderation. The wives of the Spaniards and many of their husbands who were trying to escape carrying their possessions in bundles were treated with respect in their misfortune. Their flight toward the nearby port was so disorderly and confused that many dropped their weapons, others threw off their clothing in order to run faster, believing the enemy was pursuing them, and others finally abandoned themselves to their fate cursing the cowardly and inhuman leader who had put them in this situation. Such is the picture of Caracas I saw as I approached the capital.

This is not the time to present to the world a manifesto detailing the excesses of our enemies or describing our military operations. Those will emerge from the trial that must be held and for which the necessary instructions are being issued, based on the report I have given and will convey to the honorable Congress of New Granada for her own glory and the satisfaction of America. As stated at the beginning, our intention is merely to resist slander and convey succinctly the justice of our complaints against Spain. The Cortes and the Regency of Cádiz not only viewed with unconcern Monteverde's insubordination to his general, Miyares, but they applauded his usurpation of the latter's authority, promoting him to Captain-general of Caracas. Not only did they look with indifference on the scandalous violation of the surrender at San Mateo, on the arrests and maltreatment of the citizens, the destruction of their jobs, the acts of plunder, the assassinations, and the atrocities which Monteverde, his officers, and soldiers committed and have continued to commit since they took refuge in Puerto Cabello, but even today the newspapers and journals report that the question of whether the surrender ought or ought not to be honored is still being argued in the Cortes.

Eight of the men involved in the violation remain free on the Peninsula, and in the interim Monteverde has continued to act capriciously and willfully, without restraint or fear of disciplinary action.

But there is one further fact that proves better than any other the criminality and complicity of the government of Cádiz. The Cortes established the constitution of the kingdom, which is clearly a product of the enlightenment, knowledge, and experience of its members. Monteverde regarded this constitution as something irrelevant, or as something opposed to his ideas and those of his advisors. Finally he decides to publish it in Caracas. He does so, and for what purpose? Not only to mock it but to insult it and contradict it by deeds wholly contrary to it. He invites everyone to assemble, urging calm and suggesting that the ark of peace is at hand; the naïve citizens assemble, many of them crawling out of the caves in which they were hiding; they believe he is speaking in good faith. His intent was to entrap those who had escaped, so he publishes a copy of the Spanish constitution, a document based on the holy principles of freedom, property, and security, while simultaneously sending out bands of Spaniards and Canarians to arrest and carry off ignominiously those unwary enough to have assembled to witness and celebrate its publication.

This is a truth as notorious as all of those that have been described in this paper, and it will be further explicated in the manifesto being drawn up. In the province of Caracas, the Spanish constitution has no validity; the Spaniards themselves mock it, insult it. Following its publication they make arrests without probable cause, shackle prisoners with chains and handcuffs at the whim of the commanders and judges; and put prisoners to death without legal formalities or trials, as Tízcar did in Barinas in May of this year, as [Antonio] Zuazola did in Aragua, and Boves in Espino, sending off groups of prisoners indiscriminately to jails, dungeons, and prisons, while the territorial Audiencia, following Monteverde's advice, establishes a procedure and a conduct diametrically opposed to the spirit and letter of the constitution. In view of all this, and the indifference or tacit consent of the Spanish government, can America hope to improve its lot as a dependent of that peninsula? Can America be considered criminal and insurgent in its efforts to recover its freedom? And with regard to Caracas, can anyone call into question the resolve and conduct of General Simón Bolívar and his compatriots and fellow soldiers for trying to rescue brothers, friends, and relatives from the cells, jails, dungeons, and pens where they lay oppressed, humiliated, and abused? Here we put aside the principles on which Venezuela proclaimed her freedom and independence, observing instead the long list of reasons we had for undertaking to break the yoke of her oppressors, justifying our conduct by a minimal and approximate sketch of the insults, atrocities, and crimes of Monteverde and his accomplices, especially his fellow Canarians. Those can be reduced to a few articles: the scandalous infraction of the surrender at San Mateo; the murders perpetrated throughout the province, the killing of prisoners of war, people who had surrendered, who were unarmed, simple farmers, peaceful citizens, and even people already imprisoned; the inhuman, ignominious, cruel, and brutal treatment of distinguished, decorated citizens; the occupation of haciendas and other properties; acts of plunder tolerated and authorized; the senseless, unwarranted destruction of places of employment where Americans worked; the suffering of so many devastated families; the homelessness, sadness, and weeping of the most respected women in the towns, who wandered through the streets exposed to lewd insolence and the savage behavior of the Canarians, city thugs, sailors, and soldiers.

This then, Nations of the World, is the most succinct idea I can give you at this time of my conduct in the project which I conceived to liberate Caracas from the tyrant Monteverde, under the auspices of the virtuous, humane, and generous people of New Granada. I stand before you with my weapons still at the ready, and I will not put them down until I eradicate every last Spaniard from the provinces of Venezuela that have most recently experienced the excess of their tyranny, their injustice, their perfidy, and their atrocities. I will fill with glory the campaign I have undertaken for the health of my country and the happiness of my fellow citizens, or I will die in the effort, demonstrating to the entire world that the Americans are not to be scorned or slandered with impunity.

Nations of the World: Venezuela owes you the consideration of not letting you concern yourselves with the false and misleading accounts which those scoundrels will contrive to discredit our conduct. In short order, the precise and documented manifesto of everything that happened in the year 1812 and up to the present time in these provinces will be published. Suspend your judgment for the moment, and if you wish to seek out the truth on your own, Caracas not only welcomes you but eagerly awaits the arrival in its ports of all able men who come seeking refuge among us and who can help us with their skill and knowledge, without concern for their place of origin.

Simón Bolívar

Manifesto of Carúpano

Carúpano, 7 September 1814

Simón Bolívar
Liberator of Venezuela, and Commanding General of her armies.

Citizens:

Unhappy is the leader who, responsible for the calamities or crimes occurring in his country, is called before the tribunal of the people to defend himself against accusations concerning his conduct; but happy is he who, having steered a true course among the reefs of war, politics, and public misfortune, preserves his honor intact and stands innocent before his companions in misfortune to demand a fair decision concerning his righteous actions.[5]

I was chosen by the fortunes of war to break your chains, but it must also be said that I was the instrument used by Providence to gauge the extent of your afflictions. Yes, I brought you peace and freedom, but in the wake of these priceless boons, war and slavery also accompanied me. Victory tempered by justice was our constant guide as we marched on the ruins of our illustrious capital of Caracas to wrest it from the hands of its oppressors. The warriors of New Granada preserved their laurels fresh and bright as they fought against the conquerors of Venezuela, and the soldiers of Caracas were crowned with equal fortune against the fierce Spaniards who tried to subjugate us once again. If fickle destiny caused victory to alternate between us and our enemies, it was only because an appalling dementia led the American peoples to take up arms to destroy their liberators and restore the scepter to their tyrants.

Thus, it would seem that heaven, to bring us humiliation and then glory, allowed our conquerors to be our brothers and our brothers, no one else, to triumph over us. The Army of Liberators exterminated the enemy armies, but has not been able, nor should it be able, to exterminate the people for whom it fought in hundreds of battles. It is not right to destroy men who do not want to be free, nor do we give the name of freedom to what we impose against the will of fanatical creatures whose spiritual depravity makes them love their chains as if they were social bonds.

So grieve not for yourselves but for your compatriots who, driven by the fury of discord, have immersed you in that swamp of calamities whose very aspect makes Nature tremble, an image so horrific no one could paint it for you. It was your brothers, not the Spaniards, who ripped out your hearts, shed your blood, set fire to your homes, and forced you into exile. Your cries should be directed against those blind slaves who seek to bind you with the very chains they drag behind them; do not vent your wrath on the martyrs who in the passionate defense of your freedom spilled their blood on every battlefield and confronted every danger heedless of their own safety in order to save you from death or ignominy. Be as just in your sorrow as the cause from which it stems.

Do not let your torments alienate you, citizens, to the point of regarding your protectors and friends as accomplices of imaginary crimes, either of intention or of omission. Those who govern your destiny, no less than those who work with them, had no other intention than to provide perpetual happiness for you, an achievement which for them would represent immortal glory. But if things did not turn out according to that intention, and if unparalleled disasters have frustrated this admirable undertaking, it was not because of ineptitude or cowardice; it was, rather, the inevitable consequence of an enormous project, beyond all human capacity. The destruction of a government whose origins are lost in the darkness of the ages; the subversion of established principles; the mutation of customs; the upheaval in public opinion; and finally, the establishment of freedom in a nation of slaves—these are goals impossible to achieve overnight, truly beyond the reach of any human effort. So our excuse for not having obtained what we desired is inherent in the cause we follow, because in the same way that justice justifies the audacity of having sought to implement it, the impossibility of attaining it excuses the inadequacy of the means. It is praiseworthy, it is noble, it is sublime to seek to vindicate Nature violated by tyranny; nothing is comparable to the grandeur of this action, and even when desolation and death are the reward for such a glorious attempt, there is no reason to condemn it, because we are obliged to undertake not the easily attainable but rather that which is morally authorized.

In vain have our extraordinary efforts achieved victory after victory, purchased dearly by the blood of our heroic soldiers. Then a few minor successes by our enemies sufficed to bring down the edifice of our glory, the masses being carried away by religious fanaticism and seduced by the lure of voracious anarchy. In opposition to the torch of freedom, which we presented to America as the guide and object of our struggle, our enemies have offered the incendiary torch of discord and devastation and the motivation of honor and fortune as spoils of war, powerful lures to men corrupted by the yoke of servitude and bestialized by the doctrine of superstition. How could the simple theory of political philosophy, based only on truth and nature, prevail over vice, vice armed with unfettered license limited only by one's appetite and suddenly transformed by the prestigious veneer of religion into a political virtue and a form of Christian charity? No, it is impossible for ordinary men to appreciate the high value of the realm of freedom or to choose it over blind ambition and vile greed. In this crucial matter our fate depended on the choice of our compatriots, who in their corrupted condition chose against us; the rest was a consequence of a decision that was more dishonorable than fatal and more to be lamented for its essence than for its results.

It is stupidity provoked by malice to hold public men responsible for the vicissitudes naturally occurring in a state, since in times of turbulence, catastrophe, or social turmoil it is beyond the capacity of a general or a magistrate to stem the tide of human passions stirred up by the momentum of revolutions and growing in intensity in direct proportion to the forces seeking to resist them. Even when serious errors or the violent passions of leaders frequently weaken the Republic, the harm must nonetheless be viewed objectively and its origin sought in the primitive causes of all misfortune: the frailty of the human race and the power of chance to determine events. Man is the plaything of fortune, the effects of which can often be anticipated, though never with certainty, because our realm is so remote from the higher order of things. To expect politics and war to move to the rhythm of plans we formulate in darkness guided only by the purity of our intentions and aided by the limited means at our disposal is to strive for the effects of a divine power through merely human agency.

Far from the mad presumption of considering myself guiltless in the catastrophe of my country, I suffer the opposite burden, the deep sorrow of believing myself to be the wretched instrument of her appalling miseries. Yet I am innocent, because my conscience never engaged in deliberate or malicious error, although on the other hand it may have contributed unintentionally to the harm. It is my heart that persuades me of my innocence, and this testimony is for me the most authentic, though it may seem to others to be the delirium of pride. This is why, not deigning to reply to each one of the accusations that may be alleged against me in good or bad faith, I reserve this act of reckoning, which my own vindication requires, until it can be carried out before a tribunal of wise men who will judge my conduct during my mission in Venezuela with rectitude and reason. I refer to the Supreme Congress of New Granada, the august body that commissioned me with armies to come to your aid, as they did heroically to the last man on the field of honor. It is proper and necessary that my public life be examined with care and judged impartially. It is proper and necessary that I give satisfaction to anyone I may have offended and that I be cleared of erroneous accusations of which I am innocent. This high judgment must be pronounced by the sovereign I served. I assure you that the occasion will be as solemn as possible and that my actions will be irrefutably documented. Then you will know whether I have been unworthy of your trust or whether I deserve the name of Liberator.

I swear to you, beloved compatriots, that this august title your gratitude bestowed on me when I came to take away your chains was not given in vain. I swear to you that whether I be Liberator or dead, I will always be worthy of the honor you have done me and that no human power on earth can deflect me from the course I have pledged to follow until I free you a second time, marching from the west along the route nourished with so much blood and adorned with so many laurels. Have every expectation, compatriots, that the noble and virtuous people of New Granada will fly forth eager to win new trophies, to come once again to your aid and bring you freedom, unless your own valor wins it first. Indeed, your own virtues are capable of waging successful war against that frenzied multitude who are oblivious to their own interests and honor, for freedom has never been subjugated by tyranny. Do not measure your physical forces against those of the enemy, as there is no comparison between spirit and matter. You are men, they are beasts; you are free, they are slaves. Fight, and you will win. God grants victory to those who persevere.

Bolívar

Manifesto on the Execution of General Manuel Piar

General Headquarters in Angostura, 17 October 1817

Simón Bolívar
Supreme Commander of the Republic of Venezuela, etc., etc.

To the Soldiers of the Liberating Army:

Soldiers! Yesterday was a day of sorrow for my heart.[6] General Piar was executed for his crimes against the country, for conspiracy and desertion. A just and legal tribunal has pronounced the sentence against that unfortunate citizen who, intoxicated by the favors of fortune and to satisfy his ambition, tried to bury the country amid her ruins. General Piar truly had rendered important service to the Republic, and though the course of his conduct had always been factious, his services had been rewarded generously by the government of Venezuela.

For a leader who had obtained the highest military rank, there was nothing left to aspire to. Prior to his rebellion, the second highest authority of the republic, which had been vacated due to the dissidence of General [Santiago] Mariño,[7] was about to be conferred on him; but this general, who aspired only to the supreme command, contrived the most atrocious plot a perverse soul can conceive. Piar sought not only civil war but anarchy and the most inhuman sacrifice of his fellow soldiers and brothers.

Soldiers! You know this. Equality, liberty, and independence are our motto. Has not humankind regained its rights through our laws? Have our arms not destroyed the chains of slaves? Have not the odious differences between classes and colors been abolished forever? Has it not been ordered that the wealth of the nation be fairly distributed among you?[8] Do not fortune, knowledge, and glory await you? Are your merits not richly, or at least fairly, rewarded? What then could General Piar have wanted on your behalf? Are you not equal, free, independent, happy, and honored? Could Piar have secured greater good for you? No, no, no! Piar was digging the grave of the republic with his own hands and was about to bury in it the lives, properties, and honor of the brave defenders of Venezuela's freedom, of her sons, wives, and fathers.

Heaven looked with horror on this cruel patricide. Heaven delivered him to the rigors of the law. Heaven ordained that a man who had offended divinity and the human race should no longer profane the earth or be further tolerated after his infamous crime.

Soldiers! Heaven keeps vigil over your welfare, and the government that is your father watches over you. Your general, who is your companion in arms, and who has always marched at your head and shared your dangers and hardships as well as your triumphs, puts his trust in you. Therefore, put your trust in him, confident that he loves you more than if he were your father or your son.

Declaration of Angostura

Angostura, 20 November 1818

Simón Bolívar
Supreme Commander of the Republic of Venezuela, etc.

Considering that when the Spanish government requests the mediation of the major powers in its effort to reconcile and reestablish its authority over the free and independent people of America, it is urgent that we convey to the world Venezuela's feelings and decision.[9]

That even though these feelings and that decision were embodied in the establishment of the Republic on 5 July 1811 and more specifically since the very first announcements of the proposition of the government of Madrid, it is the obligation of those representing the national government to reiterate them, giving them formal expression in solemn and legal terms.

That we are obliged to make this frank and clear declaration not only out of respect and consideration for the major powers but even more urgently to calm the spirits of the citizens of Venezuela.

Having convened a national meeting of all the civil and military authorities, including the Council of State, the Supreme Court of Justice, the governor, the vicar general of this vacant diocese, and the general staff of the armed forces, and having examined with great care the conduct of the Spanish government, we have borne in mind:

1. that the idea of cordial reconciliation was never a consideration of the Spanish government.
2. that though Great Britain twice proposed such a reconciliation from the first days of our disagreements, Spain, in defiance of all parties, rejected it.
3. that even while efforts at reconciliation were being negotiated, she blocked our ports, sent armies against us, and conspired to destroy us.

4. that having subjected Venezuela to terms of solemn capitulation, no sooner had we put down our arms than she violated every article of that armistice, sacrificing thousands of citizens whose rights had been guaranteed.

5. that waging against us a war to the death without respect for sex, age, or condition, she broke every social bond and aroused our just and implacable hatred.

6. that this hatred has been exacerbated by the atrocities she has committed and by the bad faith she has shown us at every juncture.

7. that all America, and very particularly Venezuela, is thoroughly convinced of the absolute impossibility that Spain could ever recover her authority on this continent.

8. that all America is now satisfied of her power and her resources: she is fully aware of her natural advantages and means of defense and secure in her conviction that no power on earth can ever bind her to Spain again.

9. that even if there were such a power, she is resolved to perish rather than be subjected again to a government of blood, fire, and devastation.

10. that having found ourselves in possession of the freedom and independence for which nature destined us, and which even the laws of Spain and the examples of her history authorized us to seize by force of arms, as we have in fact done, it would be an act of deranged stupidity to bow down to the Spanish government no matter what the conditions.

Due to all these considerations, the government of Venezuela, interpreter of the national will and purpose, has seen fit to proclaim to the world the following declaration:

1. that the Republic of Venezuela, by divine and human right, is emancipated from the Spanish nation and constituted as an independent, free, and sovereign state.

2. that Spain has no right to reclaim dominion over her, nor does Europe have the right to attempt to subject her to the Spanish government.

3. that Venezuela has not requested, nor will she ever request, incorporation into the Spanish nation.

4. that she has not requested the mediation of the major powers to seek reconciliation with Spain.

5. that she will never deal with Spain, in peace or war, except on terms of equality, as is the mutual practice of all nations.

6. that she only desires the mediation of foreign powers to exert their good offices on behalf of humanity, inviting Spain to draft and sign a treaty of peace and friendship with the Venezuelan nation, recognizing and dealing with her as a free, independent, and sovereign state.

7. and that, finally, the Republic of Venezuela declares that she has been engaged in a struggle for her rights since 19 April 1810, shedding the blood of most of her sons, sacrificing her wealth, her pleasures, and everything that men hold dear and sacred, in her effort to recover her sovereign rights, and that to retain her integrity, as Divine Providence has ordained, the people of Venezuela are resolved to bury themselves alive amid the ruins if Spain, or Europe, or the world seeks to subject her to the Spanish yoke.

Presented, signed by my hand, sealed with the provisional seal of the Republic, and countersigned by the secretary of state in the Palace of Government in Angostura on 20 November 1818, the eighth year of independence.

Simón Bolívar

For His Excellency the Supreme Commander,
the Secretary of State, *Pedro Briceño Méndez*

My Delirium on Chimborazo

(1822)

I was coming along, cloaked in the mantle of Iris, from the place where the torrential Orinoco pays tribute to the God of waters.[10] I had visited the enchanted springs of Amazonia, straining to climb up to the watchtower of the universe. I sought the tracks of La Condamine and Humboldt,[11] following them boldly. Nothing could stop me. I reached the glacial heights, and the atmosphere took my breath away. No human foot had ever blemished the diamond crown placed by Eternity's hands on the sublime temples of this lofty Andean peak. I said to myself: Iris's rainbow cloak has served as my banner. I've carried it through the infernal regions. It has ploughed rivers and seas and risen to the gigantic shoulders of the Andes. The terrain had leveled off at the feet of Colombia, and not even time could hold back freedom's march. The war goddess Belona has been humbled by the brilliance of Iris. So why should I hesitate to tread on the ice-white hair of this giant of the earth? Indeed I shall! And caught up in a spiritual tremor I had never before experienced, and which seemed to me a kind of divine frenzy, I left Humboldt's tracks behind and began to leave my own marks on the eternal crystals girding Chimborazo. I climb as if driven by this frenzy, faltering only when my head grazes the summit of the firmament. At my feet the threshold of the abyss beckons.

A feverish delirium suspends my mental faculties. I feel as if I were aflame with a strange, higher fire. It was the God of Colombia taking possession of me.

Suddenly, Time appears to me as an ancient figure weighed down by the clutter of the ages: scowling, bent over, bald, his skin lined, scythe in hand . . .

"I am the father of the centuries, the arcanum of fame and secret knowledge. My mother was Eternity. Infinity sets the limits of my empire. There is no tomb for me, because I am more powerful than

Death. I behold the past, I see the future, and the present passes through my hands. Oh, child, man, ancient, hero, why such vanity? Do you think your Universe matters? That you exalt yourself merely by scaling one of the atoms of creation? Do you imagine that the instants you call centuries are enough to fathom my mysteries? Do you believe you have seen the Holy Truth? Are you mad enough to presume that your actions have value in my eyes? Compared to my brother, Infinity, everything is less than the tiniest point."

Overcome by a sacred awe, I answered: "Oh, Time, how can a wretched mortal who has climbed so high not simply vanish in thin air? I have surpassed all men in fortune, because I have risen to be the head of them all. I stand high above the earth with my feet; I grasp the eternal with my hands; I feel the infernal prisons boiling beneath my footsteps; I stand gazing at the glittering stars beside me, the infinite suns; I measure without astonishment the space that encloses all matter, and in your face I read the History of the past and the thoughts of Destiny."

"Observe," he said to me, "learn, hold in your mind what you have seen. Draw for the eyes of those like you the image of the physical Universe, the moral Universe. Do not conceal the secrets heaven has revealed to you. Tell men the truth."

The apparition disappeared.

Absorbed, frozen in time, so to speak, I lay lifeless for a long time, stretched out on that immense diamond serving as my bed. Finally, the tremendous voice of Colombia cries out to me. I come back to life, sit up, open my heavy eyelids with my own hands. I become a man again, and write down my delirium.

Simón Bolívar

Letter to José Antonio Páez:
"Nor Am I Napoleon"

Magdalena, 6 March 1826

My Dear General and Friend:

I have received your very important letter of the first of October of last year, which you sent to me by way of Mr. [Antonio Leocadio] Guzmán, whom I met and listened to with some surprise, since his is an extraordinary mission.[12] You tell me that the situation in Colombia is much like that in France when Napoleon found himself in Egypt and that I should say, with him, "The conspirators are going to lose the country. I am going to save it." In truth, your entire letter is inscribed by the chisel of truth, but the truth alone is not sufficient for a plan to achieve its purpose. It seems to me that you have not judged matters and men with sufficient objectivity. Colombia is not France, nor am I Napoleon. People in France think a lot, and they know even more, the population is homogeneous, and moreover, war had the country on the edge of the precipice. France was the only country in Europe with a great republic, and France had always been a monarchy. The republican government had been discredited and reduced to a point of abyssal execration. The monsters who ran France were cruel and inept to an equal degree. Napoleon was a great and unique man, in addition to being extremely ambitious. None of that applies here. I am not Napoleon, nor do I wish to be. Neither do I wish to imitate Caesar, even less Iturbide. Such models seem unworthy of my glory. The title of Liberator is superior to any ever granted to human pride. Therefore, it is impossible to degrade it. On the other hand, our population is not French by any stretch of the imagination. The republic has uplifted the country to glory and prosperity, given it laws and freedom. The leaders of Colombia are not Robespierre or Marat. The danger ended when hope began, so there is no urgent need for such measures. Colombia is surrounded by republics, and

Colombia has never been a monarchy. A throne would be frightening as much for its height as for its brilliance. Equality would be destroyed, and the people of color would see all their rights stripped away by a new aristocracy. In short, friend, I cannot persuade myself that the project communicated to me by Guzmán makes any sense, and I also believe that those who have suggested it are men like those who exalted Napoleon and Iturbide so they could enjoy their prosperity and then abandon them when it became risky. If it should turn out that they were acting in good faith, then you should know that they are deluded, either that or partisans of extreme ideas of one kind or another.

I will tell you in all candor that this project is not good for you or for me or for the country. I do, however, believe that in the upcoming period set aside for the reform of the constitution, it may well undergo significant changes in favor of good conservative principles, and this without violating a single republican rule. I will send you a rough draft for a constitution that I have drawn up for the republic of Bolivia; in it are included every guarantee of permanence and freedom, equality and order. If you and your friends saw fit to support this project, it would be very useful if you could write in support of it and recommend it to the opinion of the people. This is the service we can proffer to the country, a service that can be admired by every one of the parties that are not extremist, or, to put it another way, those who desire real freedom accompanied by real stability. Beyond this, I do not advise you to do for yourself what I do not wish for myself, but if the people wish it, and you accept the national will, my sword and my authority will be employed with infinite pleasure to sustain and defend the decrees of popular sovereignty. This protest is as sincere as the heart of your true friend.

Bolívar

A Soldier's Death Penalty Commuted

Bogotá, 26 January 1828

Simón Bolívar
Liberator President, etc.

Having witnessed in Government Council the accord issued on the 25ᵗʰ of this month by the Superior Military Court of the Department of Cundinamarca, in which on advice of the Executive Power a commutation was granted regarding the death penalty to which artillery soldier Antonio León was condemned during the regular meeting of the Council of War in this capital on 21 August 1827 for the crimes of climbing over the barracks wall, abandoning guard duty, and aiding in the escape of the prisoner Casimiro Solanilla, this sentence having been confirmed by the same court on appeal, after examining the original trial record, the following circumstances have been considered:[13]

1. that although the crimes for which León has been convicted are punishable by the death penalty according to army ordinances, they did not cause serious harm to society.
2. that far from displaying any depravity of heart in the commission of these crimes, the prisoner has exhibited a spirit of compassion and gives indications of being capable of rehabilitation in the future.
3. that the abandonment of guard duty did not occur before the enemy, nor during a campaign, but in the jail of one of the military barracks that have been used for incarcerating prisoners under the jurisdiction of the civil tribunals and courts due to the circumstances in which this city found itself following the earthquakes.
4. Finally, that the prisoner whose escape León aided was not convicted of a capital crime. For all these reasons and using the

power conceded to the Executive Power by Article 127 of the Constitution, I have determined the following:

The death penalty to which artillery soldier Antonio León has been condemned shall be commuted to the same sentence imposed on the prisoner Casimiro Solanilla, on final appeal, by the Superior Court of Justice of Cundinamarca, to which in its military jurisdiction this decree will be communicated for appropriate action.

The Secretary of State of the War Department is charged with the execution of this decree.

Given, signed by my hand, and countersigned by the Secretary whose signature appears below, in the Palace of Government, in Bogotá, on 26 January 1828, the eighteenth year of independence.

Simón Bolívar

C. Soublette

Manifesto Justifying the Dictatorship

Bogotá 27 August 1828

Simón Bolívar
Liberator President of the Republic of Colombia, etc.

Colombians! The will of the people was given energetic expression in the political reforms of the nation. The legislative body deferred to your desires, ordering the convocation of the Great Convention so that the representatives of the people could carry out their wishes, constituting the Republic according to our beliefs, our inclinations, and our needs.[14] The people asked for nothing except what was theirs by right. However, the hopes of all the people were betrayed in the Great Convention, which at last had to be dissolved, because while some heeded the petitions of the majority, others insisted on making laws dictated by their conscience or personal opinion. The constitution of the Republic no longer had the force of law for the majority, because the convention itself had annulled it, pressing unanimously for its reform. Then the people, realizing the seriousness of the ills besetting them, reassumed that portion of their rights which they had delegated and, exercising immediately their full sovereignty, took steps to ensure their own future. This sovereign entity chose to honor me with the title of minister and authorized me, further, to be the executor of their decrees. My position as supreme leader imposed on me the obligation to obey and serve my sovereign even beyond my own capacities. It has been utterly impossible for me on such a solemn occasion to refuse to comply with the trust of the nation, a trust that weighs upon me with an immense glory, while simultaneously humbling me, making me aware of my own inadequacy.

Colombians! I accept the obligation to obey rigorously your legitimate desires. I will protect your sacred religion as the faith of all Colombians and the ethical code of good people. I will ensure that you are treated justly, that being the first law of nature and the universal guarantee for citizens. The careful management of the national treasury will be the first priority of your servants; we will take great pains to pay Colombia's debt to our generous foreign creditors. Finally, I will only retain the supreme power until such time as you order me to return it to you, and I will convene the national assembly within a year, unless you see fit to do so earlier.

Colombians! I will not speak to you of freedom, because if I keep my promises, you will be more than free, you will be respected. Besides, in a dictatorship, who can speak of freedom? Let us sympathize mutually with the people who obey and with the man who rules alone!

Bolívar

Manifesto Concerning the Installation of the Constituent Congress, the End of the Dictatorship, and Announcing the End of His Political Career

Bogotá, 20 January 1830

Simón Bolívar
Liberator President of Colombia, etc.

Colombians![15] Today I cease to govern you. I have served you for twenty years as soldier and leader. During this long period we have taken back our country, liberated three republics, fomented many civil wars, and four times I have returned to the people their omnipotence, convening personally four constitutional congresses. These services were inspired by your virtues, your courage, and your patriotism; mine is the great privilege of having governed you.

The constitutional congress convened on this day is charged by Providence with the task of giving the nation the institutions she desires, following the course of circumstances and the nature of things.

Fearing that I may be regarded as an obstacle to establishing the Republic on the true base of its happiness, I personally have cast myself down from the supreme position of leadership to which your generosity had elevated me.

Colombians! I have been the victim of ignominious suspicions, with no possible way to defend the purity of my principles. The same persons who aspire to the supreme command have conspired to tear your hearts from me, attributing to me their own motives, making me seem to be the instigator of projects they themselves have conceived, representing me, finally, as aspiring to a crown which they themselves have offered me on more than one occasion and which I have rejected with the indignation of the fiercest republican. Never, never, I swear to you, has it crossed my mind to aspire to a kingship that my enemies have fabricated in order to ruin me in your regard.

Do not be deceived, Colombians! My only desire has been to contribute to your freedom and to the preservation of your peace of mind. If for this I am held guilty, I deserve your censure more than any other man. Do not listen, I beg you, to the vile slander and the tawdry envy stirring up discord on all sides. Will you allow yourselves to be deceived by the false accusations of my detractors? Please don't be so foolish!

Colombians! Gather around the constitutional congress. It represents the wisdom of the nation, the legitimate hope of the people, and the final point of reunion of the patriots. Its sovereign decrees will determine our lives, the happiness of the Republic, and the glory of Colombia. If dire circumstances should cause you to abandon it, there will be no health for the country, and you will drown in the ocean of anarchy, leaving as your children's legacy nothing but crime, blood, and death.

Fellow Countrymen! Hear my final plea as I end my political career; in the name of Colombia I ask you, beg you, to remain united, lest you become the assassins of the country and your own executioners.

Bolívar

Letter to General Juan José Flores:
"Ploughing the Sea"

Barranquilla, 9 November 1830

My dear General:

I have received your fine letter from Guayaquil, of 10 September placed in my hands by your emissary, [José María] Urbina.[16] You cannot imagine my surprise to see that you took the trouble to send a special envoy to deliver your reply and to inform me of what is happening in the South and with your situation. I never expected that a personal letter could be the object of so much concern and benevolence. By so doing, you have surpassed the usual standard of extraordinary kindness in your dealings with me. Your friendship leaves nothing to be desired. With regard to the country, you conduct yourself like a statesman, always behaving in accordance with the ideas and desires of the people who have entrusted their destiny to you. In this case you fulfill your obligation as a leader and citizen.

I will not respond to the letter in question, because the important letter was the message delivered in person by Mr. Urbina: this procedure is diplomatic, prudent, and consistent with the nature of the revolution, for we never know in what moment and with whom we live our lives; and a voice is most flexible and lends itself to all the alterations one chooses to give it; this is politics. Urbina assures me that the desire of the South, according to the information he has brought, is final with respect to the independence of that country. Let the will of the South be carried out; keep your promises. Those people are in possession of their own sovereignty and will make of it a sack or a smock, depending on their whim. In this, nothing is determined so far, because nations are like children, who soon throw away what they have wept to attain. Neither you nor I nor anyone else knows the will of the people. Tomorrow they may kill each other, split into factions, and let themselves fall into the most pow-

erful or the most ferocious hands. Be sure, my dear General, that you and
those generals from the North[17] are going to be ejected from that country, unless you transform yourselves into France, and even that will not
suffice, because you know that all the revolutionaries of France died
slaughtering their enemies, and that there are very few monsters of that
ilk who have escaped the knife or the gallows. I will speak to you in passing and with clear intent. This young man has told me, because I asked
him, that the grand destiny of the South is in the hands of the northern
generals. This struck me as despicable even before the last revolution.
With how much more justification will they not now call this tyranny?
Even at this distance I have been hearing that they are still colonists,
creatures of foreigners; foreigners from Venezuela, others from New
Granada, others English, others Peruvians, and who knows from how
many other countries they originate. And then, what manner of men!
Some arrogant, some despotic, no doubt others simply thieves; all of
them ignorant, with absolutely no talent for administration. Yes, my dear
sir, I say this to you because I love you and do not want you to be a victim of this prejudice. I must warn you that [Vicente] Rocafuerte[18] must
already be en route to that country and that he is a man who harbors the
most sinister intentions against you and against all my friends. He is
capable of anything and has the means to carry out his designs. He is full
of the most conflicting ideas; he was one of my best friends in our tender
youth, one of my admirers until I entered Guayaquil, but then he became
my fiercest enemy for the same offenses you have committed, i.e., for
attacking La Mar and for not being from Guayaquil, and for other petty
matters and opinions. He is the most rabid federalist the world has ever
known, the antimilitarist incarnate, and something of a bully. If that gentleman lays his hands on Guayaquil, you will have much to suffer, and
beyond this, God only knows. La Mar will join him. [José Joaquín]
Olmedo idolizes him, loves only him. Use the past to predict the future.
You know that I have ruled for twenty years, and I have derived from
these only a few sure conclusions: (1) America is ungovernable, for us; (2)
Those who serve revolution plough the sea; (3) The only thing one can
do in America is emigrate; (4) This country will fall inevitably into the
hands of the unrestrained multitudes and then into the hands of tyrants
so insignificant they will be almost imperceptible, of all colors and races;
(5) Once we've been eaten alive by every crime and extinguished by
ferocity, the Europeans won't even bother to conquer us; (6) If it were
possible for any part of the world to revert to primitive chaos, it would be
America in her last hour.

The first French Revolution cut the throat of the Antilles, and the second[19] will produce the same effect on this vast continent. The sudden reaction of extremist ideology is going to provide us with all the evils we were lacking or, rather, fill out our allotment. And you will see how the whole world will succumb to the flood of demagoguery, and then, alas for the people, alas for the governments.

My advice to you as a friend is that as soon as you sense your fortune waning, step down yourself and leave your post with honor and on your own: *No one dies of hunger on land.*

I will speak to you of Colombia in more specific terms. This country has suffered a Great Revolution, and marches forward on volcanic terrain. Because a single revolution engenders a thousand others, and the first have not yet been extinguished, the history of La Ladera[20] is still being written. Of course, the southern section of the Department of Cauca is at war with all the furies from hell. There was an uprising in Río Hacha, the government troops took the city, but the bandits, led by [Pedro] Carujo,[21] are infesting the country and causing great damage. [Juan Nepomuceno] Moreno, Carvajal's murderer, has not yet acknowledged the legitimacy of the government and is using certain governmental documents to stir up trouble.[22] In the province of Socorro there was conflict between the city of Vélez and the capital, producing much mayhem and injury. The entire population, as well as the Church and the army, are supporters of the new order, but there are still some assassins, traitors, partisans of factions, and malcontents, perhaps several hundred. Unfortunately, among us, the masses are incapable of independent action, so a few powerful individuals do everything, and the multitude follows their audacity without examining the righteousness or criminality of the leaders, but then they abandon them as soon as others even more treacherous stage a surprise attack. This is the essence of public opinion and national power in our America.

The administration in Bogotá, presided over by [General Rafael] Urdaneta, goes about its business with good energy and much activity. There are those who would like to see more of the former, but there's the constitution to consider, responds Urdaneta. Still, he takes his hits now and then, but they're meted out with style, as [Juan Bautista] Arismendi said. The new general, [Florencio] Jiménez, has already marched south with fifteen hundred men to protect Cauca against the assassins of the most famous victim.[23] Let me add, like Cato the Elder: This is how I see it, and Carthage must be destroyed. When I say Carthage, you should understand that lair of monsters in Cauca. Let us avenge Sucre, and you should avenge those who *[a large stain, probably ink, blots out the next thirty or thirty-five letters]*; and finally, avenge Colombia that had its Sucre, avenge the world that admired him, avenge the glory of the army and the saintly humanity so wickedly savaged in this most innocent of men. If you are insensible to this clamor of everything visible and everything invisible, you must have suffered a drastic change of character.

The most famous liberal thinkers of Europe have published and written that *the death of Sucre is the blackest and most indelible stain on the history of the New World and that in the Old World nothing comparable had happened for many centuries.* It is up to you, then, to wash away this execrable stain, because in Pasto[24] you will find Colombia's absolution, and Jiménez with his fifteen hundred men cannot penetrate that far. This is the only sacrifice that the friends of the North demand of their friends in the South, or rather they urge them to rise to the occasion.

Finally, I will speak to you of myself: I have been appointed president by all of New Granada,[25] but not by that den of assassins in Casanare and Popayán; meanwhile, Urdaneta is exercising the executive power with the ministers elected with him. I have not accepted this revolutionary responsibility, because the election is not legitimate. Then I fell ill, which prevents me from serving, even as a subordinate. While all this is going on here, the elections are being verified according to the law, although in some places the deadline has passed. They assure me that I will receive many votes, perhaps more than anyone else, and then we will see what happens. And you can ask yourself whether a man who has drawn the previous conclusions as his only profit from his experience with revolutions is going to want to drown himself again after having emerged from the belly of the whale. The answer should be obvious.

My letter is quite long in comparison with yours, so it is time to close, and I do so by imploring you to tear up this letter as soon as you have read it, because I only wrote it out of consideration for your health, always fearing that it might fall into the hands of our enemies and that they might publish it with atrocious commentaries.

Meanwhile, accept my assurances of friendship and even more my gratitude for your former acts of kindness and loyalty toward me, and lastly, receive my heart.

Bolívar

Postscript: I have learned of [José Domingo] Espinar's insane action with the ship *Istmeña*.[26] I beg you to bear this with patience, because this brazen dictator is ill advised by his sudden promotion and by the spirit of [Juan Eligio] Alzuru.[27] Finally, one should not bicker over trifles among friends who lose their minds. I repeat that I ask this favor so that the scandals do not grow.

Bolívar's flourish

Final Proclamation of the Liberator

Santa Marta, 10 December 1830

Simón Bolívar
Liberator of Colombia, etc.

Colombians! You have been witness to my efforts to establish freedom where tyranny previously reigned.[28] I have worked without thought of personal gain, sacrificing my fortune and even my peace of mind. I relinquished my power when I became convinced that you mistrusted my detachment. My enemies took advantage of your credulity and undermined what is most sacred to me: my reputation and my love of freedom. I have been the victim of my persecutors, who have driven me to the very threshold of my grave. I forgive them.

As I disappear from among you, my affection tells me that I must make clear my final wishes. I aspire to no other glory than the consolidation of Colombia. You must all work for the inestimable good of the Union: the people offering their obedience to the current government in order to save themselves from anarchy; the ministers of the sanctuary directing their prayers to heaven; and the military officers using their swords to defend social guarantees.

Colombians! My final wishes are for the happiness of the country. If my death contributes to the cessation of factions and the consolidation of the Union, I will step peacefully into the grave.

Hacienda of San Pedro [Alejandrino], in Santa Marta, 10 December 1830, in the twentieth year of independence.

Simón Bolívar

2. INTERNATIONAL AFFAIRS

Letter to Sir Richard Wellesley: An Appeal for Support

Kingston, 27 May 1815

My dear sir:

When I had the honor of making your acquaintance in that capital [London], I vowed to satisfy the request you kindly made, to write to you about what I believed worthy of communicating to you.[1] At first I did not wish to abuse your indulgence, and I only took the liberty of intruding on your attention when I judged that the time had come to share with you the most important of the terrible and glorious events that had befallen us. After many victories had been won by the forces under my command, I made so bold as to enter into confidential communication with you. I did that then, but have not presumed a second time to take advantage of a privilege so flattering to me.

Now, for the second time, I take the liberty of addressing my thoughts to you, not to recount fortuitous events but to draw forth the sublime sentiments characteristic of an enlightened and liberal man. I write to you, esteemed friend and gentleman, in the hope that you will use your influence on behalf of a world as worthy of compassion for its innocence as it is cruelly persecuted by its enemies. Yes, dear sir, the fortunes of America are urgently in need of the support of every generous soul who knows the value of freedom and who prides himself on his defense of justice. In you, these heroic virtues shine bright. Because of this, you will listen with tenderness to the anguished cries of twenty million victims. Please deign to hear what I have to say.

The philosophy of this century, English politics, French ambition, and Spanish stupidity suddenly combined to leave America utterly orphaned and indirectly to reduce her to a state of passive anarchy. Some thinkers were inspired to recommend independence, reasonably anticipating the support of the British nation, the cause being just. Most of the people in these nations were docile and followed the path of good. But once Spain had recovered from her initial shock, because England gave her cause to hope,[2] she directed her attention not to recovering her former possessions and conquering in order to possess; instead, with fire and sword in hand, her purpose is to reduce this half of the world to desolation a second time, since she is too impotent to hold onto it. The balance of world power and the interests of Great Britain are perfectly in accord with the salvation of America! My land offers vast opportunities to her defenders and friends! Sciences, arts, industry, culture, everything that currently constitutes the glory of the European continent and arouses the admiration of its people will find swift passage to America. England, almost exclusively, will see prosperity flow back to her shores from this hemisphere which must depend, almost exclusively, on her as benefactress.

This is the final period of our existence unless a powerful nation lends us support of every kind. What a sadness! We have an enormous power that must collapse on its own unless strong, skillful craftsmen help construct the edifice of our freedom. Vast regions furrowed by mighty rivers, inexhaustible springs of agricultural and mercantile riches, these will all be rendered null by Spanish malice. Entire provinces are transformed to deserts; others are become frightful arenas of bloody anarchy. Passions have been aroused by every stimulus, fanaticism has turned people's minds into volcanoes, and extermination will be the result of these chaotic elements.

I was witness, dear friend, to the devouring flame that is swiftly consuming my unfortunate land. Unable to extinguish it despite innumerable and unheard of efforts, I have come out to sound the alarm to the world, to beg for help, and to announce to Great Britain and to all humanity that a large part of the human race is going to perish and that the most beautiful half of the earth is going to be reduced to a state of desolation.

Please view with indulgence these emotional transports, which must seem like the exaggerations of a madman rather than expressions of hard truth and reasonable predictions of what is to come. But no, it is no more than a faithful representation of what I have seen and what is inevitable, unless Great Britain, the liberator of Europe, friend of Asia, and protector of Africa, consents to be the savior of America.

If I still had a shred of hope that America could triumph on her own, no one would have been more eager than I to serve my country, rather than humiliate it by seeking protection from a foreign power. This is the cause of my departure from the mainland. I come to seek aid. I will seek it in your proud capital; I will march all the way to the North Pole, if need be; and if everyone is deaf to the voice of humanity, I will have fulfilled my duty, although in vain, and I will return to die fighting in my country.

I flatter myself that the glory that has brought such brilliance through military and political exploits to your distinguished family will also have extended its well-deserved favors to you, as I ardently hope, and as one might reasonably expect due to the eminent qualities shining in your person. Please forgive, sir, these testimonies of my respectful affection and of the high regard that makes me your most attentive and obedient servant, who kisses your hands.[3]

Simón Bolívar

Letter to Baptis Irvine, Agent of the United States of America to Venezuela: Debating Neutral Rights

Angostura, 20 August 1818

Dear Agent:

Although your note dated 17 August, which I had the honor of receiving yesterday, can only be regarded as a preliminary outline or preparation for the response you offer to my letter of 6 August, I believe it is wise to formulate in advance certain reflections that spring from the very principles you acknowledged in that note.[4]

You consider my indignation with respect to the supporters or allies of our fierce enemies to be just, but you add that it is unfair to expect neutral merchants to abandon their profession in order to take sides politically. Without arguing this point, I insist that I see no need for a neutral to embrace this or that faction just to keep from abandoning his profession, nor do I think it possible to apply this principle to ports under blockade without destroying the rights of the warring nations. If the usefulness of neutral nations is the origin and basis for allowing them to continue trading with powers at war, the latter not only can advance the same rationale against the common practice of trading with ports under blockade but can also point out the harm that results from the prolongation of a campaign or a war that could otherwise be ended through surrender or through the imposition of a limited siege. Impartiality, which is the essential ingredient of neutrality, vanishes in the act of aiding one party against the clearly expressed will of the other, which justly opposes such action and which moreover has not asked for help.

The conduct of France and England in the final years of their famous struggle is quite apropos in support of this opinion. But I do not seek to justify my opinion, because I do not believe that our current situation fits that category, nor do I need further arguments beyond the very ones you offer. The doctrine cited by Vattel,[5] which is without doubt the most liberal for neutral parties, not only offers powerful support to the justice of Venezuela's conduct in the condemnation of the sailing ships *Tigre* and *Libertad*.[6] It also prompts me to recall events I would prefer to forget so as not to have to lament them. I refer to the conduct of the United States of North America with respect to the independents of South America and to the strict laws promulgated for the purpose of preventing any kind of aid that we might have sought there. Contrary to the leniency of American laws, we have seen imposed a penalty of ten years in prison and a fine of 10,000 pesos, which is the equivalent of a death penalty, against the virtuous citizens who wished to abet our cause, the cause of justice and freedom, the cause of America.

If free trade for the neutrals consists of supplying both sides with the means to wage war, why is this prohibited in the North? Why, in addition to this prohibition, is there the additional imposition of severity to the penalty, without precedent in the annals of North America? Do you not declare yourselves against the independents when you deny them what the law of neutrality permits them to request? This prohibition can only be understood as directed against us, who were the only ones in need of protection. The Spaniards had everything they needed, or there were other sources they could turn to. We alone were forced to turn to the North, first because you were our neighbors and brothers, and second because we lacked the means and connections to negotiate with other powers. Mr. Cobbett[7] has thoroughly demonstrated in his weekly the partiality of the United States toward Spain in this conflict. To deny one side the supplies it lacks and without which it cannot pursue its aims when its enemy has abundant supplies is the same as condemning it to surrender, and in our war with Spain that is the same as sending us to the gallows, to order our execution. The result of the prohibition against securing arms and supplies makes that partiality clear. The Spaniards who did not need them acquired them with ease while those heading for Venezuela were blocked.

The extreme repugnance and sorrow with which I recall these actions prevent me from further describing them. Only the need to justify the government of Venezuela could have forced me to give expression to complaints I have sought to stifle up to now and which I would have buried in silence and oblivion if they had not been needed at this time in order to negate the arguments with which you have tried to prove the illegitimacy of the chains used to immobilize the sailing ships *Tigre* and *Libertad*.

For the moment, however, I wish to assume hypothetically that impartiality has been maintained. What could we deduce from this? Either it is necessary to deny us the right to blockade and lay siege, or it is necessary to say that neutral ships can enter and leave the ports that have been temporarily excluded from commerce by a decree of blockade now in effect. In the first case, it would be necessary to deny us the rights others claim, thus placing no obligation on others to respect them. And it would be no less atrocious to uphold the second opinion, which goes against all the practices and laws of nations.

I could elaborate endlessly on the observations I have made, but since it is not my intention to respond definitively until such time as I have read and considered your reply, which has just arrived, I will wait until then to expound these same points and add others that I omit now so as not to burden your attention.

With all due respect I remain your attentive and obedient servant,

Bolívar

Invitation to the Governments of Colombia, Mexico, Río de la Plata, Chile, and Guatemala to Hold a Congress in Panama

Lima, 7 December 1824

My great, good friend:

After fifteen years of sacrifices dedicated to the freedom of America, in order to achieve a system of guarantees that can serve both in peace and war as shield for our new destiny, it is now time for the bonds of interest uniting the American republics, formerly Spanish colonies, to be provided with a foundation to perpetuate, if possible, the duration of these governments.[8]

To establish that system and consolidate the power of this grand political body will require a sublime authority that will give direction to the policies of our governments, whose influence will ensure uniformity of principles, and whose name alone will calm troubled waters. An authority so august can only exist in an assembly of plenipotentiary representatives appointed by each one of our republics and convened under the auspices of the victory won by our arms against Spanish power.

Profoundly persuaded of the urgency of these ideas, in 1822, as president of the Republic of Colombia, I invited the governments of Mexico, Peru, Chile, and Buenos Aires to form a confederation and to convene in the Isthmus of Panama or some other site acceptable to a plurality of these governments a congress of plenipotentiaries of each state "to serve as advisors in moments of great conflict, as facilitators of communication in the face of common dangers, as faithful interpreters in public negotiations during difficult times, and lastly as mediators of our differences."

On 6 July of that year, the government of Peru entered into a treaty of alliance and confederation with the plenipotentiary of Colombia, whereby both parties pledged to offer their good offices to the governments of America formerly under Spanish control so that when all had signed the same pact a meeting of the general assembly of the confederated states could be held. A similar treaty was signed in Mexico on 3 October 1823 by Colombia's special ambassador to that state, and there are good reasons to expect that the other governments will bow to the wisdom of their own best interests.

To further postpone the general assembly of plenipotentiaries of the republics who are already members of the confederation, until such time as the others see fit to join, will be to deprive ourselves of the advantages that such an assembly will produce from the moment of its installation. These advantages increase extraordinarily in light of the support that will come from the political world and especially from the European continent.

The meeting of the plenipotentiaries from Mexico, Colombia, and Peru will be delayed indefinitely unless action is taken by one of the parties to the treaty, or unless we convene a new and special convention to set the time and place suitable to this grand purpose. In light of the difficulties and delays entailed by the physical distance between us, in addition to solemn motives springing from our common interests, I am resolved to take this step for the purpose of encouraging without further delay this meeting of our plenipotentiaries, while the remaining governments are engaged in preliminary matters concerning the appointment and briefing of their representatives, steps that we have already taken.

With respect to the timetable for the inauguration of the Congress, I will be so bold as to suggest that there can be no reason not to hold it within six months of this date; and I will also flatter myself to presume that the burning desire inspiring all Americans to exalt the power of the world of Columbus will alleviate the difficulties and delays needed for the official preparations and lessen the distance separating the capitals of each country from the site of the Congress.

It seems to me that if the world had to choose its capital, the Isthmus of Panama would be ideal for this august purpose, situated as it is in the center of the globe, looking toward Asia on one side and toward Africa and Europe on the other. The Isthmus of Panama has been offered for this purpose[9] in the existing treaties by the government of Colombia. The Isthmus is equidistant from the farthest reaches of the continent and could thus be the provisional site for the first Congress of the confederated states.

Deferring, for my part, to these considerations, I feel greatly inclined to send the delegates of this Republic to Panama as soon as I have the honor of receiving the desired response to this circular. Nothing could so truly satisfy my heart's desire as the willing agreement by the confederated governments to participate in this most solemn of all American acts.

Should Your Excellency decline to participate in it, I foresee enormous delays and difficulties at a time when the momentum of world events is accelerating everything, with the potential to swiftly exacerbate any adverse consequences to our detriment.

Once the initial discussions of the plenipotentiaries have been held, the permanent site of the Congress, as well as its range of authority, can be determined in a solemn manner by the majority; at that time, everything will have been accomplished.

The day on which our plenipotentiaries exchange credentials will mark the beginning of an immortal period in the diplomatic history of America. A hundred centuries from now, when posterity seeks the origin of our public law, and they recall the treaties that consolidated their destiny, they will look with awe on the protocols of the Isthmus. There, they will find the outline of our first alliances, which will trace the progress of our relations with the rest of the world. Then the Isthmus of Corinth will pale in comparison with that of Panama!

God keep Your Excellency!

Your great and good friend,

Bolívar

Minister of Foreign Relations, *José Sánchez Carrión*

Letter to General Francisco de Paula Santander: The Brazilian Empire, Upper Peru, North Americans, and Other Problems

Arequipa, 30 May 1825

My dear General:

I have instructed my secretary general to inform you of the Portuguese invasion of Chiquitos in Upper Peru and to forward to you a copy of the barbaric and insolent demands of the Portuguese commander.[10] General Sucre has replied to him in similar terms, no doubt overcome by the feeling of outrage such an abominable atrocity must have caused him. However, I do not approve of the use of such language, because a new outbreak of war cannot be in anyone's interest and will destroy the remnants of our meager fortunes. I presume that the commander may have acted without consulting his government, and if the emperor has indeed ordered him to do such a thing, that may be just another in the long list of mad things he does from day to day. This event needs to be considered from a number of perspectives.

The emperor may, of course, have taken this action on his own, in which case there may be no consequences. But if the emperor has been in consultation with the Holy Alliance, then the matter is far more serious, because the allies are too strong and have a vital interest in the destruction of the new American republics. This kind of aggression against our republics is opposed by England and by all the liberal governments of the New World. This being so, it must be understood that only through a major war can our destruction be achieved. Consequently, extensive preparations would alert us to plans for waging such a war, yet we have not observed any such preparations in Europe. Public funds are rising. England, France, and Russia are busy protecting the emancipation of the Greeks. This is a matter of the greatest interest to Russia, whereas France is immersed in the problem of the indemnification of her emigrés, which is also of interest to all the aristocrats, who favor peace so they can be reimbursed for the property confiscated during the revolution. As these circumstances are apparently so favorable to us, if the emperor should continue to harass or even invade us, such an absurd action would inevitably prove counterproductive. Under no circumstances, therefore, would the Holy Alliance have advised him to take these hostile measures, because that would destroy his commerce, his cause, and risk his removal from the throne. For these reasons I believe that the invasion of Chiquitos must have been a thoughtless action initiated by commander [Manoel José] Araújo [e Silva]. If it was the emperor who initiated it, without consulting the Holy Alliance, it was an impulsive, foolish act of no consequence. However, if it happened on advice of the Holy Alliance, then it is a matter of great seriousness and dire transcendence. We must in that case prepare ourselves for a protracted conflict with most of Europe. I believe that the first step we should take, if the Holy Alliance is meddling in our affairs, is to have Peru and Buenos Aires immediately occupy Brazil. Then Chile should occupy Chiloé,[11] while Colombia, Guatemala, and Mexico prepare to defend themselves, and all of America should form a solid front to deploy their combined forces to any area that is attacked or threatened.

For the formation of this league and this pact, the meeting of the confederated states in the Isthmus is more urgent than ever, in order to take the appropriate anticipatory measures dictated by the circumstances. Even if this congress were no more than a general headquarters for the sacred league, its utility and importance would be immense. Therefore, we must work swiftly to bring it about. There is one further consideration: England will make every effort to prevent any sort of conflict among us, or between us and the Europeans, because England is primarily interested in America as a lucrative commercial zone, which can only be exploited if peace is maintained. For this reason I am of the opinion that we should consult the English representatives and perhaps even the government concerning their assessment of the nature, origin, and consequences of this incident. I also believe that no hostile action should be taken against Brazil until after the incident has been thoroughly analyzed.

I have written to the Peruvian Council of Government urging that they contact the Brazilian government asking for an explanation of this invasion by their troops, and that they ask the English ministers and agents for advice in the matter. I also believe it would be helpful for you to make the same request of our representatives in Europe, for we need to be very cautious in a matter of such transcendence. I have written also to the Council of Government pointing out how useful it would be to persuade the Chilean government to move up its occupation of Chiloé, with the understanding that island might otherwise be occupied by some foreign power harboring hostile intentions against us. Not even England would object, since it is the port of call for ships rounding the cape and its occupation would offer invaluable advantages to her trade in the Pacific.

I have begun this letter even though the post from your city will not come until tomorrow and return the next day. For now the only thing that occurs to me is the matter of Brazil, and the peaceful state of things in Peru, where everything proceeds as circumstances allow, until such time as the new constituent congress and constitutional government are definitively established.

On 10 June, I leave for Cuzco to have a look at that country and to arrange matters on a provisional basis, as is urgently needed. In July I will go to Upper Peru to establish a provisional government for that country in keeping with the resolution of the congress in Lima.

The provinces of Upper Peru were formerly under the Presidency and Audiencia of Charcas; it has a population of over a million and almost two million pesos of public revenue for the government. It is divided into six provinces, situated at approximately 700 leagues from Buenos Aires, which is its only port and its only capital as of this date.[12] Public opinion favors the creation of a state like those in Chile and Guatemala (which are in all respects similar to Upper Peru): they want an independent state subject only to the American federation. I believe this is reasonable and even necessary for the prosperity of those provinces. Otherwise, this region will sink into a state of anarchy like that in Buenos Aires. There, the province of Buenos Aires is occupied by the Portuguese on the Banda Oriental,[13] the Indians from the Pampa infest the countryside surrounding the city, and a small town named Santa Fe has declared itself independent of its capital. Thus, Buenos Aires is little more than a Hanseatic city without a league or province. The provinces of Salta and Mendoza are the only ones that have sent their delegates to the congress in Buenos Aires. But these two provinces are subdivided into four or six parts, so the entire state of Río de la Plata consists truly of only two provinces and the city of Buenos Aires. The province of Paraguay is occupied by a certain [José Gaspar Rodríguez de] Francia, who has kept it in a virtual state of quarantine for the last fourteen years. It doesn't belong to anyone, and it has no government, except for a tyrant who is enemy to the entire world, dealing with no one, persecuting everyone; anyone who enters there never returns. So Humboldt's companion, the unfortunate Bonpland,[14] is still held prisoner there. Paraguay is closer to Charcas than to Buenos Aires, so it would be easier to launch an attack with troops from Upper Peru than with those from Buenos Aires. Buenos Aires is a city that wants war with no one and operates on the principle that each province should run itself as it sees fit, this according to General [José Ildefonso] Alvarez [de Arenales], the representative from Buenos Aires in Peru, and General [Juan Antonio Alvarez de] Arenales, a dependent of the same government who rules in Salta.[15] The government of Buenos Aires has no desire to control the provinces of Upper Peru, knowing it lacks the means to do so, as well as men capable of governing a large state. The government of Río de la Plata will be content to rule the provinces already represented in the congress of Buenos Aires, aware that they are much easier to govern without the vexing problem of Upper Peru, which will always resist annexation into a political union offering no benefits.

All of this means that we can anticipate a new state in the American federation, one that will favor us because it will owe us its existence and its freedom, whereas the Río de la Plata will become our enemy out of envy rather than rivalry, since there can be no rivalry between entities so unequal. Peru will be satisfied with the provinces already under her control. This republic is possessed of extensive territory and wealth, with more than enough resources to ensure prosperity. God willing, she will find the men she needs to govern her.

The congress will meet on 10 February; then I will be free of all further obligations in this country and will be able to dispose of myself as I see fit.

It is now 7 June. This letter was interrupted until today, as I waited to finish until after the post had arrived.

Today I had the pleasure of receiving your most pleasant and flattering communication. First, the article from *La Estrella* on the independence of Colombia and Mexico with the editorial from the same paper about the confidence with which England can proceed without any fear of reaction from Europe. Second, I am pleased at your assurance that France, Holland, Sweden, and Denmark will soon recognize us. I was already quite confident in this regard as you must have seen in my note, and this is now confirmed for me by Holland's recognition of all our states.

I was also quite pleased by your permission to offer promotions to our poor companions in Ayacucho. They all need encouragement, and many have received no recognition at all because there was truly nothing to offer.

The assurances you offer concerning peace and security in Colombia are what interest me most in your letters, for it is undoubtedly a great consolation to know that, in the midst of everything, the republic is going to survive after so many disasters. However, amid all these fair winds I perceive a frightful precipice. You speak of retiring from public service because of stomach problems. No, friend, you must not, you cannot retire. You are the one man crucial to the prosperity of the republic. You must die in office, as I must die on the battlefield. Without you, what will become of Colombia? What will become of our army and my glory? I will tell you frankly that if you had not been there to support me with your skill and energy, my project would have been run aground long ago. Moreover, I believe that, on my own, without you, it would never have turned out so well. I am no administrator, nor could I have endured the sedentary demands of an office. By the same token, I would have destroyed the work of my companions in arms without your strong character and your capacity for administering public business. So I repeat: You are the indispensable man of Colombia.

The assignment you offer to General Sucre[16] seems admirable to me, but at the same time I believe that this must not be, because I need him for everything, so I cannot do without him under the current circumstances.

The business of boundaries and payment to Colombia will be fully arranged before my departure, no matter who is assigned to represent our rights. If you can persuade him to return, [Joaquín] Mosquera[17] is the ideal man for the job; if not, someone else will do. General Sucre has been appointed to assume command in Upper Peru, which consists of five magnificent departments, and I still need him in Lima as president of the Council of Government, because General La Mar is unwilling to accept the position. For this reason, General Sucre cannot be used at this time for diplomatic matters. [José Gabriel] Pérez is also qualified to take on the assignment you are offering to Sucre, but only after he finishes his work as my secretary general of Peru. The payment and the boundaries will be arranged as you wish, as I know that Colombia's claims are just.

If you cannot use the three thousand men I have offered you, communicate this to the minister of state in Lima so that he doesn't send them to you in August, as I have ordered. In this country Colombian troops are not resented, at least for the time being; later, who knows? We have thirty-five hundred men in Upper Peru, where they love us because we defend them against the designs of their neighbors. In this city there are three thousand men and another fifteen hundred in Lima, although a quarter of those are Peruvian prisoners from Ayacucho. Thus, fewer than five or six thousand true Colombians are still quartered here, and the country loves them because they regard them as well-disciplined soldiers. If you need two or three thousand Peruvians to quiet the black factions, put in a request for them to the Council of Government, as I said previously. But if you do not want them, write immediately, for at the end of August they are scheduled to set out, as I said earlier.

I have seen the plan for a general federation extending from the United States to Haiti. I found it unwise in its membership but admirable in its ideas and concept. Haiti, Buenos Aires, and the United States are ill chosen, each of them for powerful reasons. Mexico, Guatemala, Colombia, Peru, Chile, and Upper Peru have the potential to form a superb federation. Guatemala, Chile, and Upper Peru will concur with our wishes. Peru and Colombia are of a single mind, and only Mexico is isolated physically from the rest of the federation, which has the advantage of being homogeneous, compact, and solid. The Americans from the North and those from Haiti, simply because they are foreigners, are too heterogeneous in character to fit in. Therefore, I will never agree to invite them to take part in our American system. While thinking about this, I have read the 19 January issue of the Caracas paper, *El Colombiano,* profiling the candidates to the presidency, and I was outraged to see the ingratitude with which those gentlemen treat you, after the miracle you have worked to create laws in a country of slaves and establish freedom in the midst of war, revolution, and chains. We will see if another can do as well. As for me, my mind is quite made up, first of all, to reject the presidency under any circumstances; even more so should they appoint anyone other than you vice president; because I know that no matter how much ability, talent, and virtue another citizen might have, what is, is, and what is not, is not. That is, you are an excellent vice president, the only one I have known. Accordingly, however much I respect Briceño,[18] and as you know I idolize him, I don't want to switch horses in the middle of the Orinoco, when you have braved its waters well enough to rescue me from its waves. Those people seem determined to sink in sight of shore, so to speak. Good luck to them if that happens. For my part, I have met my obligations as best I could, and if they choose not to stay on course, I will wash my hands with Pilate. My mind is made up, and you can be sure I will not waver.

It is my hope that in New Granada they will treat you as you deserve, unless it turns out that the envious proliferate there as well.

I am telling [Juan Paz del] Castillo to reduce his battalions in the South to cadres. I will do the same here with the troops from Peru in order to reduce expenses and still maintain security and the morale of the troops. I recommend this system to you, should you wish to adopt it.

Yours with all my heart,

Bolívar

P.S. In Chile, anarchy is rampant. Freire has gone to Concepción and Pinto to Coquimbo.[19] The province of Santiago is governed by its intendant. They say that the congress of Chile is going to send a delegation to draft O'Higgins again; they say that in that country there is a large faction supporting me, and another, much smaller faction against me.

On rereading your letter, I see that you are appointing Father [Manuel Benito] Rebollo to the great American Congress. I know him and know that he is very talented. But what will the delegates from the other nations say on seeing a man of the cloth? They'll say we have no real statesmen.

Thoughts on the Congress to Be Held in Panama

(1826)

The Panama Congress will assemble all the representatives of America and a diplomatic agent of the government of His Britannic Majesty.[20] This Congress seems destined to form the largest, most extraordinary, and most powerful league ever seen on the face of the earth. The Holy Alliance will be inferior in power to this confederation, provided Great Britain chooses to take part in it. The well-being of the human race would benefit immensely from such an alliance, and America and Great Britain would reap extraordinary benefits. Relationships between political entities would be given a code of public law to govern international conduct.

1. The New World would be made up of independent nations bound by a common law that would regulate foreign relations and provide guarantees for their survival through a general and permanent congress.
2. The existence of these new states would be given new guarantees.
3. Spain would make peace out of respect for England, and the Holy Alliance would grant recognition to these emerging nations.
4. Domestic order would be preserved intact between the different states and within each one of them.
5. None would be weaker or stronger than any other.
6. A perfect balance would be established in this new and authentic order of things.
7. The power of all would come to the aid of any member nation under attack from a foreign enemy or from anarchist factions.

8. Differences in origin and color would lose their importance and effect.

9. America would no longer fear that horrific monster which has devoured the island of Santo Domingo, nor would she fear the numerical preponderance of the native populations.

10. Social reform, in effect, would be achieved under the holy auspices of freedom and peace, but England would necessarily have to take responsibility for holding steady the fulcrum of this equilibrium.

Great Britain would undoubtedly derive considerable advantage from this arrangement.

1. Her influence in Europe would increase progressively, and her decisions would come to coincide with those of destiny.

2. America would serve her as an opulent commercial domain.

3. America would be the center of her relations with Asia and Europe.

4. The English would be considered as equal in status to American citizens.

5. Mutual relations between the two countries would in time come to coincide entirely.

6. The character and customs of the British would become models for Americans to strive for in the future.

7. With the passage of centuries, it might be possible that a single federated nation would dominate the globe.

Such thoughts are on the minds of some of the most distinguished Americans, who await impatiently the beginning of this project at the Congress of Panama, which could well be the occasion to consolidate the union of the new states with the British Empire.

Simón Bolívar

Letter to General Lafayette:
On George Washington

Lima, 20 March 1826

Dear General:

I have been honored to look for the first time on the noble features of [George Washington] the man who did so much good on behalf of the New World.[21] I owe this honor to Colonel Mercier, who delivered to me your precious letter of 13 October of last year. I experienced a mysterious exhilaration on learning in the newspapers that you have had the generosity of heart to honor me with one of the treasures from Mount Vernon. The portrait of Washington, some mementos, and one of the monuments to his glory are to be presented to me by your hands in the name of the brothers of that great citizen, first son of the New World. There are no words to tell you how my heart treasures this gift and how much glory your high regard instills in me. Washington's family honors me beyond any aspirations my imagination could conceive, because Washington presented by Lafayette is the crown of all human rewards. He was the noble protector of social reforms, and you were the citizen-hero, the champion of freedom, who with one hand served America, and with the other, the Old World. Ah, what mortal could ever be worthy of the honors that you and Mount Vernon see fit to lavish on me! My consternation is equal to the immensity of the gratitude I offer you, conjoined to the respect and veneration all men owe to the Nestor of human freedom.

With highest regard, I remain your respectful admirer,

Bolívar

Letter to Colonel Patrick Campbell, British Chargé d'Affaires: "Plague America with Miseries"

Guayaquil, 5 August 1829

My dear Colonel and friend:

I have the honor of acknowledging receipt of your kind letter of 31 May, posted from Bogotá.[22]

I must begin by thanking you for the many kind sentiments you have expressed toward Colombia and toward me throughout your letter. Is there any limit to the debt of gratitude we owe you? I am overwhelmed by all that you have thought and done to sustain the country and the glory of her leader since your arrival among us.

The British minister resident in the United States[23] honors me excessively when he says that he has hope only for Colombia, because only in Colombia is there a Bolívar. What he does not know is that his physical existence and health are much debilitated and that Bolívar is at death's door.

What you have seen fit to tell me regarding the new plan to name a European prince as successor to my authority does not catch me entirely by surprise, because some inkling of this had been communicated to me, though quite mysteriously and somewhat timidly, since my way of thinking is well known.

I am not sure how to respond to you concerning this idea, which is objectionable for many reasons. You must know that, for my part, I have no objection, resolved as I am to step down during the next session of Congress, but who could possibly temper the overweening ambition of our leaders and the fear of inequality among the common people? Does it not seem likely to you that England would be resentful were a Bourbon to be chosen?[24] Can you imagine the opposition that would come from the new American states, and from the United States, which seems destined by Providence to plague America with miseries in the name of Freedom?[25] I can almost foresee a general conspiracy against poor Colombia, already the target of excessive envy by all the American republics. Every newspaper would join the crusade against the accomplices of this betrayal of freedom, against the addicts of the Bourbon cause and the violators of the American way. The flames of discord would be ignited in the south by the Peruvians, in the Isthmus by the Guatemalans and the Mexicans, and in the Antilles by the Americans, and by the liberals everywhere. Santo Domingo[26] would not respond passively but would call on her brothers to make common cause against a prince from France. Everyone would turn against us, but Europe would do nothing to support us, because the New World is not considered worth the expense of a Holy Alliance. At the very least, we have good reason to believe this, judging by the indifference with which Europe looked on as we struggled to emancipate half of the known world, soon to become the most productive source of European prosperity.

Finally, I am far from opposing the reorganization of Colombia in accordance with the institutions proven by Europe in her wisdom and experience. On the contrary, it would bring me great delight and renew my will to assist in a task that might well lead to our salvation and that would succeed if we had the support of England and France. With these powerful allies we would be capable of anything; without them, no. For this reason, I will wait to offer my opinion until we know how the governments of England and France feel about the proposed change of system and our choice of a dynasty.

I assure you in all sincerity, dear friend, that I have expressed all my thoughts on this matter, holding nothing back. Please make use of them as befits your duty and the welfare of Colombia. These are my only conditions. Meanwhile, receive the deep affection of your most attentive and obedient servant,

Bolívar

3. Social and Economic Affairs

Decree for the Emancipation of the Slaves

Carúpano, 2 June 1816

Simón Bolívar
Commander in Chief and Captain General of the Armies of Venezuela
and New Granada, etc.

To the Inhabitants of Río Caribe, Carúpano, and Cariaco

Greetings:

Considering that justice, policy, and the country imperiously demand the inalienable rights of nature, I have decided to formally decree absolute freedom for the slaves who have groaned under the Spanish yoke during the three previous centuries.[1] Considering that the Republic needs the services of all her children, we must impose on these new citizens the following conditions:

Article 1—Every healthy man between the ages of fourteen and sixty shall appear in the parish church of his district to enlist under the flag of Venezuela, within twenty-four hours of the publication of this decree.

Article 2—Old men, women, children, and invalids shall be exempt from this day forth from military service and exempt as well from any domestic or field service in which they were previously employed for the benefit of their masters.

Article 3—The new citizen who refuses to bear arms in fulfillment of the sacred duty to defend his freedom shall be subject to servitude, not only for himself but also for his children under the age of fourteen, his wife, and his aged parents.

Article 4—The relatives of the military occupied in the army of liberation shall enjoy the rights of citizens and the absolute freedom granted to them by this decree in the name of the Republic of Venezuela.

The present regulation shall have the force of law and be faithfully executed by the Republican Authorities of Río Caribe, Carúpano, and Cariaco.

Signed into law in the General Headquarters of Carúpano on 2 June 1816.

Bolívar

Redistribution of Properties as Compensation for Officers and Soldiers

10 October 1817

Simón Bolívar
Commander in Chief of the Republic, and Captain General of the Armies of Venezuela and New Granada

Considering that the first obligation of the government is to reward the services of the virtuous defenders of the Republic who, selflessly sacrificing their lives and property for the freedom and happiness of the country, have fought and continue to fight the disastrous war for independence, while neither they nor their families have the means to support themselves; and considering that in the territory occupied by the forces of the Republic, and in the territory still to be liberated, now in possession of the enemy, there are substantial properties owned by Spaniards and royalists, which according to the decree and ordinance published on the third of September of the current year should be seized and confiscated, I have decided to decree and do hereby decree the following:[2]

Article 1. All real estate and property that in accordance with the decree and ordinance cited above has been seized and confiscated, or which is scheduled for seizure and confiscation, and which has not been diverted or cannot be diverted into the national treasury, shall be redistributed and awarded in bonuses to the generals, commanders, officers, and soldiers of the Republic, according to the terms stipulated below.

Article 2. As the ranks obtained in battle are an indisputable proof of the level of service performed by each one of the individuals in the army, the redistribution of property referred to in the preceding article shall be awarded in proportion to that service, as follows:

General-in-chief	$ 25,000
Divisional general	$ 20,000

Brigadier general	$ 15,000
Colonel	$ 10,000
Lieutenant colonel	$ 9,000
Major	$ 8,000
Captain	$ 6,000
Lieutenant	$ 4,000
Second lieutenant	$ 3,000
First and second sergeant	$ 1,000
First and second corporal	$ 700
Private	$ 500

Article 3. The officers, sergeants, corporals, and privates who are promoted after the redistribution shall have the right to claim the difference between the amount they received when they held the previous rank and that to which they are entitled by the last rank conferred on them and which they held at the time of the final redistribution.

Article 4. If the value of the property available for redistribution has been estimated to be insufficient to cover these bonuses, the government offers to make up the difference from any other national property found to be available and particularly from uncultivated public lands.

Article 5. If before or after the property has been redistributed, the government sees fit to reward the distinguished or exceptional valor, service, or act of a soldier, it shall be empowered to do so by conceding any of the aforementioned properties, regardless of the rank of the recipient or the amount stipulated in the table in Article 2.

Article 6. In the event that a soldier has merited or been granted the reward referred to in the preceding article, he shall not have the right to claim the share assigned to him in Article 2 if the value of the property awarded to him is greater than that stipulated for his rank.

Article 7. When the value of the properties available for redistribution exceeds the amount stipulated for the different ranks, the government shall ensure that this property is distributed according to the best interests of all, for which purpose several or many individuals may join together and petition that such property be shared among them.

Article 8. The redistribution shall be carried out by a special committee, which shall be appointed in due course and which shall adhere to the regulations published for this purpose.

Article 9. The government reserves to itself the immediate direction of this committee.

To be published, communicated to the appropriate parties, and forwarded to the general staff in order that it be inserted in the order of the day, which shall be circulated throughout the divisions and battalions of the army of the Republic for their satisfaction.

Issued, signed by my hand, sealed with the official seal of the Republic, and countersigned by the undersigned secretary of the supreme government in the general headquarters of Santo Tomás de la Nueva Guyana on 10 October 1817, the seventh year of the Republic.

Simón Bolívar

J. G. Pérez, Secretary

Letter to General Francisco de Paula Santander: On Slave Recruitment

San Cristóbal, 18 April 1820

Most Excellent Sir:

I am honored to respond to Your Excellency's query of 2 April regarding the renting of the salt mines and the instructions of General [Manuel] Valdés, in which he speaks, according to Your Excellency, of announcing the liberation of the slaves in Cauca province.[3]

The article reads as follows: "All slaves fit for military service shall be recruited into the army." If I am not mistaken, this has nothing to do with liberating the slaves, but rather with the power given to us by the law as stipulated in Article 3: "However, those called up into military service by the president of the Republic, or who perform some distinguished service, shall immediately be given their freedom."[4]

I respond to all your observations with this reference to the law. But, as is my custom, I shall explain my orders.

I have ordered that slaves fit for military service be recruited. It should be understood that this means only those needed for military service, as an excessive number of them would be more harmful than useful.

The military and political reasons for ordering the recruitment of slaves are quite obvious. We need strong, hardy men who are accustomed to inclement weather and fatigue, men who will embrace the cause and the career of arms with enthusiasm, men who identify their own cause with the public interest and who value their lives only slightly more than their deaths.

The political reasons are even more powerful. The liberation of the slaves has been instituted by law and by fact. The congress has considered the words of Montesquieu: *In moderate governments political freedom makes civil freedom precious, and anyone deprived of the latter still lacks the former: he sees a happy society in which he has no part; he finds security guar-*

anteed for others but not for him. Nothing so lowers us to the condition of beasts as seeing free men but not being one. Such people are enemies of society, and they become dangerous in numbers. It is not surprising that in moderate governments the state has been brought into turmoil by the rebellion of slaves or that this rarely happens in despotic states.

It is, then, clearly demonstrated by political maxims based on historical example that a free government that commits the absurdity of maintaining slaves shall be punished by rebellion and in some cases by extermination, as in Haiti.

In effect, the law passed by Congress is in all aspects wise. What could be more suitable or more legitimate than to obtain freedom by fighting for it? Can it be just that only free men should die for the emancipation of the slaves? Would it not be better that the latter win their rights on the field of battle and that their dangerous numbers be reduced through a powerful and legitimate action?

In Venezuela we have seen the free population die and the slaves survive. I don't know if this is politic, but I know that if in Cundinamarca we fail to utilize the slaves, the result will be the same.

Thus, availing myself of the powers granted me by the law of emancipation of the slaves, I repeat my previous orders: Let the army of the South recruit as many slaves fit for military service as it needs, and let 3,000 unmarried young men be sent to the army of the North. Regarding the latter, I strongly insist.

Bolívar

Decrees on Indian Rights, Lands, and Tribute

1. DECREE ABOLISHING PERSONAL SERVICE IMPOSED ON THE NATIVE PEOPLES: NEW STATUTE GOVERNING THEIR WORK

Rosario de Cúcuta, 20 May 1820

Simón Bolívar
Liberator President, etc.

Wishing to correct the abuses practiced in Cundinamarca in most of the native villages, against their persons as well as their communal lands and their freedom, and considering that this segment of the population of the republic deserves the most paternal attention from the government because they were the most aggrieved, oppressed, and humiliated during the period of Spanish despotism, in view of the provisions of canonical and civil laws, I have decided to decree and do hereby decree:[5]

Article 1. All the lands whose titles identify them as part of the communal reserves [*resguardos*] shall be returned to the Indians as the legitimate owners, despite any legal claims alleged by the current landholders.

Article 2. The liens against these reserves, having no approval from the authority empowered to grant it, now or in the past, shall be declared null and void even if they have subsisted since time immemorial.

Article 3. Once the usurped land has been restored to the reserves, the *Jueces políticos*[5] shall allot to each family as much land as it can reasonably farm, taking into consideration the number of people that make up the family and the total extent of the reserves.

Article 4. Should there be surplus acreage after the reserve lands have been parceled to the families as specified above, it shall be leased at auction by these same *jueces políticos* to the highest bidder with the best collateral, giving preference in case of equal bids to those currently in possession.

Article 5. The families, or family members, shall not be permitted to lease the allotment they own without first informing the *juez político,* so as to avoid any damage and fraud that might ensue.

Article 6. The income from the lands leased according to the provisions of Article 4 above shall be applied in part to the payment of tribute and in part to the payment of the salaries of teachers in the schools to be established in each town. Each teacher shall earn an annual salary of 120 pesos if the rental income equals or exceeds this amount; if it amounts to less, the entire sum shall be for the teacher.

Article 7. The *juez político,* in consultation with the priest of each town, shall appoint these teachers and notify the provincial governors of these appointments so that they can notify the governor of the department.

Article 8. The political governors of the provinces shall establish the regulations to be observed in the schools of their respective provinces, detailing the methods to be used in teaching and education.

Article 9. All children between the ages of four and fourteen shall attend the schools, where they shall be taught reading, writing, arithmetic, the principles of religion, and the rights and obligations of men and citizens in Colombia according to the laws.

Article 10. When the money for teachers' salaries has been deducted, the remaining income from land rental shall be applied to the payment of tribute, deducting this sum from the general total owed by the town so benefited on a pro rata basis.

Article 11. In order that these operations shall be carried out with all the method, order, and precision required for the general benefit of the towns, the *jueces políticos* shall be obliged to keep a running account of the rent monies and shall present this along with the account of the tributes to the respective administrators of the public treasury.

Article 12. Neither the priests, nor the *jueces políticos*, nor any other person, employed by the government or not, shall be allowed to exploit native peoples in any manner at any time without paying them a wage previously stipulated in a formal contract witnessed and approved by the *juez político.* Anyone violating this article shall pay double the value of the service performed, and the *jueces políticos* shall exact this fine without exception in favor of the aggrieved person for any complaint, however slight; when the *jueces políticos* themselves are the violators, the political governors shall be responsible for exacting said fines.

Article 13. The same provisions of Article 12 apply to religious confraternities whose cattle shall not be pastured on reserve lands unless they pay rent, nor shall they be herded by Indians except under the terms laid down in Article 12.

Article 14. As of this moment, certain scandalous practices that are contrary to the spirit of religion, to the discipline of the church, and to all law shall be terminated without exception, including the practice of denying the sacraments to parishioners who have not paid dues for guild membership or for maintenance of the priest, as well as the practices of obliging them to pay for festivals in honor of the saints and demanding parish fees from which Indians are exempted in consideration of the stipend given to the priests by the state. Any priest found to be violating the provisions of this article by continuing these abuses shall suffer the full rigor of the law, and the *jueces políticos* shall monitor the conduct of the priests, notifying the government of the slightest infraction observed in this regard so that appropriate action can be taken.

Article 15. The Indians, like all other free men in the Republic, can come and go with their passports, sell their fruit and other products, take them to the market or fair of their choice, and practice their craft and talents freely as they choose to do so and without impediment.

Article 16. Not only shall the present decree be publicized in the usual manner but the *jueces políticos* shall instruct the Indians as to its content, urging them to demand their rights even though it be against the judges themselves and to initiate action against any infraction committed.

Article 17. The vice president of Cundinamarca is charged with the observation and execution of this decree.

Issued in the General Headquarters of Rosario de Cúcuta, on 20 May 1820, tenth year of the Republic.

Simón Bolívar

11. Proclamation of the Civil Rights of Indians and Prohibition of Their Exploitation by Officials, Priests, Local Authorities, and Landowners

Cuzco, 4 July 1825

Simón Bolívar
Liberator President of the Republic of Colombia, Liberator and Supreme Commander of Peru, etc.

Considering:

 I. That equality among all citizens is the basis of the constitution of the Republic;[7]

 II. That this equality is incompatible with the personal service that has been imposed on native peoples, and equally incompatible with the hardships they have endured due to the miserable conditions in which they live and the ill treatment they have suffered at the hands of officials, priests, local authorities, and even landowners;

 III. That in the assignment of certain public works and services the Indians have been unfairly burdened;

 IV. That they have been denied wages on fraudulent grounds for the work in which they have been traditionally involved, either willingly or by force, whether it be the working of mines or farm labor or crafts;

 V. That one of the burdens most harmful to their existence is the payment of excessive and arbitrary fees that are commonly assessed them for the administration of the sacraments, I have decided to decree and do hereby decree:

 1. That no person in the state shall demand personal service of the Peruvian Indians, either directly or indirectly, without first negotiating a free contract stipulating the wage for the work.

 2. That the department prefects, intendants, governors and judges, ecclesiastical prelates, priests and their subordinates, landowners, and owners of mines and workshops are prohibited from working the Indians against their will in *faenas, séptimas, mitas, pongueajes,* and other types of domestic and common labor.

3. That when public works are ordered by the government for the general benefit of the community, this burden should not fall on Indians alone but all citizens should be drafted proportionally according to their numbers and abilities.

4. That the political authorities, through the mayors or municipalities, shall arrange for distribution of supplies, provisions, and other materials for the troops or any other purpose without burdening the Indians more than other citizens.

5. That the labor of workers in the mines, workshops, and haciendas should be paid in cash according to the wage specified in the contract, without forcing them to accept other forms of pay against their will and at levels below that commonly paid for such work.

6. That the scrupulous observance of the preceding article shall depend on the vigilance and zeal of the intendants, governors, and the territorial deputies for mining.

7. That the Indians shall not be forced to pay higher parochial fees than those stipulated in existing regulations or those legislated in the future.

8. That the parish priests and their assistants cannot negotiate these fees with the Indians without the mediation of the intendant or governor of the town.

9. Any neglect or omission in the observance of the preceding articles shall be cause for popular complaint and shall result in specific charges being brought before the courts.

10. The provisional secretary general is responsible for the execution and observance of this decree.

To be printed, published, and circulated.

Issued in Cuzco on 4 July 1825, the sixth and fourth years[8] of the republic.

Simón Bolívar

By order of His Excellency, *Felipe Santiago Estenós*

III. RESOLUTION ON THE REDISTRIBUTION OF COMMUNAL LANDS

Cuzco, 4 July 1825

Liberator President of the Republic of Colombia, vested with Supreme Authority, etc., considering:

I. That despite the stipulations of previous laws the distribution of lands has not been carried out adequately;[9]

II. That the majority of Indians have had no opportunity to enjoy land ownership;

III. That large tracts of these lands, which ought to be owned by the Indians, have been usurped under various pretexts by the caciques and collectors of tribute;

IV. That the provisional use granted them under the Spanish government has been extremely prejudicial to the development of agriculture and the prosperity of the state;

V. That the constitution of the republic does not acknowledge the authority of the caciques but rather that of the intendants of provinces and governors of their respective districts, I have decided to decree, and do hereby decree:

1. That the provisions of articles 3, 4, and 5 of the decree issued in Trujillo on 8 April 1824,[10] concerning the redistribution of communal lands be carried out forthwith.

2. Included in the land to be redistributed shall be those sections appropriated by the caciques and tribute collectors by virtue of their office, those lands being clearly identified by those commissioned to sell and distribute them.

3. The extent, redistribution, and sale of lands in each province shall be carried out by persons of integrity and intelligence whose names shall be presented as candidates to the prefect by the departmental junta holding jurisdiction, the junta to determine the fees and authority granted to those carrying out this commission.

4. Article 2 above does not refer to caciques who have inherited or who have legitimate claims and who have been granted absolute ownership of lands assigned to them during redistribution.

5. The caciques who do not own any land of their own shall receive through their wives and each of their children five

topos[11] of land or an equal area in places where the term *topo* is unfamiliar.

6. Each native citizen, regardless of sex or age, shall receive one topo of land in fertile places with adequate water.

7. In barren regions without adequate water, they shall receive two topos.

8. The Indians whose lands were taken from them under the Spanish government in order to pay the so-called pacifiers of the revolution of year 14,[12] shall be compensated in the redistribution to be made of communal lands by one-third more land than that to be assigned to others who have not suffered such a loss.

9. That the absolute ownership granted to the Indians designated in article 2 of the aforementioned decree be understood to be inalienable until year 50, and never taken by mortmain, under penalty of nullity.

10. The provisional secretary general is charged with the responsibility to carry out and fulfill this decree.

To be printed, published, and circulated.

Executed in Cuzco on 4 July 1825.—the sixth and the fourth years of the republic.

Simón Bolívar

By order of His Excellency, *Felipe Santiago Estenós*

Note: Article 5 of this decree was amended as follows:[13]

His Excellency the Liberator has ordered that the five topos of land, which Article 5 of the decree executed in Cuzco on 4 July of last year allots to the wife and each of the children of the caciques, also be allotted to the cacique himself, as if the article referred to reads as follows: *The caciques will receive, for themselves, for their wife, and for each of their children, and so on.*

By order of His Excellency, I have the honor of communicating this to you so that it shall be brought to the attention of the Council of Government for its proper fulfillment.

I am, Minister, your most attentive and obedient servant.

Felipe Santiago Estenós

To the Minister of State of the Department of Government

iv. Resolution That Colombian Indians Pay a Tax Called "a Personal Tribute From Indigenous Peoples"

Bogotá, 15 October 1828

Simón Bolívar, Liberator President, etc.

Considering:

i. That it is an indispensable obligation of all Colombians to contribute to the cost of running the State, either directly or indirectly, and that not even the indigenous peoples are exempt from this obligation;[14]

ii. That though the statute of 4 October 1821 decreed that they should make contributions equal to those of all Colombians, this provision, far from improving their condition, has made it worse and aggravated their penury;

iii. That the majority of the indigenous people themselves prefer and many have asked permission to make a personal contribution that will exempt them from the charges and fees assessed the other citizens, I have decided in consultation with the Council of State to decree the following:

Title 1
Names, Amount, and Payment Schedule of the Indian Tribute

Article 1. Indigenous Colombians shall, from their eighteenth birthday until the day they turn fifty, pay a tribute to be called "personal tribute from indigenous peoples."

Article 2. This annual tribute, amounting to three pesos, four reales, is to be paid equally by all.

Paragraph 1. Those Indians who in addition to communal or reservation lands [*resguardos*] own property valued at 1,000 pesos or more in real estate or personal property will not be assessed this tribute but will be subject instead to the ordinary taxation paid by all citizens in common.

Paragraph 2. Exceptions will also be made for all Indians who are permanently disabled or seriously ill to the point of not being able to work and earn a salary, providing this impossibility has been previously established by the competent authority through the legal procedures justifying this declaration of exemption in advance to the tax collector.

Article 3. The personal tribute from Indians must be paid in two installments, on 30 June and 31 December of each year; in the current year the installment for one semester only will be collected, this falling due at the end of December.

Title 2

Concerning the Tax Collectors, Their Duties, Security Bond, and Compensation

Article 4. The collection of the Indian tribute shall be the responsibility of persons or employees appointed by the government.

Article 5. All those appointed to this position shall guarantee one-fourth of the amount estimated to be collectable in their district, and in addition to the obligation secured by their personal property they will submit a security bond sufficient to satisfy the respective intendants who must give their approval, in consultation with the Treasury Board.

An affidavit of the receipt of the security bond shall be forwarded to the Office of the Auditor of the Treasury and another to the treasurer, at the cost of the tax collector.

Article 6. The tax collectors shall visit personally the parishes or sites designated in their commission for the collection of taxes due them, and accompanied by one of the parochial mayors or the parish priest and conducting themselves with the civility dictated by prudence so as not to cause anxiety, the two of them, in the presence of the registry and the parish archives, will enter the names and ages of all male Indians in a general registry, which with their three signatures will be submitted to the Office of the Auditor of the Treasury, another copy being submitted to the respective treasurer, and this procedure shall be repeated every five years.

Article 7. From the general registry the tax collectors shall draw specific lists of the Indians to be taxed, notarized by the collector, the parish mayor, and the priest, which shall be used for collecting the tribute, these lists being updated each year with precise data on new contributors.

Article 8. The treasurer shall deliver to the tax collectors the signed books in which they are to enter the detailed account of the collection according to parish and the number of contributors and the copies of the receipts that must be given to them by the collectors, duly notarized. The forms or receipts will contain the name of the Indian paying tribute, the parish, home, or hacienda where he lives, and the amount paid, this information being filled out by the collector in the spaces designated on these forms.

These will be issued by the auditors of the Treasury, who will turn them over to the treasurers for the purpose indicated.

Article 9. When a tribute payer dies, the tax collectors shall record this on the lists and in the collection book, demanding to see the death certificate, which will be given to them by the priests without exception.

In the event that the death certificate is not found or when an Indian is absent without any information concerning his existence, the death or absence shall be verified by sworn testimony of a mayor and priest of the parish or by information of witnesses on official forms.

Article 10. If any Indian has changed residence, the tax collector into whose district he has moved shall demand of him the tribute that he owes, recording this on his lists and advising the collector of the previous residence so his name can be removed from that list.

Article 11. The tax collectors are required to provide punctual accounts of the amount of money they collect to the respective treasurers who, informed of the progress of the collections on a monthly basis, will be in a position to take the necessary actions against those who refuse to pay or delay in doing so.

Article 12. Each year the collectors shall submit to the treasurers a notarized account of the total amount of tribute collected no later than March of the following year, keeping however a running tally as the money is collected and ascertaining the entire amount one month prior to the submission of the account.

In proof of the accuracy of the account they will also submit the lists and collection books, and the certificates or documents verifying the death or absence of the Indians or their exemptions from payment, with sworn statements from the tax collector concerning tributes still uncollected after the exhaustion of all diligent effort, thus justifying legally the impossibility of the collection and the unused payment forms being returned.

Article 13. The treasurers shall examine and finalize the accounts submitted by the collectors of Indian tribute no later than three months following their submission.

Article 14. Six percent of all monies collected shall be set aside for the tax collectors, without further emoluments or allowances for expenses.

Title 3
Concerning the Exemptions Granted to the Indians

Article 15. The Indians shall be exempted from all military service, unless they choose to enlist voluntarily in the corps of veteran soldiers. They shall be exempted from paying parochial fees and other national taxes of any kind.

In order to exercise the exemption from paying sales tax, it is necessary that any item they sell, trade, or barter be their own property, including harvest, crops, livestock, and handicraft, or be the property of other Indians. But should they sell anything belonging to any person subject to sales tax, they must declare and so indicate, following the instructions of the tribute office.

Article 16. In all negotiations involving Indians, and in civil or criminal actions initiated among themselves or with other citizens, either communities or individuals, they shall be regarded as paupers, in virtue of which they will be charged no fees by secular and ecclesiastical courts and judges.

Article 17. The Indians cannot be subjected to any kind of service by any class of person without paying them the wage customarily paid for such service throughout the country.

Title 4
Concerning Council Leaders and Other Indian Employees

Article 18. The lesser officials and employees of the Indian parishes will be continued in their posts for purely economic matters.

The duties of these employees are as follows:

1. To supervise the conduct of their subordinates in order to avoid excesses in consumption of alcohol and in other activities;
2. To advise the tax collectors concerning Indians who have left the parish and those who have come from other parishes;
3. To lend their influence and efforts in the collection of the personal tribute when the person charged with that responsibility appears in the parishes, informing the tribute payers of his arrival so that payment can be made on the initial demand;
4. To notify the priests in a timely manner when an Indian falls gravely ill so that he can be provided with the necessary spiritual and corporal aid.

Title 5
Concerning the Reservations or Indian Lands

Article 19. In the parishes where there are communal lands or reservations, each Indian family shall be provided with the land necessary for his home and personal cultivation, in addition to the communal land needed to graze his livestock and other purposes.

Article 20. Wherever there is a surplus of land, this can be leased to benefit the Indian community at a public auction presided over by the governor of the province and witnessed by the protector of the community, Indian bidders being favored over other citizens provided that they are leasing the land for themselves and that they offer the necessary security.

Article 21. The priests and protectors shall encourage the Indians as subtly as possible to practice communal farming of a large enough portion of the surplus land of the reserve in order to invest the proceeds precisely for their own benefit.

Title 6

Concerning the General and Individual Protectors of the Indians

Article 22. The court prosecutors [*fiscales*] shall serve as general protectors or guardians for Indians, and whenever one of the latter, either individually or as part of a group, comes to him asking for representation before the government or the superior courts in matters pertinent to Indian rights, these protectors shall provide such representation without any delay that might prejudice the matter.

Article 23. The court prosecutors acting as general protectors shall represent to the government whatever they consider useful and advantageous to the Indians, to their civilization, their welfare, and the preservation of their communal lands, without allowing anyone to usurp or alienate their rights or property.

Article 24. The court prosecutors shall serve as particular protectors of the province in which the Court resides, and in each one of the other provinces or provincial capitals there shall be a protector appointed by the prefect on the governor's recommendation.

Article 25. The provincial protectors shall defend the person and properties of the Indians and the concessions and privileges granted them by this decree and by the existing laws, attesting to their action on official paper and without exacting fees or any charges whatsoever.

Article 26. The protectors shall promote by any means within their power the establishment of schools for the education of the children of the Indians, and they shall urge the parents to send them to these schools as frequently as possible.

Article 27. They shall represent to the courts through the prosecutors and petition the government through the respective governor, asking whatever they consider fair and beneficial to the Indians of their province.

Article 28. The protectors, during their term of office, shall be exempt from all council duties.

Article 29. In cases where the protectors are unable to intervene on behalf of an Indian, the court or judge shall appoint provisionally the necessary defender or defenders in the absence of attorneys for the poor, the defenders so named being obligated to defend them gratis as they would paupers.

Article 30. Based on a determination of the government and any previous information that may be requested of the respective intendants, a fee or allowance shall be allotted to the local protectors to compensate them for their work.

Title 7
Concerning the Stipends for the Priests and the Observance of This Decree

Article 31. The priests in charge of Indian parishes shall receive the stipend of 183 pesos, 2 reales.

Article 32. The priests who receive some part of the *novenos* or tithes shall not be given the designated stipend, but should that amount be less than the stipend, it is to be supplemented up to the amount of 183 pesos, 2 reales.

Article 33. The law of 11 October 1821 concerning Indians is hereby annulled in all its parts.[15]

Article 34. The present decree shall be gradually implemented in whole or in part, according to subsequent instructions to be issued by the respective secretary.

Article 35. In provinces where implementation of this decree has not been mandated, the government, depending on local circumstances, shall dictate through special decrees the procedures to be observed.

The cabinet secretaries of state of the Departments of the Interior and the Treasury are hereby charged with the responsibility for implementing and supervising the observance of the specific articles of this decree falling under their jurisdiction.

Signed into law in the Palace of Government in Bogotá, the capital of the Republic, on 15 October 1828.

Simón Bolívar

For His Excellency the Liberator President, Secretary of the Interior, *José M. Restrepo.*
Secretary of the Treasury, *Nicolás M. Tanco.*

Application of Capital Punishment to Officials Who Have Taken Money from Public Funds

Lima, 12 January 1824

Simón Bolívar
Liberator President, etc.

Considering:

First, that one of the principal causes of the disasters in which the Republic has become embroiled was the scandalous waste of its funds by certain officials who have had access to them;[16]

Second, that the only way to eradicate this disorder completely is to dictate harsh and extreme measures, I have decided to issue this decree at once;

Decree:

Article 1. Any public official convicted in summary court of having misapplied or stolen more than ten pesos from the public funds shall be subject to capital punishment.

Article 2. The judges assigned jurisdiction in such a case, according to law, but who fail to adhere to this decree shall be condemned to the same penalty.

Article 3. Any citizen can charge public officials with the crime specified in Article 1.

Article 4. This decree shall be posted in all the offices of the Republic and taken in account in all commissions issued to officials who are in any way involved in the handling of public funds.

It shall be printed, publicized, and circulated.

Signed into law in the Dictatorial Palace of Lima on 12 January 1824, fourth year of the Republic.

Simón Bolívar

By order of His Excellency, *José Sánchez Carrión*

Measures for the Protection and Wise Use of the Nation's Forest Resources: Bolívar as Ecologist

Guayaquil, 31 July 1829

Simón Bolívar
Liberator President of the Republic of Colombia, etc.

Considering:

First, that the Forests of Colombia, those owned publicly as well as privately, represent an enormous treasure in wood suitable for all types of construction as well as dyes, quinine, and other useful substances for medicine and the arts.[17]

Second, that throughout the region we are experiencing excessive harvesting of wood, dyes, quinine, and other substances, especially in the forests belonging to the state, with disastrous consequences.

Third, that to avoid these, it is necessary to establish regulations for the effective protection of public and private property against violations of every kind, having seen the reports compiled for the government on this matter and heard the report of the Council of State,

I hereby decree:

Article 1. The governors of the provinces shall designate in each canton, through elected judges or other trustworthy persons, common lands belonging to the Republic, specifying in writing their boundaries and botanical properties, such as precious woods, medicinal plants, and other useful substances, ordering this information to be recorded in the public archives with another copy forwarded to the prefecture.

Article 2. They shall immediately make it known in each canton that no one can harvest precious wood or timber for the construction of commercial boats from vacant or state lands without prior written permission from the governor of the respective province.

Article 3. These permits shall never be issued free of charge, but shall be subject to a graduated fee to be determined by the governor in consultation with experts who shall submit a regulation to this effect for the approval of the prefecture.

Article 4. Anyone who harvests quinine, precious wood, and timber for construction from the state forests without the proper permit, or who harvests more than the amount specified in the permit, shall incur a fine of from 25 to 100 pesos, which shall be applied to the public funds, and shall, further, reimburse the cost of harvested or damaged property, based on the assessment of experts.

Article 5. The prefects of the maritime departments shall take special care to conserve the timber in the state forests, especially that which can be used for the naval forces, and to ensure that only the specified amount is harvested, or that which will bring a profit to the public revenues.

Article 6. The governors of the provinces shall prescribe regulations that are simple and accommodated to the local circumstances so that the harvesting of wood, quinine, or plants for dyes is conducted in an orderly fashion that will improve the quality of the forests and promote greater commercial profits.

Article 7. Wherever quinine or other substances useful as medicines are present, a supervisory junta shall be established to oversee an area considered appropriate by the respective prefect; this junta shall be composed of at least three persons and, whenever possible, one of them shall be a medical doctor. The members of the junta shall be appointed by the prefect, on nomination by the respective governor, and they shall serve in this capacity as long as their conduct warrants.

Article 8. Anyone who intends to harvest quinine and other substances useful as medicines from forests owned by the state or by individuals shall be inspected in their operations by one or two commissioners appointed by the supervisory junta, salaries or expenses to be paid by the entrepreneur or entrepreneurs. The junta and the commissioners shall ensure:

First, that the limits specified in the permit to harvest quinine and to extract other substances useful as medicines shall not be exceeded.

Second, that the extraction and other preparations shall be done according to the regulations drawn up by the faculties of medicine in

Caracas, Bogotá, and Quito, in a simple guidebook they are to compile that will have as its object the prevention of the destruction of the plants that produce these substances, which moreover are to be handled with all essential care in their preparation, bottling, etc., so that their price and commercial value will be maximized.

Article 9. In ports where no supervisory junta has been established, the inspection stipulated in Article 8 shall be carried out by intelligent persons appointed to this task by the governor, their report rigorously expressing the quality of the quinine or substance that has been examined. Should this requirement not be satisfied with the appropriate rigor, customs will not issue a stamp to register said substance, and should it be discovered that extraneous bark or substances lacking the necessary beneficial properties have been mixed with it, this shall be noted, the governor or customs administrator being so informed in order that shipment can be blocked.

Article 10. The faculties of medicine of Caracas, Bogotá, and Quito and the department prefects shall each provide the government with a report proposing measures to improve the extraction, preparation, and sale of quinine and other substances available for harvest in the forests of Colombia for medicinal use or for the arts, making all necessary recommendations for the increase of this important aspect of the public wealth.

The secretary of state in the Office of the Interior is charged with the execution of this decree.

Simón Bolívar

For His Excellency the Liberator President of the Republic, the Secretary General, *José D. Espinar*

4. EDUCATION AND CULTURE

Method to Be Employed in the Education of My Nephew Fernando Bolívar

(1822?)

The education of children should always be appropriate to their age, inclinations, spirit, and temperament.[1]

As my nephew is above twelve years of age, he should apply himself to learning modern languages, without neglecting his own. The dead languages should be studied after he has learned the living languages.

Geography and cosmography should be the earliest knowledge acquired by a young man.

The study of history, like languages, should begin with the contemporary period and then gradually move back in time to the dark ages of fable.

It is never too early to begin the study of natural sciences, because they teach us the technique of analysis in everything, moving from the known to the unknown, and in that way we learn to think and reason with logic.

But the student's ability to perform calculation should be kept in mind, for not all are equal in their aptitude for mathematics.

In general, everyone can learn and understand geometry, but this is not true of algebra and integral and differential calculus.

Rapid memorization always impresses as a brilliant faculty, but it may redound in detriment to comprehension; so the child who demonstrates too great a facility in retaining his lessons by memory should be taught those things that will force him to think, such as problem solving and setting up equations. On the other hand, those who are slow of retention should be taught to memorize and to recite passages selected from the great poets. Both memorization and calculation can be improved through practice.

The memory should be exercised to the extent possible but should never be strained to the point of weakening it.

The study of statistics is necessary in the times we are living, and I wish for my nephew to learn this science.

If he chooses to do so, he will receive instruction in mechanics and civil engineering, but not against his will, should he show a disinclination to study those subjects.

There is no need for him to learn music unless he develops a passion for this art; he should, however, acquire a rudimentary knowledge of line drawing, astronomy, chemistry, and botany, delving more or less deeply into those sciences according to his inclination or enjoyment of one or more of them.

The teaching of good manners or social habits is as essential as the acquisition of knowledge. For this reason, special care should be taken to have him learn the values and manners of a gentleman by reading the letters of Lord Chesterfield to his son.[2]

Morality derived from religious maxims and from the practical preservation of health and life is a subject that no teacher can neglect.

Roman law, as the basis of universal legislation, must be studied.

As it is most difficult to judge where art ends and science begins, should his temperament incline him to learn an art or trade, I will celebrate his decision, for there is an abundance of doctors and lawyers among us, but we lack good mechanics and farmers, which are what the country needs to advance in prosperity and well-being.

Dance, which is the poetry of motion, imparting grace and flexibility to the individual, as well as being a hygienic exercise in moderate climates, should be practiced if it appeals to him.

Above all, I recommend that you instill in him the enjoyment of cultivated society where the fair sex exerts its beneficial influence, as well as that respect for men of superior age, knowledge, and social position that makes youth fascinating by linking it to aspirations for the future.

Simón Bolívar

Decree on the Installation of Several Normal Schools Based on the Lancasterian System

Lima, 31 January 1825

Simón Bolívar
Liberator President of the Republic of Colombia, empowered with dictatorial authority in the Republic of Peru, etc.

Considering:
    I. That the Lancasterian system is the only rapid and efficient method of promoting public education;[3]
    II. That by introducing it into each of the departments it will be diffused without delay into the entire territory of the Republic,
    I have decided to issue the following decree:

1. In the capital city of each department a normal school will be established, modeled on the Lancasterian system.
2. The prefects, entering into an accord with the municipalities of their respective capital, will provide a precise estimate of the funds needed for this purpose.
3. Each province will send a minimum of six students to the school located in its department, so that they can later introduce this curriculum into the capital and other towns in the respective province.
4. The intendants, in cooperation with the municipalities, will select students with the greatest potential to be sent to the normal school. From the funds budgeted for public education, a subsistence allowance will be provided to students who are poor.

5. The Minister of State in the Department of Government and Foreign Relations is charged with the responsibility for executing this decree, which is to be printed, published, and distributed.

Signed in the Dictatorial Palace, in Lima, on 31 January 1825, fourth year of the Republic.

Simón Bolívar

By order of His Excellency, *José Sánchez Carrión*

Letters to José Joaquín de Olmedo:
Critique of the "Victoria de Junín"

I.

Cuzco, 27 June 1825

Dear friend:

A few short days ago I received on the road two of your letters and a poem: The letters are from a politician and a poet, but the poem is from an Apollo.[4] Neither the heat of the tropics, all the fires of Junín and Ayacucho, nor all the lightning bolts sent down by the Father of Manco Capac[5] have ever produced a more intense conflagration in the mind of a mortal. You open fire . . . where no shot has ever been fired before; you scorch the earth with the sparks from the axle and wheels of a chariot of Achilles that never passed through Junín; you take possession of all the characters: you turn me into a Jupiter, Sucre into a Mars, La Mar into an Agamemnon or a Menelaus, Córdova into an Achilles, Necochea into a Patrocles or an Ajax, Miller into a Diomedes, and Lara into a Ulysses.[6]

Each one of us is given our divine or heroic shadow to shield us with its protective wings like a guardian angel. You fashion us after your poetic and fantastic style, and to extend this fiction and fable into the realm of poetry, you exalt us with your false deification the way Jupiter's eagle lifted the tortoise up to the heavens only to drop it onto a rock to crush its floundering legs: In short, you have lifted us up to such sublime heights that we are flung into the abyss of nothingness, a vast and shimmering array of lights covering the pale reflection of our opaque virtues. Thus, my friend, you have pulverized us with the lightning bolts of Jupiter, the sword of Mars, the scepter of Agamemnon, the lance of Achilles, and the wisdom of Ulysses. If I were not as generous as I am, and if you were not the poet you are, I might think you had deliberately written a parody of the *Iliad* using the heroes of our puny farce. But I don't really believe that. You are a poet, and you know quite well, as did Bonaparte, that from the sublime to the ridiculous there is but a short step, and that Manolo[7] and the Cid are brothers, though sons of different fathers. An American will read your poem as Homerian canto; a Spaniard will read it as a canto from Boileau's[8] *Facistol*.

For all of this, I offer you my boundless gratitude.

I have no doubt that you will carry out your mission to England with dignity; so convinced was I of this that after turning my gaze on every corner of the Empire of the Sun, I found no diplomat capable of representing Peru and negotiating on her behalf more skillfully than you.[9] I sent a mathematician along to keep you from concluding, in a transport of poetic truth, that two plus two equaled four thousand;[10] our Euclid is there to keep our Homer alert, so he does not look with his imagination but with his fingers, and to prevent him from being charmed by harmonies and metrical patterns, keeping his ears tuned instead to the crude, harsh, astringent prose of politicians and publicans.

I came yesterday to the classic land of the sun, of the Incas, of fable and history. Here the true sun is gold; the Incas are the viceroys or prefects; the fable is Garcilaso's history; history is the relation by Las Casas of the destruction of the Indies.[11] An abstraction made of pure poetry, it calls to mind noble ideas, profound reflections; my soul is dazzled by the presence of primitive nature, evolved on its own, forming creations from its own elements based on the model of its intimate inspirations, without any admixture of foreign works, or alien counsel, or the whims of the human spirit, or the contagion of the history of crime and the absurdities of our species. Manco Capac, Adam of the Indians, left his Paradise on Lake Titicaca and formed an historic community, without a single element of sacred or profane fable.

God made him a man, he established his kingdom, and history has spoken truthfully because the monuments of stone, the broad, straight roads, the innocent customs, and authentic tradition make us witness to a social creation of which we have no concept or model or copy. Peru is unique in the history of mankind. It seems this way to me because I am here, and everything I have just said to you, more or less poetically, seems obvious to me.

Please be so kind as to share this letter with Mr. Paredes. I offer you the sincere expression of my friendship.

Bolívar

II.

Cuzco, 12 July 1825

My dear friend:

Day before yesterday I received your letter of May 15, which struck me as extraordinary because you take the liberty of making me a poet without my knowledge and without my consent.[12] As all poets are obsessive, you insisted on endowing me with your tastes and talents. Since you have gone to all that trouble, I will do as that fellow did whom they cast as king of a farce and who said: "Since I'm king, I'll mete out justice." Don't complain, then, about my mistakes because, having no knowledge of the profession, I'll strike out blindly with my cudgel in imitation of the king of the farce who scarcely left a puppet with his head on straight. Those he missed he had arrested. So let's get to it.

I've heard that Horace wrote a harsh letter to the Piso family severely criticizing metrical composition, and his imitator, M. Boileau, has taught me a few precepts that a man without any metrical sense can use to rip and truncate anyone who speaks rhythmically and melodiously and with controlled dignity.

I'll start by pointing out a flaw in oratory, since I don't like to start out praising only to end up savaging. I'll save my panegyrics for the conclusion of the work, which in my opinion well deserves them, so get ready to hear immense truths or, to put it more accurately, prosaic truths, since you know quite well that a poet measures truth differently than we men of prose. I'll follow my teachers.

You must have erased a great number of verses that I would have found prosaic or humdrum; either I have no ear for music, or these are . . . pure declamation. Forgive my boldness, but you gave me this poem and I can do with it as I will.

After this, you should have let the song ferment like wine until it could be savored chilled and delicious. Haste is a great fault in a poet. Racine took two years to compose fewer verses than these you've written, and that's why he is the purest writer of verse in modern times. The plan for this poem, although truly good, has a serious formal defect.

You have provided a very small frame to hold a colossus who occupies the entire space and covers the other characters with his shadow. The Inca Huaina-Capac is the apparent subject of the poem: He's the genius, the wise one, the hero, the end-all. On the other hand, it does not seem appropriate for him to proffer indirect praise to the religion that destroyed him; and it seems even less appropriate, even if he has no interest in being returned to his throne, to give preference to intrusive foreigners who while being the avengers of his blood are nonetheless the descendants of those who annihilated his empire: This abdication will not sit well with anyone. Nature prevails over all other rules, and this is not a natural action. Allow me also to point out to you that this Inca genius, who must be lighter than air, since he comes from the sky, comes across as overly talkative and complex, something the poets were unable to forgive in good king Henry in his harangue to Queen Elizabeth, and you are well aware that Voltaire had a reputation for generosity but was nonetheless criticized.[13]

The introduction to the poem is grandiloquent: it is Jupiter's thunderbolt splitting the earth to blast the Andes, which are forced to endure my unparalleled exploits in the battle of Junín. Apropos here is one of Boileau's precepts, who praised the modesty with which Homer begins his divine *Iliad*: He promises little and gives much. The valleys and mountains proclaim the earth: The repetition here is not pretty, and the soldiers proclaim the general, since the valleys and the mountain are the very humble servants of the earth.

Stanza 360 seems a bit prosaic. Perhaps I'm mistaken, and if so, why did you make me king?

Let's quote a verse so there can be no misunderstanding; verse 720, for example:

Que al Magdalena y al Rímac bullicioso [to the Magdalena and the torrential Rímac]

And another, verse 750:

Del triunfo que prepara glorioso [Of the glorious triumph here prepared]

Plus others that I won't quote in order not to seem harsh and ungrateful to one who sings my praises.

The tower of San Pablo will be your Mt. Pindo, the torrential Thames your Helicon: There you'll find your spleen-song, and consulting Milton's ghost you'll neatly apply your own devils to us. With the shades of many other illustrious poets, you'll find better inspiration than in the Inca, who, if truth be known, probably wouldn't know how to sing anything but sad Quechuan *yaravís*. Pope, your favorite poet, will give you some instruction for correcting some of those lapses that afflicted even Homer from time to time. You'll pardon me if I take after Horace in the enunciation of my oracular findings. That famous fault-finder waxed indignant because the author of the *Iliad* nodded off from time to time. And you know very well that Vergil regretted having given birth to a daughter as divine as the *Aeneid* after having worked for nine or ten years engendering her. So, my friend, it takes a lot of polish to polish the works of men. I can see land now; my critique is done, or should I say, I'm done striking out blindly.

I confess to you humbly that the versification of your poem seems sublime to me: Some genius pulled it forth from you and raised it to the heavens. You sustain throughout most of the poem a lively and constant warmth; some of the inspirations are truly original; the thoughts are noble and beautiful; the thunderbolt that your hero lends to Sucre is superior to the loan of Achilles's arms to Patroclus. Stanza 130 is extremely beautiful: I can hear the whirlwind roaring and see the axles burning: That's Greek, that's Homeric. In the presentation of Bolívar in Junín one can see, if only in profile, the moment before the clash between Turnus and Aeneas. The role you give to Sucre is warlike and grand. And when you speak of La Mar, I'm reminded of Homer singing to his friend Mentor. Although the characters are different, the case is similar. And, besides, isn't La Mar like a warrior Mentor?

Dear friend, allow me to ask: Where did you find the inspiration to sustain a song so powerfully from beginning to end? Victory lies in the conclusion of the battle, and you have won it because you concluded your poem with sweet verses, lofty ideas, and philosophical thoughts. Your return to the battlefield is Pindaric, and I liked it so much I would call it divine.

Press forward, my dear poet, in the lovely career the Muses have opened to you with your translation of Pope and your song to Bolívar.

Forgive, forgive me, friend; the fault is yours, since you cast me as a poet.

Your dear friend,

Bolívar

Circular on Educational Reform: Bentham Treatises Banned from All Colombian Universities

Bogotá, 12 March 1828

Simón Bolívar
Liberator President, etc.

Taking into consideration several reports that have been addressed to the government advising against the use of the treatises on civil and criminal legislation, written by Jeremy Bentham, for the teaching of the principles of universal legislation, these reports being supported by the General Direction of Studies,[14]

I decree:

Article 1. The Bentham legislative treatises shall not be taught in any of the universities of Colombia, Article 168 of the General Plan of Studies being hereby amended.

Article 2. Article 227 is also amended, and in the classes on jurisprudence and theology the General Direction shall be permitted to make substitutions in the basic texts, on advice of the report to be read at the meeting of the governing board of the university, which the professors of the school of law are to attend. In the universities where the General Direction of Studies is not in residence, the respective subordinate directors shall be permitted to make similar substitutions in the basic texts designated for use in said plan, informing the General Direction in order that it be brought to the attention of the Executive Power.

Article 3. In any branch of jurisprudence and theology where a basic text appropriate for instruction is not available in print, the respective professors shall dictate to their students a new course following the guidelines disposed in Article 28 of the General Plan of Studies.

Article 4. As it is very important that there be an abundance of basic texts, especially in areas in which there are currently none available for Colombian youth, the General Direction shall encourage the assistant administrators and universities to have the most capable professors draft texts for certain courses, which shall be printed with monies drawn from the funds of the universities, the costs being reimbursed subsequently from profits produced by the sale of the books.

The Secretary of State in the Office of the Interior shall be charged with the execution of this decree.

Simón Bolívar

The Secretary of State of the Office of the Interior, *J. M. Restrepo*

Prohibition of Secret Societies

Bogotá, 8 November 1828

Simón Bolívar
Liberator President, etc.

Having learned from experience, both in Colombia and in other nations, that secret societies serve the specific purpose of instigating public upheavals that disturb the peace and the established order, that concealing all of their operations behind the veil of mystery they lead us to the fundamental conclusion that they are neither good nor useful to society, and by the same token that they seed mistrust and alarm among all those who are uninitiated into the objects used in their ceremonies, the judgment of the Council of Ministers follows.[15]

Decree:

Article 1. All secret societies or guilds are prohibited in Colombia, whatever their denomination.

Article 2. The governors of the provinces, acting on their own and through the chiefs of police of the cantons, will dissolve and prevent meetings of the secret societies, first carefully ascertaining whether any exist in their respective provinces.

Article 3. Any person giving or renting his house or property to a secret society will incur a fine of 200 pesos, and each of those attending will be fined 100 pesos for the first and second offense, twice that amount for the third and subsequent offenses; those who cannot pay the fine will be sentenced to jail for two months for the first and second offense, and for the third and subsequent offenses the sentence will be doubled.

Paragraph 1. The governors and chiefs of police will apply these penalties to violators in a swift and summary manner, without possibility of appeal.

Paragraph 2. The fines will be used to cover expenses incurred by the police, under the direction of the governors of the provinces.

The Minister serving as Secretary of State of the Department of the Interior is charged with the execution of this decree.

Simón Bolívar

The Minister serving as Secretary of State of the Department of the Interior, *J. M. Restrepo*

Notes

I. The Major Political Texts

1. *Escritos*, IV, 116–27. Though commonly referred to as the Cartagena Manifesto, the precise title of this document is *Memoria dirigida a los ciudadanos de la Nueva Granada por un caraqueño*. Its initial publication was in pamphlet form, in Cartagena, early in 1813.

2. Since the province of Caracas so overshadowed the others in population and wealth, and the city of Caracas similarly overshadowed other towns of Caracas province itself, there was widespread demand that the province be subdivided for the sake of better balance among the component parts of Venezuela's federal union. Though Congress acceded to the demand, the measure could not be carried out before the collapse of the First Republic.

3. The empire "lost" by Spain in this case is Spain itself, which by 1812 had fallen largely into the hands of French forces and their Spanish collaborationists.

4. Bolívar here uses the name *Colombia* in the sense pioneered by the Venezuelan "Precursor," Francisco de Miranda, as referring to Spanish America generally. In later usage it comes to refer to the area of northern South America that had formed the Viceroyalty of New Granada and in 1819 was declared the Republic of Colombia, corresponding to present-day Venezuela, Colombia, Ecuador, and Panama (and normally referred to, in retrospect, as Gran Colombia).

5. This analysis of Spanish America's past experience, present condition, and future prospects, which is known in Spanish simply as *Carta de Jamaica*, was addressed to a British subject then resident on the island who has been identified as Henry Cullen. It was clearly Bolívar's intent that the letter be brought to the

attention of the larger British community in Jamaica and of English speakers elsewhere, for which purpose it was translated, apparently, by John Robertson, a British military officer who became one of his friends and supporters during West Indian exile. It was first published in Kingston, in the *Jamaica Quarterly Journal and Literary Gazette* of July 1818, under the title "Letter to a Friend, on the Subject of South American Independence." The original Spanish-language manuscript has been lost, and the first known publication in Spanish was in 1833, in the *Colección de documentos relativos a la vida pública del Libertador* compiled by Francisco Javier Yanes and Cristóbal Mendoza (in vol. XXI, appendix). The translation given here is based on that found in *Escritos*, VIII, 222–48; the English version and Spanish variations, along with extended commentary, can be found in the same volume of *Escritos*, 75–221.

6. The Viceroyalty of New Spain, whose capital was Mexico City, included the Captaincy-General of Guatemala, corresponding to all of Central America except Panama.

7. William Walton (1784–1857), a British publicist, wrote on Spanish and Spanish American affairs and collaborated with Venezuelan patriot agents in London.

8. The Abbé Guillaume Thomas Raynal (1713–96), a French critic of Spanish colonial policy, was widely read in Latin America despite the aspersions he also cast on the New World and its inhabitants.

9. Antonio de Herrera y Tordesillas (1559–1625) and Antonio de Solís y Rivadeneyra (1610–86) were two of the principal Spanish chroniclers of the conquest and colonization of America.

10. The references to Fernando VII are at first glance confusing, since he appears as both usurper and victim of usurpation. In March 1808, Fernando succeeded his father Carlos IV, when a protest movement caused the latter to abdicate the throne; subsequently, Napoleon lured both father and son to Bayonne in France, where Fernando was induced to abdicate in turn, initially in favor of his father but in practice to clear the way for Napoleon to impose his brother Joseph as king of Spain.

11. The Mexican revolutionary priest Fray Servando Teresa de Mier Noriega y Guerra (1763–1827).

12. José María Blanco (1775–1841) was a Spanish liberal who took refuge in England (where he was better known as Joseph Blanco-White) and gave sympathetic treatment to the Spanish American revolutionists in his publication *El Español*.

13. The French priest and publicist Dominique de Pradt, usually referred to simply as the Abbé de Pradt (1759–1837), was another supporter of the Spanish American cause who would become an apologist for and correspondent of Bolívar.

14. The Araucanian Indians of southern Chile were never fully conquered until after Chile became independent.

15. Charles–Irénée Castel (1658–1743) was a French writer who in his ecclesiastical capacity was the Abbé de Saint-Pierre.

16. José de Acosta (1539–1600) was a Jesuit naturalist who traveled extensively in Spanish America during the first century of colonial rule and wrote the *Historia natural y moral de las Indias* (1590).

17. Delivered at the inauguration of the Congress of Angostura on 15 February 1819, this address was first published, in incomplete form, in the *Correo del Orinoco*, 20 and 27 February, 6 and 13 March 1819. An early English version was published almost simultaneously, as a pamphlet, at Angostura, and a Spanish version revised by Bolívar himself was printed at Bogotá in April 1820. The translation given here is based on the version in *Escritos*, XV, 315–46. Both English and assorted Spanish versions and commentary are found in the same volume, 95–346.

18. Cundinamarca was the name assumed by the former province of Santafé, in a rhetorical tribute to New Granada's Native American antecedents, although it is actually of Quechua origin rather than derived from one of the Chibcha tongues spoken by the original inhabitants of the area. It would at times be applied to New Granada as a whole and today is the name of the Colombian department surrounding Bogotá. It was "pacified" by Bolívar in December 1814, when he forcibly compelled it to join the United Provinces of New Granada.

19. Constantin-François Chasseboeuf, Comte de Volney (1757–1820), was a French scholar and liberal thinker and contemporary of Bolívar.

20. Lazare Carnot (1753–1823), French Revolutionary general and administrator.

21. "Active" citizens, in what was a common usage among legislators and constitution-makers of the period, were those endowed with all citizenship rights, including the suffrage; "passive" were inhabitants who enjoyed basic guarantees but were not full participants in the political process.

22. Bolívar's address together with the text of his draft constitution was published in Lima in 1826, as *Proyecto de Constitución para la República de Bolivia y discurso del Libertador*. It was republished the same year in Bogotá and in 1827 in London in English translation. The address and proposed text are taken here from vol. I of *El pensamiento constitucional hispanoamericano hasta 1830* (Caracas, 1961; Biblioteca de la Academia Nacional de la Historia, 40), 171–221, where the changes introduced by Bolivia's national constituent assembly are indicated by means of footnotes. All substantive changes—as distinct from those of purely routine or technical nature—will also be shown in the notes to this translation.

23. The reference is to Emmanuel-Joseph Sieyès (1748–1836), French clergyman and revolutionist.

24. As spelled out in the text of the constitution, the vice president did not inherit by being next in bloodline to the president but in the sense that he would automatically succeed to the presidency on the incumbent's death: In effect, he was adopted as heir by the president.

25. Since Bolivia did in fact have a coastline, we see here a curious, though not entirely surprising, lapse on Bolívar's part. To be sure, that coastline (lost to Chile in the War of the Pacific later in the nineteenth century) was largely uninhabited and undeveloped at the time of Bolívar's writing; for overseas trade Bolivia thus relied on ports in Peru and Argentina.

26. At this point the Bolivian assembly incorporated an additional chapter and article:

Of the Religion

Article 6. The Apostolic Roman Catholic Religion is the religion of the Republic, to the exclusion of any other public cult. The government will protect and cause it to be respected, recognizing the principle that there is no human power over a person's conscience.

27. The Bolivian assembly amended this to read, "Those who fought for freedom in Junín or Ayacucho."

28. The Bolivian assembly changed this article to read: "All those who have until now been slaves and who are liberated as a consequence of the publication of this Constitution; but they shall not be allowed to leave the house of their former owners, except in the manner to be determined by a special law."

29. This also was changed to read: "To know how to read and write well; this qualification will only be required after the year 1836." The delayed application of a literacy test was a common feature of early Latin American constitutions (with French Revolutionary precedents). It was ostensibly to give those who were illiterate only because the colonial regime had failed to provide sufficient schools time to overcome the deficiency.

30. In the constitution as finally adopted, there was to be one elector for every 100 Bolivian citizens, not every 10.

31. Here the Bolivian assembly inserted the requirement that electors, at least, had to be literate even before 1836.

32. Although the assembly stopped short of abolishing the traditional patronato or system of state control over church administration, one of the changes it made in this article was to provide that the electors should nominate priests and vicars directly to "the ecclesiastical authority" rather than to the "Executive Power."

33. Here the Bolivian assembly inserted: "2. Profess the religion of the Republic."

34. The wording finally adopted was slightly more practical: "in peace and war, and in person when necessary."

35. Here again the Bolivian assembly made a very practical change in the constitutional text, giving the president authority to leave the capital city without first getting legislative permission. Similar leeway was granted the vice president in its final version of Article 90.

36. In the version finally adopted, this was changed to: "The power to judge

pertains exclusively to the tribunals established by law." The alteration appears to suggest a higher regard for the judicial branch than that shown by the Liberator himself, who in his address to the Convention of Ocaña (the document that appears next in this compilation) would state that the judicial function is really a subtype of the executive.

37. Presumably "popular action" refers to the functions of petition and complaint assigned to the provincial electoral assemblies.

38. This recurso, in traditional Spanish jurisprudence, was an appeal permitted outside normal judicial channels of a court decision already handed down in final instance. The procedure was an invitation to executive interference in judicial matters and was therefore a frequent target of institutional reformers in postindependence Spanish America.

39. This article appears to suffer from careless drafting. In the version finally adopted, the number of justices of the peace was reduced and the alcaldes were eliminated.

40. The Bolivian assembly filled in the blank by specifying that there should be a ten-year trial period, as also required in Colombia's Constitution of 1821.

41. *Obras*, III, 789–96; first printed in *Gaceta de Colombia*, 1 May 1828.

42. In actual fact, the constitution as written required a two-thirds vote of the members present to override an executive veto and more than two-thirds of the total membership in order to hold a session. Hence in practice it would take at least two-ninths of the congressmen to override.

43. The reference is to Manuel José Hurtado, named by Vice President Santander to negotiate the foreign loan that was actually obtained in London in 1824. Hurtado was widely criticized for the terms that he accepted as well as for the seemingly excessive commission he received from Colombia for his services. The damage done by his "extended stay in Europe" is less obvious, although he did unwisely leave á portion of the loan funds in the hands of the British financial firm that served as intermediary in raising the loan and which in 1826 went bankrupt, carrying with it the Colombian money. (It should perhaps be noted for the record that at the time pesos were generally equivalent to United States dollars.)

44. The reference here is to Peru, whose independence was achieved with the help of Colombian arms but was now enmeshed in a series of diplomatic and other controversies with Colombia, leading to the brief war of 1828–29 between the two countries.

45. No reliable estimate of Gran Colombian losses in the war of independence has ever been made, but clearly the figure given here, roughly equivalent to one-fifth the total population, is grossly inflated for rhetorical effect.

46. *Obras*, III, 841–47. This essay was written in Quito, for anonymous publication as a newspaper article or pamphlet. Under the title *Una mirada sobre la América Española*, it was published in Caracas in 1829.

47. The actual date of establishment of a governing junta in Buenos Aires was 25 May 1810.

48. Hero of the defense of Buenos Aires against the British invasions of 1806–7, Liniers was no longer viceroy when the revolution there got under way in May 1810. Attempting to organize a counterrevolutionary movement in Córdoba in the Argentine interior, he was captured and summarily executed.

49. In what is now Bolivia, the Desaguadero was the farthest point reached by a revolutionary expedition sent from Buenos Aires and led by Castelli. He was an "expeditionary philosopher," as noted below, in that he was a civilian lawyer who represented the more radical wing of the Argentine revolution. Indeed, he and his collaborators managed to alarm Bolivian whites through their appeals to the Indian masses while sowing even wider alarm with their seeming irreligiosity. Contrary to what Bolívar has to say, the survivors of that expedition were not pursued quite "all the way to Córdoba."

50. A militia officer and political moderate with strong ties to the interior provinces, Cornelio Saavedra presided over the ruling junta set up in Buenos Aires in May 1810; he was soon forced out by his political rivals.

51. Rivadavia became chief minister of Buenos Aires province under Rodríguez but was not governor himself; instead, he briefly became president of a precariously united Argentina.

52. Lavalle was a leader of the Unitario party, which had supported Rivadavia. In December 1828, Lavalle rose against Governor Dorrego and had him executed. Previously he had served as a member of the Argentine expeditionary forces taken by San Martín to Peru, e.g., in fighting near Ica, as noted perhaps unfairly in the next paragraph.

53. Supreme director of the United Provinces of Río de la Plata, 1816–19.

54. José Miguel Carrera for a time headed the patriot regime established in Chile. After the Spanish reconquest in 1814, he took refuge in Argentina, where along with his brothers Juan José and Luis he became enmeshed in the factional disputes of the Argentine revolutionists.

55. This highly uncomplimentary reference is to Vicente Guerrero, a prominent guerrilla leader in the Mexican struggle for independence, who became president in 1829, only to be overthrown the following year.

56. In reality the first Mexican emperor, Agustín de Iturbide, on his overthrow in 1823 was allowed to go peacefully into exile with a generous pension. He was executed only when he returned to Mexico without authorization the following year.

57. Another revolutionary guerrilla leader and first president of the Mexican Republic, Guadalupe Victoria was no longer holding that office when Guerrero committed the crimes Bolívar accuses him of.

58. In Spanish *léperos*, the derogatory term applied to vagrants and petty criminals infesting the streets of Mexico City.

59. The Convention of Girón, of 1 March 1829, was signed the day after the Colombian victory over invading Peruvian forces in the Battle of Tarqui and

temporarily put an end to hostilities between the two countries. What was "despicable" to Bolívar was the bad faith shown by Peru in failing to honor it.

60. The Argentine officer Rudecindo Alvarado led the ill-fated expedition into southern Peru that ended in defeat in early 1823 at the Battles of Torata and Moquegua.

61. Although Torre-Tagle was already in potentially treasonous correspondence with the Spaniards, Callao was lost in February 1824 (and indirectly Lima as well) as the result of an essentially spontaneous mutiny by the Callao garrison.

62. A New Granadan officer acting ostensibly out of constitutionalist convictions, José Bustamante led a mutiny in January 1827 among Colombian forces still stationed in Lima against the mainly Venezuelan and Bolivarian higher officers. This contributed to the collapse of the Peruvian government, set in place by Bolívar on returning to Colombia the previous year.

63. Born in Cuenca in what is now Ecuador, La Mar was thus by birth a native of Gran Colombia despite his Peruvian military position.

64. The Third Division, after its mutiny under Bustamante in Lima, returned to Colombian territory at Guayaquil and there endeavored, in the end unsuccessfully, to overthrow the authorities loyal to Bolívar.

65. *Obras*, III, 812–17.

66. *Decretos*, III, 137–44. The decree in question established a framework for the functioning of Bolívar's final dictatorship and made clear that it was only a temporary solution, pending the convocation of a new congress to prepare a revised constitution.

67. Here Bolívar presumably has in mind the proclamation of the Peruvian general Antonio Gutiérrez de Lafuente, leader along with Agustín Gamarra of a successful revolution in Peru, denouncing the previous government headed by José La Mar for its unjust war against Colombia. The new administration very quickly made peace with the Colombians.

68. This statement refers to the uprising of José María Córdova and his followers in Antioquia in 1829 and is just a little disingenuous: Córdova was wounded in the Battle of Santuario but received the coup de grace only after his defeat, from an English officer in Bolívar's service, at a nearby house where he had taken refuge.

69. In effect, by this time dissidents favoring Venezuela's outright separation from the Colombian union had already taken control in Caracas.

II. Lesser Bolivarian Texts

1. Political and Military

1. *Escritos*, IV, 14–16. This obviously should not be taken as a literal transcription of Bolívar's words, which were not written down at the time. The version given here is one apparently handed down by Simón Rodríguez and published in

Homenaje de Colombia al Libertador Simón Bolívar en su Primer Centenario,
1783–1883 (Bogotá, 1884), 74. There are, of course, other versions, and the lengthy
first paragraph, in particular, may be taken with reservations as to Bolívar's exact
authorship.

2. *Escritos*, IV, 305–7. This was published, with minor alterations, by the print-
er Juan Baillío, in Caracas, probably also in 1813.

3. *Escritos*, V, 124–35. First published as *Exposición sucinta de los hechos del*
Comandante español Monteverde durante el año de su dominación en las Provincias de
Venezuela (Caracas, 1813). The original apparently is lost.

4. A slightly intemperate reference to Miranda, named dictator by the republican authorities in a desperate and ultimately unsuccessful effort to stave off
defeat. Bolívar held him personally responsible for the capitulation that ended
Venezuela's First Republic and was one of the officers who, by arresting him, pre-
vented his escape from the country.

5. *Escritos*, VI, 390–95.

6. *Escritos*, XI, 253–54.

7. The reference is to the abortive attempt by Mariño and others earlier in the
year, at the so-called Congresillo of Cariaco, to withdraw Bolívar's supreme
authority.

8. The "order" that Bolívar speaks of here is his own recent decree for the distribution of confiscated properties to members of the patriot armed forces; it is
reproduced below.

9. *Escritos*, XIV, 495–97.

10. *Escritos*, XXIII, 233–34. The original is missing, but composed at some
point in 1822—the first copy bearing the date of 13 October 1822—during Bolívar's
stay in what is now Ecuador. He obviously did not scale Mount Chimborazo,
Ecuador's highest, to its 6,267-meter summit, and even the attribution of this
composition to Bolívar has been questioned by some. But its authenticity as one
of his writings is accepted by most Bolivarian scholars, and neither is there reason
to doubt that he did ascend part way. The document was first published in 1833,
in vol. XXII of Francisco Javier Yanes and Cristóbal Mendoza, *Colección de docu-*
mentos para la vida pública del Libertador de Colombia y del Perú, Simón Bolívar.

11. The French scientist Charles-Marie de La Condamine (1701–74) had visited what is now Ecuador as part of an expedition to measure the length of a
degree at the Equator. The German naturalist Alexander von Humboldt
(1769–1859) visited the same area in the course of his travels through much of
Spanish America in the late colonial period.

12. *Obras*, II, 322–23. The letter of Páez to which it is an answer is reproduced
on pp. 324–26 of the same volume. The carrier of the letter, Antonio L. Guzmán,
was one of the Venezuelans who strongly opposed the national administration
headed in Bolívar's absence by Vice President Santander; he later was a founder
of Venezuela's Liberal Party.

13. *Decretos*, III, 16–17.

14. *Obras*, III, 808–9.

15. *Obras*, III, 817–19 (which appends a slightly different draft of the same).

16. Different versions of this letter exist. The present version is not that of *Obras*, III, 501–4, as reconstructed from extant fragments by Vicente Lecuna, but that contained in the second (posthumous) edition of Lecuna, comp., *Cartas del Libertador* (Caracas, 1969), VII, 585–89, and originally published by Federico Stagg y Caamaño, "El general Flores," in the *Boletín Histórico* of the Fundación John Boulton (Caracas), 1 (December 1962): 17–21. The "emissary" who had brought the letter from Flores that Bolívar is answering was an Ecuadoran officer who in the mid-nineteenth century became president of his country.

17. That is, Venezuelans like Flores himself, many of whom were holding command positions in the "South," or present-day Ecuador.

18. The Ecuadoran patriot Rocafuerte had been serving as an agent of independent Mexico in London and had been fulsome in praise of Bolívar, but he came to see Bolívar's dictatorship as essentially a betrayal of republican principles and was to that extent now aligned with Bolívar's political opponents.

19. The so-called July Revolution of 1830 overthrew the restored Bourbon monarchy of Charles X and sparked a number of other revolutions (not necessarily successful) in the rest of Europe.

20. In the battle of La Ladera, November 1828, José María Obando and José Hilario López routed the Bolivarian loyalist Tomás C. de Mosquera as part of their (ultimately unsuccessful) revolt against Bolívar's dictatorship. Now they were at it again, fighting to overthrow the government of General Rafael Urdaneta, who came to power when a military uprising forced out the New Granadan moderate Joaquín Mosquera—who had succeeded to the Colombian presidency at the final resignation of Bolívar.

21. This was the same Venezuelan officer who had been highest ranking military conspirator in the attempt on Bolívar's life of September 1828; after release from prison, he returned to Venezuela and from there accepted a summons to help the resistance in Río Hacha against the intrusive Urdaneta regime.

22. A Santanderista caudillo of the New Granadan *llanos*, Moreno refused to recognize the Urdaneta government and went so far as to call for the annexation of Casanare to now-independent Venezuela. The Carvajal mentioned here is Lucas Carvajal, a Venezuelan-born hero of independence who was assassinated in Casanare.

23. The "victim" in question is Antonio José de Sucre, whose assassination was blamed by Bolívar's supporters on Obando and López, both of whom were now actively resisting Urdaneta.

24. It was near Pasto that Sucre was murdered, as he was returning from Bogotá to Quito, where he proposed to make his home.

25. Bolívar had in fact been urged to resume power by Urdaneta and his faction, and by public pronouncements in many parts of New Granada, but he had hardly been "appointed by all of New Granada."

26. The Panamanian officer Espinar seized power on the Isthmus and for a time ruled it as a de facto autonomous state; he provided the armed schooner *Istmeña* to be used in an attempt to undermine the control of Flores in Ecuador. This last was ostensibly in support of the Liberator, but Bolívar correctly diagnosed it as an essentially trouble-making exercise.

27. Alzuru was a Venezuelan colonel serving on the Isthmus and, for the moment, a collaborator of Espinar.

28. *Obras*, III, 823–24.

2. INTERNATIONAL AFFAIRS

1. *Escritos*, VIII, 10–13.

2. The reference here, of course, is to Great Britain's aid against Napoleon in Europe, which gave Spain hope not only of surviving the invasion by French forces but of going on to suppress the colonial insurrections.

3. The Spanish text ends simply with the abbreviation "Q.B.S.M.," here spelled out in translation.

4. *Escritos*, XIV, 207–10. This letter was part of an extensive series of exchanges on the subject of maritime claims, with letters from Bolívar to Irvine starting on 29 July (ibid., 125–27) and culminating 12 October 1818 (ibid., 376–78). In them Bolívar shows increasing irritation with the North American, and in the last letter he effectively breaks off negotiations. Curiously, none of these letters appear in what has been the most complete set of Bolívar's writings in English translation, the *Selected Writings of Bolívar*, as compiled by Vicente Lecuna and edited by Harold A. Bierck (2 vols., New York, 1951). In Spanish, the letter's opening salutation reads "Señor Agente."

5. Emmerich de Vattel (1714–67), the Swiss jurist and diplomat who in *Le droit des gens* (1758) sought to apply natural law principles to international relations.

6. These two United States ships were seized by the Venezuelan navy for attempting to run the blockade that the patriots had declared against the port of Angostura while it was still in royalist hands. The episode gave rise to the most serious of the disagreements between Bolívar and Irvine.

7. William Cobbett (1763–1835), English political writer and radical thinker.

8. *Obras*, II, 50–52.

9. Naturally here "this purpose" is not the same as "this august purpose" noted in the preceding sentence, i.e., to serve as capital of the world; it is simply to serve as seat of the proposed congress.

10. *Obras*, II, 141–47. On the "Portuguese [*sic* for Brazilian] invasion" of the province of Chiquitos in Upper Peru or modern Bolivia, which in fact was the work of a regional commander acting without authorization from the emperor in Rio de Janeiro, see Ron L. Seckinger, *The Brazilian Monarchy and the South American Republics 1822–1831* (Baton Rouge, 1984), 73–79.

11. The island of Chiloé, off the coast of southern Chile, was a royalist redoubt left still unconquered after the defeat of royalist forces in Chile's central valley and the setting up of an independent government.

12. Or more precisely, capital of the Viceroyalty of Río de la Plata to which Charcas had belonged.

13. That is, the present Uruguay, occupied during the wars of independence by Portuguese forces and inherited in 1822 by the new Brazilian empire.

14. Bolívar had met the French scientist Aimé Bonpland (1773–1858), who was also a collaborator of the German naturalist Alexander von Humboldt, while living in Paris before the start of the independence movement. Bonpland had gone to Paraguay for scientific purposes but was detained by order of Dr. Francia on suspicion of being somehow in league with the dictator's numerous foreign and domestic enemies.

15. The former of the two Argentines mentioned was not actually a general but *comandante* and was a representative of Buenos Aires specifically in Upper Peru; he was the son of the latter.

16. Santander had proposed appointing Sucre as Colombian plenipotentiary to Peru, hoping to take advantage of the prestige he acquired at Ayacucho in order to obtain a favorable settlement of boundary disputes and of Colombian claims for reimbursement for expenses incurred in helping to liberate Peru. He made the proposal in a letter to Bolívar of 6 March 1825 (*Cartas Santander-Bolívar*, 6 vols. [Bogotá, 1988–90], IV, 323).

17. Mosquera had earlier served as Bolívar's agent to Peru (before going there in person), Chile, and Buenos Aires.

18. Pedro Briceño Méndez, the Venezuelan general who had been serving as Colombia's secretary of war, was one of those mentioned as a candidate for vice president in 1826 in opposition to the reelection of Santander.

19. Ramón Freire and Francisco Antonio Pinto were both Chilean liberal leaders who had helped to overthrow the government of Chile's own Liberator, Bernardo O'Higgins.

20. *Obras*, III, 756–57. This document was not dated but is thought to have been drafted early in 1826. It was first published by Vicente Lecuna as *Un pensamiento sobre el Congreso de Panamá: Obsequio de Vicente Lecuna a los delegados al II Congreso Científico Panamericano* (Washington, 1916).

21. *Obras*, II, 334–35. This letter was published in the *Gaceta de Colombia*, 25 February 1827. As it indicates, George Washington's family had presented to Lafayette, for transmission to Bolivar, a gold medal dedicated to Washington, a portrait, and some strands of his hair.

22. *Obras,* III, 278–79.

23. Col. Bedford H. Wilson, who was one of the British volunteers who had previously served in Bolívar's forces.

24. The installation of a prince of the French—not Spanish—Bourbon line was the most widely discussed of various possibilities for establishing a monarchy in Colombia at the death or resignation of Bolívar.

25. It may be of interest to note, as a curious sidelight, that a few United States scholars have tried to water down this, the most scathing comment Bolívar ever made about their country, by the simple expedient of removing a comma; it then

reads, "the new American states and the United States, which seem [now plural] destined...." He thus would be lumping the United States together with the independent Latin American nations, expressing his exasperation with them all indiscriminately. See, e.g., William R. Shepherd, "Bolívar and the United States," *Hispanic American Historical Review* (August 1918): 279. Indeed, Bolívar himself possibly did not dictate the comma, yet his particular annoyance with the United States at this point is beyond question.

26. Meaning, of course, Haiti, or the former French colony of Saint-Domingue, although as a matter of fact it had at this point temporarily absorbed the former Spanish colony of Santo Domingo.

3. SOCIAL AND ECONOMIC AFFAIRS

1. *Escritos*, IX, 185–87.

2. *Escritos*, XI, 219–21.

3. *Escritos*, XVII, 218–20. This letter is more often reproduced with the date of 20 April 1820 (as in *Obras*, I, 424–25), which also happens to be the date of an incomplete copy—lacking the discussion of motives—that is included in the *Memorias del General O'Leary*, vol. XVII, 137.

4. The article is from a law of 22 January 1820, adopted by the Congress of Angostura, which reaffirmed general emancipation of slaves as an objective but left it for some future legislature to determine how this should be done. The law endorsed Bolívar's offer of freedom to slaves who performed military service on behalf of the Republic but also made the specific pledge (which would hardly have been to Bolívar's liking) to return fugitive slaves who entered Colombia from foreign countries. The entire measure may be found in *Correo del Orinoco*, 5 February 1820.

5. *Escritos*, XVII, 372–75, where the measure is taken directly from *Decretos*, I, 194–97. In this and subsequent decrees the Native Americans were consistently referred to either as *naturales* ("natives") or as *indígenas*, the term *indio* being carefully avoided in an early attempt at political correctness. Since the term *native* standing by itself can be ambiguous, and *indigene* has an awkward ring in English, the term *Indian* is employed instead in these translations.

6. Although *Juez político* literally means "political judge," it was not a judicial office. Instead, the *Juez político* was the agent of the national executive at the municipal level. The position was subsequently given the more appropriate title of *Jefe político*.

7. *Decretos*, I, 407–8.

8. This "republican" dating refers to the sixth year since the proclamation at Angostura in 1819 of the Republic of Colombia and fourth since San Martín's formal declaration of independence in Peru in July 1821.

9. *Decretos*, I, 410–12.

10. *Decretos*, I, 295–96. This decree dealt generally with the sale of government-owned lands and only in part with the distribution of Indian common

lands. Unlike the decree reproduced here, it set no limit on the Indians' alienation of formerly communal property once it was distributed to them.

11. The *topo* was a measurement of approximately 1.5 leagues.

12. An uprising led by the cacique Mateo Pumacahua, which had some support among creoles and mestizos of the Cuzco region but was primarily an Indian movement.

13. This clarification was inserted in the Peruvian *Gazeta del Gobierno*, 8 September 1825, just two weeks after publication of the original decree.

14. *Decretos*, III, 171–78. This decree was not applied in Venezuela, at least not the provisions relating to reestablishment of the tribute. See David Bushnell, "The Last Dictatorship: Betrayal or Consummation?" *Hispanic American Historical Review* (February 1983): 90, n. 86.

15. The law in question had ordered abolition of the tribute in all Colombian territory.

16. *Decretos*, I, 283.

17. *Decretos*, III, 349–51.

4. EDUCATION AND CULTURE

1. *Escritos*, II, 267–68. This document, undated but in view of the reference to Fernando Bolívar's age apparently written toward the end of 1821 or in 1822, was first published in *La Opinión Nacional* of Caracas, 24 July 1883.

2. Philip Dormer Stanhope (Lord Chesterfield), *Letters to His Son* (1774), a well known manual of social deportment.

3. *Decretos*, I, 354.

4. *Obras*, II, 153–55. Copies of this and the following letter, in the personal archive of Olmedo's father-in-law, Martín Icaza, were first published in *Los Andes* (Guayaquil), 11 June 1870.

5. Manco Capac, legendary founder of the Inca civilization, was a semidivine being; accordingly, his "father" was the sun god, Inti.

6. In addition to Antonio José de Sucre, Bolívar here lists the Peruvian officer born in what is now Ecuador, José La Mar; the New Granadan José María Córdova; the Argentine Mariano Necochea; the British volunteer William Miller; and the Venezuelan Jacinto Lara, all of whose contributions to the victory of Junín had been noted in Olmedo's poem.

7. The leading character of a popular sainete or farce of the same name (1769) by the Spanish dramatist Ramón de la Cruz.

8. The French poet and literary critic Nicolas Boileau-Despréaux (1638–1711).

9. Bolívar had named Olmedo as Peruvian agent in London, for the primary purpose of raising a foreign loan.

10. Bolívar named the Peruvian medical doctor and mathematician José Gregorio Paredes as Olmedo's fellow commissioner.

11. Bolívar here refers to Inca Garcilaso de la Vega (1539–1616), the chronicler of Peruvian antiquities, and Bartolomé de Las Casas, the Dominican friar best

known for his scathing denunciations of Spanish atrocities toward the Native Americans (1474–1506).

12. *Obras*, II, 174–76.

13. The Henry in this case is not Elizabeth's father, Henry VIII, but her French contemporary, Henry IV, as featured in Voltaire's epic poem *La Henriade*. The harangue in question fills all the work's "Chant deuxième" and part of "Chant troisième," with a prolix recital of the problems afflicting France.

14. *Decretos*, III, 53–54. The General Direction of Studies was the agency entrusted with implementing the General Plan of Studies issued by Vice President Santander for all Colombian higher education in 1826.

15. *Decretos*, III, 201–2.

Select Bibliography

Anna, Timothy. *The Fall of the Royal Government in Peru.* Lincoln, NE, 1979.

Arnade, Charles. *The Emergence of the Republic of Bolivia.* Gainesville, FL, 1957.

Belaunde, Víctor Andrés. *Bolívar and the Political Thought of the Spanish American Revolution.* Baltimore, MD, 1938.

Bierck, Harold A. *Vida pública de Don Pedro Gual,* Caracas, 1947.

Brading, David A. *Classical Republicanism and Creole Patriotism: Simón Bolívar (1783–1830) and the Spanish American Revolution.* Cambridge, 1983.

Bushnell, David. *The Santander Regime in Gran Colombia.* Newark, DE, 1954.

Carrera Damas, Germán. *Boves: aspectos socioeconómicos de la guerra de independencia.* Caracas, 1972.

——. *El culto a Bolívar.* Caracas, 1969.

Cussen, Antonio. *Bolívar and Bello: Poetry and Politics in the Spanish American Revolution.* Cambridge, 1992.

Earle, Rebecca A. *Spain and the Independence of Colombia 1810–1825.* Exeter, UK, 2000.

Fisher, John, Allan J. Kuethe, and Anthony McFarlane, eds., *Reform and Insurrection in Bourbon New Granada and Peru.* Baton Rouge, 1990.

Fundación Polar. *Diccionario de historia de Venezuela.* 3 vols., Caracas, 1968.

Gutiérrez, Alberto. *La iglesia que entendió el Libertador Simón Bolívar.* Bogotá, 1981.

Hasbrouck, Alfred. *Foreign Legionaries in the Liberation of Spanish South America.* Reprint ed., New York, 1969.

Hispanic American Historical Review, vol. 63, no. 1 (February 1983). Special issue dedicated to Bolívar on the bicentennial of his birth.

Hoover, John P. *Admirable Warrior: Marshal Sucre, Fighter for South American Independence*. Detroit, 1977.

Izard, Miquel. *El miedo a la revolución: la lucha por la libertad en Venezuela (1777–1830)*. Madrid, 1979.

Jaramillo, Juan Diego. *Bolívar y Canning 1822–1827*. Bogotá, 1983.

Lecuna, Vicente. *Crónica razonada de las guerras de Bolívar*. 3 vols., New York, 1950.

Liévano Aguirre, Indalecio. *Bolívar*. 1st ed., Medellín, 1971.

Lucena Salmoral, Manuel. *Características del comercio exterior de la provincia de Caracas durante el sexenio revolucionario (1806–1812)*. Madrid, 1990.

——. *Vísperas de la independencia americana: Caracas*. Madrid, 1986.

Lynch, John. *The Spanish American Revolutions, 1808–1826*. 2d ed., New York, 1986.

Madariaga, Salvador de. *Bolívar*. London and New York, 1952.

Masur, Gerhard. *Simon Bolívar*. 2d ed., Albuquerque, NM, 1969.

McFarlane, Anthony. *Colombia Before Independence*. Cambridge, 1993.

McKinley, Michael P. *Pre-revolutionary Caracas: Politics, Economics, and Society, 1777–1811*. Cambridge, 1985.

Mijares, Augusto. *The Liberator*. Trans. John Fisher, Caracas, 1983.

Moreno de Angel, Pilar. *Santander: biografía*. Bogotá, 1989.

Murray, Pamela. "'Loca' or 'Libertadora'?: Manuela Sáenz in the Eyes of History and Historians, 1900–c. 1990." *Journal of Latin American Studies*, vol. 33, part 2 (May 2001): 291–310.

O'Leary, Daniel F. *Bolívar and the War of Independence*. Austin, TX, 1970.

Páez, José Antonio. *Autobiografía*. Facsimile ed., 2 vols., New York, 1946.

Parra-Pérez, Caracciolo. *Historia de la Primera República de Venezuela*. 2d ed., 2 vols., Caracas, 1959.

——. *Mariño y la independencia de Venezuela*. 4 vols., Madrid, 1954–56.

Polanco Alcántara, Tomás. *Simón Bolívar: ensayo de interpretación biográfica a través de sus documentos*. Caracas, 1994.

Restrepo, José Manuel. *Historia de la Revolución de la República de Colombia*. 4th ed., 6 vols., Medellín, 1969.

Robertson, William S. *The Life of Miranda*. 2 vols., Chapel Hill, NC, 1929.

Rodríguez Villa, Antonio. *El teniente general don Pablo Morillo, primer Conde de Cartagena, Marqués de La Puerta*. 4 vols., Madrid, 1908–10.

Stoan, Stephen. *Pablo Morillo and Venezuela, 1815–1820*. Columbus, OH, 1974.

Tovar, Hermes. "Guerras de opinión y represión en Colombia durante la independencia (1810–1820)." *Anuario Colombiano de Historia Social y de la Cultura*, no. 11 (1983), 187–233.

Valencia Tovar, Alvaro. *El ser guerrero del Libertador*. Bogotá, 1980.

Van Aken, Mark J. *King of the Night: Juan José Flores and Ecuador, 1824–1864.* Berkeley, 1989.

Waddell, D.A.G. *Gran Bretaña y la independencia de Venezuela y Colombia.* Caracas, 1983.